How to Be Your Own
Marriage Counselor

How to Be Your Own

MARRIAGE COUNSELOR

A Commonsense Guide
to Marital Happiness

Michael C. Venditti, M.D.

CONTINUUM | New York

To my beloved Marianne
and our children Michael, Rita,
Marilouise, and David.
O that everyone could share
a love so great and a life
so full—thus was the inspiration
for this book.

1980
The Continuum Publishing Corporation
815 Second Avenue, New York, N.Y. 10017

Library of Congress Cataloging in Publication Data

Venditti, Michael C 1929–
How to be your own marriage counselor.
1. Marriage. I. Title.
HQ728.V44   646.7'8   80–16181   ISBN 0–8264–0013–2

Grateful acknowledgment is made to the following people whose
combined efforts and encouragement have contributed immeasurably to making
this book a reality:

Dr. Albert Campbell whose editing helped to make it readable;

My office staff who worked many hours overtime to convert my spoken words
into readable type;

My many friends and patients who have shared their problems with me over
the years and have taught me through experience the realities of life and
marriage;

Mario A. Castallo, M.D., whose early confidence in me helped to make it all
possible.

M.C.V.

Contents

Foreword   xi

Questionnaire   xiii

Introduction   xix

Part I | The Anatomy of Marriage

1 Marriage as a Way of Life   3

2 Courtship   7

3 The Marriage Contract   11
  To Have and to Hold
  For Richer, for Poorer
  In Sickness and in Health
  For Better, for Worse
  Until Death Do Us Part
  I Now Pronounce You Man and Wife

4 The Wedding Day   19

5 Honeymoon, Sexual Adjustment, and Family Planning   22
  Sexual Adjustment
  Family Planning and Birth Control

6 Early Marriage Until the First Pregnancy   37

7 The Subject of Children   41

8 Life with Children   45
  Pregnancy
  The Infant and the Preschool Child

The Years from the Beginning of School to Puberty
Adolescence to Maturity
When the Children Leave Home

9 From the Time Children Leave Home Until Retirement   53

10 After Retirement   55

11 The Elderly Retired Couple   58

Part II | The Problems of Marriage

Introduction   63

1 Boredom   65

2 Problems Associated with Housekeeping
and Home Maintenance   68

3 Interference from Family and Friends   72

4 Bickering   75

5 Infidelity   80

6 Unequal Development   84

7 Marriages with Built-in Inadequacies   90

8 Marriage in Which One Mate Has Been
Transplanted from His Native Environment   95

9 Jealousy   98

10 Financial Problems of Marriage   101

11 Alcoholism   105

12 Marriage with a Depressed Mate   115

13 Adjusting to Menopause   120

14 Male Involutional Syndrome or
Male Menopause   125

15 Peer Pressure and Media Pressure
Against the Stable Marriage   130

16 Homosexuality   134

17 Coping with the Problems of
Having a Permanent House Guest   137

18 Problems Associated with
Geographic Change   141

19 Coping with the Problems and
Failures of Children   144

20 Problems of Children from a Previous Marriage   146

21 Role Sharing and Role Reversal in Marriage   154

22 Carelessness, Laziness, and Procrastination   157

23 The Role of Drugs in Marriage   159

24 The Subject of In-Laws   164

25 Sexual Maladjustment and Frigidity   167

    Primary Frigidity   167
       Medical and Physical
       Hostility toward the Opposite Sex
       Unpleasant Premarital Experience
       Poor Sex Education
       Sexually Incompatible Partnership
       Fear of Pregnancy
    Secondary Frigidity   173
       Fear of Pregnancy
       Loss of Mutual Respect
       Lack of Self-respect and Self-confidence
       Lack of Privacy
       Fatigue
       Lack of Imagination and Interest
         in Love Play
       Impotence and Loss of Libido
       Lack of Mutual Physical Attraction
       Physical and Mental Illness
       Old Age
       Infidelity as a Cause for
         Sexual Maladjustment

Part III | Golden Rules of Marriage

    Introduction   191

Rule   **1** Keep the Marriage Dynamic   191

Rule   **2** Be Courteous at Home   192

Contents

Rule 3 Never Belittle Your Mate 192

Rule 4 Always Let Your Mate Be Number One 193

Rule 5 Call Your Mate by Name or a Pet Name 194

Rule 6 Don't Hesitate to Praise Your Mate in Public 195

Rule 7 Resolve Today's Problems Today 195

Rule 8 Bend but Don't Break 196

Rule 9 Plan Ahead 197

Rule 10 Avoid Sore Points 197

Rule 11 Stay Attractive 198

Rule 12 Be Reliable 199

Rule 13 Never Promise More than You Can Produce 199

Rule 14 Admit Your Own Shortcomings 200

Rule 15 Be Pleasant 200

Rule 16 Be Appreciative 201

Rule 17 Give Enough of Yourself to Your Family 202

Rule 18 Don't Play with Temptation 203

Rule 19 Don't Expect Your Mate to Be
Something that He or She Is Not 203

Rule 20 Keep Yourself Interesting 204

Rule 21 Don't Neglect Your Sex Life with Your Mate 204

Rule 22 Be Tolerant of Your Mate's Interests
And Recreation—Within Reason 205

Rule 23 Do Not Permit Yourself to Be
Unhappy in Your Job 206

Rule 24 Keep Healthy 207

Rule 25 Work Toward Providing Your Family
with an Adequate Home 207

Rule 26 Don't Nag 209

Rule 27 Never Criticize Your Mate's Family 209

Rule 28 Keep a Little Spice and Surprise
in Your Life   210

Rule 29 If You Love Your Mate and Children,
Tell Them So Frequently   211

Rule 30 Permit No More than One Family Per Home   212

Rule 31 Keep Your Bad Moods to Yourself   213

Rule 32 Don't Abuse Alcohol   214

Rule 33 Be Optimistic   215

Rule 34 Don't Intentionally Bore or
Irritate Each Other   215

Rule 35 Make the Most of Your Time Off   216

Rule 36 Never Compare Your Mate with Anyone Else 217

Rule 37 Always Consult Your Mate Before
Making an Important Decision   218

Rule 38 Never Criticize Your Mate Without
Acknowledging Your Own Inadequacies
at the Same Time   218

Rule 39 Always Acknowledge Your Mate's
Efforts and Improvements   219

Rule 40 Keep Current Friends and Interests   219

Rule 41 Live within Your Means   220

Rule 42 Avoid Violence at All Cost   220

Rule 43 Insist on Privacy in Your Family   221

Rule 44 Never Hold a Grudge   222

Rule 45 Go to Bed at the Same Time   223

Rule 46 Share Your Successes and Glories
with Your Mate   223

Rule 47 Live Each Phase of Life to Its Fullest   224

Rule 48 Don't Put Off the Decision About
Having Children Too Long   225

Rule 49 Be Willing to Give 90 percent in Hopes
          of Getting 10 percent in Return   225

Rule 50 Keep Some Fun and Good Humor
          in Your Marriage   226

Rule 51 Keep Physically Active and Fit   226

Rule 52 Never Hesitate to Admit Your Mistakes
          and Apologize for Them   227

Rule 53 Make Love Not War   228

Rule 54 Consider Having a Family Pet   228

Rule 55 Reevaluate Your Marriage Every Six
          Months and Plan Improvements   228

Rule 56 Eliminate Your Irritating Traits   229

Rule 57 Consider Having an Adequate Spiritual Life   230

Rule 58 Have a Regular Date Night   230

Rule 59 Select an Interested Family Physician
          and Be a Faithful Patient   231

Rule 60 Never Give Up Hope   232

Conclusion   233

Foreword

This text has been designed to provide a comprehensive understanding of the various phases of marriage. In addition, it offers insight into understanding the problems of marriage. It also offers a set of rules that will help you to solve specific marital problems and at the same time will enrich all marriages and life in general.

I strongly recommend that you take time to answer the questionnaire at the end of the foreword and, by so doing, evaluate your own marriage. If there are problems that show up, refer to the pages that address themselves to your own special problems.

Ideally, you would be wise to fill out the questionnaire every six months. This will help you to monitor your marriage and note any signs of underlying troubles before they become serious. If you do this and then reread the appropriate sections at least every six months thereafter, you will develop the knack of being your own marriage counselor.

After filling out the questionnaire, read the entire text from the beginning. When you have completed it, establish a self-study program whereby you assign yourself one golden rule from Part Three to read daily and reinforce in your life. Remember that this book is written for those who wish to be their own marriage counselor. It is my hope therefore that you will be open-minded in accepting my explanations and suggestions. And it is my hope also that you will be willing to assume most, if not all, of the responsibility for rectifying the problems in your marriage, regardless of whose initial fault it seems to be. In other words, in answer to the question "How can I help to improve my marriage?" let the text be your guide. But by no means should you use the text as a weapon with which to browbeat your mate. If both of you are sincerely interested in making your marriage better with the aid of this text, your chances for success will be many times greater. That would be a bonus. The important thing is that YOU enthusiastically embrace the program as I have outlined it here, and resolve to do your utmost to make yourself the very best marriage partner that you can possibly be.

Do not worry that any suggestion might be urging you toward being too selfless. We all know that it is better to give than to take. The spirit of giving, sharing, understanding, loving, and humility is usually contagious in the long run. You will note that throughout the text it is suggested that you add your own comments. Why not pick up a looseleaf notebook for this purpose and keep a record of your comments and reactions? Or, you could slip your comments between the appropriate pages of this book. You may feel this is unnecessary and awkward at first, but I encourage you to do it anyway; the text will be even more beneficial.

And now please fill out the questionnaire, and let's get on with the task of understanding and enriching your marriage.

A Questionnaire To Help Determine
The Health of Your Marriage

Please consult the reference pages.   *Reference Pages*

1. Do you feel you are doing the best you can as a husband or wife?
1–60, 84–89, 112–114, 147–151, 182–230

2. Are you happy with the mood of your home?
59–79, 130–133, 137–140, 144–159, 182–230

3. Are you happy with the physical makeup of your home?
209–210, 212–214, 215–216, 217–218, 220–221, 225–230

4. Are you content with your current economic status at your phase of life?
108–111, 149–151, 195, 201–202, 203–204, 212–213, 215–216

5. Are you compatible with your in-laws?
9–10, 19–21, 72–74, 137–140, 156–160, 185–186, 205–207, 209–210, 217–218

6. Are you and your mate sexually compatible?
xix–36, 45–48, 65–67, 75–94, 112–136, 151–155, 160–180, 183–230

7. Are your children rewarding to you?
41–52, 68–71, 144–145, 149–151, 185–186, 191–192, 195, 197–198, 203–205, 209, 212–213, 220–221, 223–224, 225–226, 227–228

8. Are you usually free of boredom?
65–67, 75–79, 84–89, 112–119, 130–133, 149–151, 170–178, 183–192, 193–194, 196–197, 200–205, 207–209, 210–213, 215, 219, 222, 223

9. Do you consider your mate an interesting person?

65–67, 75–79, 84–89, 112–119, 130–133, 149–151, 170–178, 183, 192, 193–194, 196–197, 200–205, 207–209, 210–213, 215, 219, 222, 223

10. Are you happy with your own current level of achievement in life?

xix–64, 65–79, 84–94, 108–133, 144–229

11. Knowing what you do at this point, if you were not already married, would you choose to marry your present mate?

xix–232. Please reread the book and assign yourself three golden rules daily.

12. Are you contented within your community?

65–79, 95–97, 115–118, 130–133, 143–144, 149–151, 156–160, 183, 192, 195, 199–200, 201–205

13. Do you feel that you are making your mate happy?

xix–232. Please reread the book and assign yourself three golden rules daily.

14. Do you intend to remain married to your present mate until death do you part?

11–21, then read entire text.

15. Do you feel that your parents are contented with you and your mate?

19–21, 72–74, 128–129, 137–140, 157–158, 164–166, 186, 193–194, 199, 204, 206–208, 212–217, 220–221, 224–225

16. Do your children consider you a good parent?

41–54, 68–71, 137–140, 144–145, 157–163, 191–194, 197–202, 207, 212–215, 220–222, 224–227, 231–232

17. Do you consider yourself at least an equal partner in marriage?

xix–18, 68–71, 84–94, 98–104, 154–158, 191–233

18. Do you feel that you are an asset to your partner, socially and career-wise?

3–61, 63–64, 75–79, 98–104, 130–133, 154–158, 191–233

19. Are your in-laws content with you and your mate?

19–21, 68–74, 84–89, 137–140, 157–158, 164–166, 192–194, 199–202, 204, 209–210, 220, 222–223

20. Do you consider yourself emotionally well?

15–16, 115–129, 144–153, 157–163, 176–178, 195–201, 203–204, 206–207, 213–220, 222–224, 226–234

21. Does your mate consider you emotionally well?

Same as #20.

22. Do you consider yourself physically well?

15–16, 115–119, 125–129, 159–163, 169–187, 198, 204, 207, 213–216, 221–222, 223, 224, 229–230, 231–232

23. Does your mate consider you physically well?

Same as #22.

24. Would you consider it wrong for your mate to be unfaithful to you?

3–18, 130–133, 230

25. Would you consider it wrong for you to be unfaithful to your mate?

Same as #24.

26. Do you consider yourself completely free of jealousy toward your mate?

98–100, 154–156, 169–187, 191–232

27. Do you consider your mate to be completely free of jealousy toward you?

Same as #26.

28. Is your family life free of bickering?

65–79, 84–94, 98–100, 101–104, 115–129, 157, 191–232

29. Do you consider your marriage to be better than most?

Read the entire text from first page.

30. Do you respect your mate as a person?

3–21, 65–94, 98–100, 115–133, 137–140, 154–163, 191–232

31. Does your mate respect you as a person?

Same as #30.

32. Do you have fun on a regular basis?

3–10, 84–94, 130–133, 157–158, 167–187, 198, 200–201, 204–206, 210–212, 213–214

33. Are your vacations satisfactory?

219–220, 224, 226–227, 230–231

34. Do you and your mate handle stress well together?

Read entire text from first page.

35. Are you satisfied with your spiritual life?

230

36. Is your mate your best friend?

65–67, 75–79, 84–94, 98–100, 144–145, 191–232

37. Is your mate free of habits that irritate you?

3–59, 65–71, 75–94, 98–100, 115–133, 154–156, 157–163, 191–232

38. Do you and your mate spend at least one waking hour per day alone?

63–94, 137–140, 193–194, 197, 202, 203–206, 207–209, 210–214, 215–217, 221–224, 226, 229–231, 233

39. Do you and your mate kiss hello and good-bye?

7–10, 63–64, 75–83, 98–100, 194–195, 198, 200–204, 204–205, 210–212, 213–214, 215, 217, 221–224, 225–228, 228–231, 233

40. When your mate is away, are you eager for his or her return?

65–67, 75–79, 84–94, 115–133, 157–163, 191–232

41. Do you consider your mate attractive?

7–10, 75–79, 84–89, 98–100, 115–124, 157–158, 167–189, 193–194, 198–201, 203–204, 204–205, 209, 210–211, 213–214, 217–219, 223–224, 225–226, 230–232

42. Do you consider your mate as physically attractive as he or she was five years ago?

Same as #41.

43. Do you feel that your mate considers you attractive physically? — 80–94, 98–100, 115–133, 157–158, 167–187, 191–232

44. Do you consult your family physician at least once a year? — 207, 226–227, 231–232

45. Are you happy with your family physician? — 231–232

46. Do you put your mate before your children and family in the event of conflict? — 11–18, 72–74, 144–145, 154–156, 193–195, 203–204, 217, 219, 223–224, 230–231

47. Are you considerate of your mate? — 11–18, 72–74, 144–145, 154–156, 193–195, 203–204, 217, 219, 223–224, 230–231

48. Is your mate considerate of you? — 11–18, 80–94, 98–100, 115–133, 154–163, 168–186, 195–205, 209, 213–216, 218–219, 225–228, 228–231, 233

49. Were you happy with the anniversary, birthday, and Christmas presents that your mate gave you last year? — 101–104, 199–200, 201–202, 203–204, 210–211, 217, 220, 225–226

50. Did you put a great deal of effort into the birthday, anniversary, and Christmas presents that you gave your mate last year? — 101–104, 199–200, 201–202, 203–204, 210–211, 217, 220, 225–226

51. Have you surprised your mate with something special in the past week? — 101–104, 199–200, 201–202, 203–204, 210–211, 217, 220, 225–226

52. Has your mate surprised you with something special in the past week? — 101–104, 199–200, 201–202, 203–204, 210–211, 217, 220, 225–226

53. Do you consider yourself an interesting person? — 65–67, 75–94, 98–100, 115–133, 191–232

54. Do you consider your mate an interesting person?   65–67, 75–94, 98–100, 115–133, 191–232

55. Are you on a self-improvement campaign?   65–67, 75–94, 98–100, 115–133, 191–232

56. Do you make the most of every day?   65–71, 84–94, 157–158, 197, 199–200, 204, 206–207, 209–210, 216–217, 219–220, 224, 230

57. Does your mate utilize his or her time to maximum advantage?   67–71, 84–94, 157–158, 197, 199–200, 204, 206–207, 209–210, 216–217, 219–220, 224, 230

58. Are you and your mate happy with your circle of friends?   206–207, 216–217, 219–220

59. Do you and your mate contribute adequately to the community?   199–200, 207–209, 216–217, 230

60. Do you feel that you were properly prepared for your present phase of marriage?   3–59, 80–83, 164–166, 207–209, 220, 225, 228–229, 230–233

61. Are you happy with the number of children you have?   29–36, 41–52, 144–145, 225

62. Do you touch and hold hands freely with your mate?   7–10, 167–187, 198, 204–205

63. Do you and your mate have interesting conservations?   7–10, 65–67, 75–79, 115–119, 191–192, 204, 209, 210–211, 218–219, 223–224, 226, 230–231

64. Do you consider your knowledge of sex adequate?   22–36, 167–187, 204–205

Introduction

Over a decade ago, I became concerned because many of my patients were increasingly plagued with marital problems and were frustrated in their efforts to get meaningful help. The time-honored sources of marital counseling, such as their own families, clergy, and even professional marriage counselors seemed to be inadequate at solving problems. The reasons why the professionals were inadequate ranged from busyness to lack of interest, and, often, to lack of training. Furthermore, either one or both partners often resented the inconvenience, embarrassment, and expense involved in seeking outside help for their difficulties. They therefore ignored or tolerated them with resentment until their marriage was on the brink of disaster.

As an interested and involved family physician, I spent many hours working with troubled couples, and I like to think that I was helpful. At the same time, it was obvious that most people did not come to me until their problems were practically beyond help or even beyond hope. And when help could be rendered, it was also apparent that couples would continue to come to me only until the immediate crisis was over. In short, I was rendering an emergency service, but I was neither solving nor preventing marital problems.

The only way to achieve that purpose, I decided, was to provide a reference text that would outline the various phases of marriage from courtship to old age, so that couples could understand the dynamics of marriage and therefore know what to expect. Most crises can be predicted and prevented. Such a text would also review the most common problems of marriage and offer workable solutions. And finally, it was necessary to provide a set of rules to follow in order to enrich the marriage and try to prevent problems from developing in the first place. In short, I wanted to give my patients a guide to help them be their own marriage counselors.

During the past ten years the divorce rate in the United States has actually doubled, although more people than ever before are getting married. The latest statistics reveal that 94.4 percent of all men between the ages of forty-five and fifty-four have been married and 95.7 percent of all women in this age group have been married.

Divorce, separation, and incompatibility have become so commonplace that they constitute a major theme in our music, theater, and politics. Not only have these *abnormal* conditions come to be accepted as almost normal but they are celebrated as "the thing to do" if you believe the media brainwashing. The net result, however, is that the security of our youth has been compromised. And in our youth lies our future—indeed our survival. As their very home life and parental models have been distorted, so have their attitudes toward tradition, authority, discipline, respect, and morals. The word *morals* has virtually disappeared from our language. Ultimately, society as we know it now may not survive—unless something is done to restore stability and commonsense to marriage and family.

In my opinion, it is not possible to have a happy, healthy, productive society composed of unstable families. I endeavored therefore to find a self-help marriage text that would serve to enrich and strengthen the family. Such a text would have to be written in layman's language for the average person and offer a commonsense practical approach to marriage. Since I was unable to find such a book to recommend, I decided to write one—based on my own twenty years' experience as a family physician —with the hope that my observations of families in sickness and in health, in richer and poorer times, and on their better and worse days would serve the purpose. Why not? After all, who other than a family physician could possibly be equipped with experience enough to offer a practical, commonsense guide to marriage and prepare people to be their own marriage counselors.

The text is divided into three parts. Part One is a review of the various phases of marriage from courtship to old age. Feelings, motivations, and potential problems are discussed. Please reread this section from time to time and make notes of your own experiences.

Part Two is a review of the most common problems of marriage with some detailed examples and suggested solutions. Read it over and refer to it occasionally, especially if you feel that any symptoms of discontent are developing in your marital relationship. Add your own examples of problems and their solutions. Draw on your own experiences, those of your family, and of your friends.

Part Three is a list of the golden rules of marriage. I suggest that you enroll yourself in a continual self-improvement program. Read a rule or two a day and attempt to apply it to your daily life. When you have finished the list, start over again, and again, and again. You will probably have some golden rules of your own that you would like to add. If so, make note of them. It is my hope to guide you to a life of love, happiness, and excitement in marriage rather than just peaceful coexistence.

My assumption will be that any two people who have chosen to marry have experienced love and that they wish to share the balance of their lives together. It will also be assumed that the reader is humble and mature enough to analyze and admit his or her shortcomings, as well as be determined enough to wage a continual self-improvement campaign to enrich the marriage. If these prerequisites are met, the success of this text is virtually guaranteed.

All of the stories in the text are based on actual facts. I have, however, changed the names, occupations, and all other identifying elements in order to ensure the privacy of those involved.

My philosophy is that marriage is a sacred act that changes individuals forever. With marriage, one's essential being changes from that of single individual to that of one half of a husband-wife combination. As such, the couple is charged with the privilege and responsibility of sharing all facets of life and with the right to bring children into the world. Because of these sanctions, marriage is meant to be permanent!!! Good luck, and I hope this book helps you to enjoy a lifetime of happiness together.

Part I

The Anatomy of Marriage

Love is ideal; marriage is real.
—*Goethe*

·1·
Marriage as a Way of Life

Have you ever wondered why such a high percentage of people in all times and places have chosen to marry? I myself have never heard of any parents wanting their son or daughter to remain single. And yet the unmarried life seems so much more glamorous. After all, it is filled with freedom and is infinitely easier. Why do you think, then, that people sell themselves into the bondage of marriage—a bondage that requires the man to be gainfully employed and the woman to manage the home and perhaps also to contribute to the economy of the family—for the rest of their lives? Why is it that a young man chooses to give up spending his entire income on himself, having free time, and freedom from responsibility? Why does a young woman, equally carefree, choose to accept a twenty-four-hour-a-day, seven-day-a-week job as wife, mother, and homemaker? (More and more, such a homemaker must in addition have a profession of her own.) Certainly the life-style of a career woman, whose job usually requires only eight hours of effort each day and offers a paycheck that is hers and hers alone, would seem attractive to many women.

It is not that they dislike the single life but that they would prefer a happy married life. Plato had the fanciful idea that each person is born with only half a soul. God, he thought, had given one half of the soul to a man; the other half to a woman. Men and women long to marry in order to reunite the soul. Maybe he was right? It is true that when two people become one in marriage, a child can result from that union. In this view, the man and the woman are charged with carrying on God's creation.

The urge in each person to be married is a primal one predicated on the following factors:

1. Each well-adjusted person from a well-adjusted family brings into adulthood a learned response that impels him to imitate his parents: he also will seek the happiness of family life.

2. All humans have an inherent drive to love and be loved uniquely by another person. This drive toward such a relationship is exemplified in an often-observed phenomenon of childhood. Most children fantasize that they have a certain boyfriend or girlfriend even though it is often a secret love and not outwardly expressed. This psychological need culminates in the young person's first experiences in dating.

3. The desire to have children preexists in the human mind. Christianity, as well as the other great religions, teaches us that God created man in His own image, so that man could love Him, honor Him, and reflect His goodness. Given God's purpose in developing the human race, it certainly takes but little imagination to realize that there is in each of us a fundamental desire to procreate children in our own likeness—we too, like the well-adjusted person in #1. above, imitate God the Parent, God the Father.

4. The social milieu of modern American life is such that, for the most part, all the activities of mature adult society are for couples only. It is rare to find a social gathering of any kind that a person can attend alone comfortably. The possible exception is activities that are expressly for singles—but the titles of such activities belie their true nature: most are organized for the primary purpose of enabling single people to meet romantic partners.

5. Marriage is the world's safest old-age insurance. Many people will argue for the exciting advantages of freedom for the young, but very rarely will anyone advocate growing old alone. It may sound calculating, but it is really practical and ultimately reasonable to make the sacrifices required to establish a sound marriage when you are young; otherwise, you are almost certainly destined to have a lonely old age.

6. The most popular reason given for marrying is the most dramatic one—life is more fun that way. Life is more fun if you have someone to love. Life is more fun for a man to have a wife to share his thoughts and dreams, compensate for all his inadequacies, and share his bed. Likewise, life is more fun when a woman has a husband to offer her economic security and physical protection. A woman needs someone to open tight jars for her, replace broken windows, shovel the walks. She also needs warmth and affection, and the opportunity to achieve motherhood. Assuredly, the main

reason why people marry is that life is more fun that way; but it can only be fun if the marriage is a good one.

7. Everyone has need for sexual satisfaction. The desire for sexual satisfaction is an obvious fact of life, one which seems to be instinctive and varies in intensity from person to person. Some people seem to be able to take it or leave it, while others are virtually driven by it to the point of irresponsibility. But the yearning for sexual satisfaction *with love* and as an expression of love is an altogether different urge and a different satisfaction when it is ultimately achieved. It represents the most complete form of acceptance of one person for another, and the physical thrill involved is the culmination of romance between a man and a woman who are indeed in love.

Unfortunately, many people today participate in sexual activity without love and become confused by the letdown which follows. For after surrendering their bodies completely, there is often a rejection, which is manifested by being left alone after the sex act is completed. There is no question that one of the prime reasons to want to be married is the craving for sexual satisfaction with love.

As for the reasons why the rate of marriage failure is so high, I think the following factors are significant:

1. The availability of birth-control measures and the encouragement to limit the size of families has made marital partners much less dependent on each other.

2. The necessity for two incomes in many families, generated by inflation, has changed the woman's role in the family. Modern appliances, prepared foods, ready-made clothes, and expanded opportunities in business for women have also decreased the interdependence that husbands and wives previously shared.

3. The relaxation of laws and social stigma previously associated with divorce.

4. The mobile society of our times has separated young couples from their parents and families; also, there is less peer pressure on couples to work out the solution of their marital problems. Statistics show that the divorce rate is significantly lower in societies that do not move around so much.

5. Media pressure seems to glorify divorce and infidelity as never before.

6. Religions have become more lax in their attitudes about marriage and divorce.

Your own experience has probably indicated other societal changes that have made it difficult for marriage to survive. Doubtlessly, you have other thoughts and observations about the causes of failure in marriage. If so, please make note of them for future reference.

Thus far, I have endeavored to list the basic reasons why people want to be married and why the overwhelming majority do marry. If you are willing to accept these reasons as valid, it follows that you must accept the profound fact that marriage is a culmination of the basic desires of healthy mature human beings.

In subsequent chapters, as we review the hardships of marriage, we shall refer to these fundamentals that make people decide to dedicate their lives to being husbands and wives in the first place. We shall see over and over again that the most frequent reasons for marriage failures are that the basic desires in marriage have never been fulfilled or have been periodically neglected.

I am sure that the lists I have given above will not be entirely adequate for everyone. Each of you will have your own special reasons for desiring to be married. As you rethink your reasons for wanting to be married, please write them down. You will find that it will be invaluable as you get into the book and start evaluating the strong and weak points of your own marriage. Go ahead, write down why you want to be married. At the same time, you might want to note whether or not each reason has been satisfied in your own marriage. If not, why not, and what can you do to make it better? Go ahead! Jot down your own comments.

Now that we recognize the motivations for happy marriage and some of the pressures that are currently making it difficult to achieve, we are ready to embark on a survey of courtship and marriage in its many phases.

·2·

Courtship

Romeo:
If I profane with my unworthiest hand
This holy shrine, the gentle fine is this:
My lips, two blushing pilgrims, ready stand
To smooth that rough touch with a tender kiss.

Juliet:
Good pilgrim, you do wrong your hand too much
Which mannerly devotion shows in this;
For saints have hands that pilgrims' hands
   do touch,
And palm to palm is holy palmers' kiss.
                                        —*Shakespeare*

The time of courtship is surely the most exciting time of life. Certainly, more has been written and sung about courtship than about any other subject. So exciting is it that I never cease to be fascinated by the fact that most traditional love stories are really courtship stories, ones that almost invariably end with marriage, and close with the magic words, "And they lived happily ever after."

If we are to accept these stories as being indicative of reality, the true excitement of courtship is the pursuit and conquest of the loved one. I would be the last to be found guilty of debunking this wonderful myth, for no one—unless it be you, the reader—loves romance more than I do. I am convinced that there is no excitement that rivals the early realization that one may have found his or her lifelong partner. The seeker is overcome by an incomparable exhilaration. And even the fictional romances cannot do justice to that feeling. There is simply no substitute for the real thing.

In the following pages, I shall attempt to analyze courtship for the purpose of establishing a norm by which we might evaluate courtship as preparation for the ensuing marriage. In establishing a link between the two, we shall be able to understand the strong and weak points of the subsequent marriage.

Courtship can best be defined as the period of shopping for a mate. It is sometimes a long and arduous task—but a delightful one. I believe it starts the very first time that a child feels the slightest attraction for someone of the opposite sex. From this time on, courtship manifests itself daily. Everyday this young person makes conscious and subconscious observations of the opposite sex, looking for the particular qualities he or she desires in the future mate. Again, this "window shopping" precedes the actual bargaining by many, many years. The reading of love stories, early dating, dancing, coed parties, the singing of love songs to oneself—all of these activities are exercises in courtship. Some people are meticulous evaluators and examine every aspect of potential mates; others rely on a more general impression.

Courtship takes all forms. How and why people find each other is a subject as diverse as people themselves. Basically, however, it can be divided i ·to three phases, (1) early attraction and introduction (getting to know each other); (2) the surge of love that makes the relationship and the experience unique and superior to all other interpersonal experiences; and (3) commitment to prepare for marriage.

Each phase must be adequately fulfilled in order to prepare properly for marriage, and if each phase is not fulfilled, problems will eventually ensue!

During the phase of *early attraction* and *introduction*, a genuine affection should really exist. Mere practicality and convenience is not enough to build a love relationship on. Likewise, an honest familiarization is essential. It is impossible to develop true, realistic love for a person without a realistic knowledge of his or her full character and personality, both its strong and weak points. An understanding of the person's philosophy, background, and goals is equally important.

Only after the first phase is fulfilled can a realistic second phase, *the surge of love*, be initiated. Most people, however, have an imaginary ideal mate long before they ever meet a realistic contender for the position. Since love is blind, a person often overlooks the potential mate's faults.

During the second phase the partners become completely absorbed in each other. They crave to be together at every opportunity to play, pet, talk, and plan. Some romances are more passion-filled than others, obviously since the personalities of people vary so. The disturbing situation, however, is when people attempt to force themselves to be in love without the true surge of love. Although they may simulate love, it may lack the depth necessary for durability.

Phase three, *commitment to prepare for marriage*, can be successfully reached only upon the satisfactory establishment of the first two phases. The results of marriage preparations, without complete familiarity and the surge of love, can be a disaster, for they are its very foundation.

In one form or another, preparations for marriage should include:

1. An agreement on a compatible philosophy to live by.
2. An agreement for complete sexual surrender.
3. A commitment to fidelity.
4. A mutually agreed upon place to live.
5. An agreement upon a plan for children.
6. Complete acceptance of each other with intent to stay together permanently.

If I had my way, all candidates for marriage would be presented with the following questionnaire to consider before deciding whether or not they really wanted to commit themselves. Why don't you fill it out and analyze your own answers?

1. Are you compatible with your prospective partner's family? Why? If not, what can be done about it?
2. What is your family's attitude toward your partner? Why? If they do not like your prospective mate, what can be done about it?
3. Are your economic goals compatible?
4. Do you know your partner well enough?
5. Does your partner have offensive traits? Could you live with them if they could not be corrected?
6. Are your attitudes toward children compatible?
7. Are you compatible with your partner's vocation? (It could be your main competition.)
8. Do you anticipate any problems in establishing a completely satisfactory sexual relationship? If so, why not see your family physician for help before problems arise?
9. Are there any major points of disagreement? Can anything be done to resolve them prior to taking marriage vows?

10. Is this love relationship everything you ever hoped it would be? Would it be worth waiting until you are more certain?

11. Do ideas flow freely between you? Do you talk to each other without inhibition?

12. Could you adjust yourself to your partner's background and culture without compromising your own character, personality, and happiness?

13. Are you eager to be married or just eager to get away from your present situation?

14. Were either you or your partner ever previously married or involved in a serious courtship that ended unsatisfactorily? What would keep history from repeating itself?

It might strike you as somewhat silly to review courtship as I have for readers who probably are already married. The purpose was to present the basic essentials leading up to marriage, in the hope that recognizing an unfulfilled courtship might offer some understanding of the eventual difficulties that might arise, and aid in the development of a plan for their solution.

Please do not be discouraged if you feel that problems later on in marriage are the result of inadequate courtship. It is never too late to start rebuilding if you can determine what is lacking in the foundation.

Truly, a really good marriage is one of perpetual courtship, and it is never too late to begin courting anew.

> *First, thou shalt be young and free*
> *In thy days of liberty,*
> *Then again be wooed and won. . . .*

·3·

The Marriage Contract

The most binding contract you can ever sign is the marriage contract; no other contract is so all-inclusive and so permanent. It deserves, therefore, all the thought that you can possibly give it. You should study the words of the contract very carefully and think about the meaning behind the words. And you should not hesitate to get professional advice if you are perplexed.

It is typical of patients who are complaining about marriage to say, "Why didn't someone tell me what I was getting into?" I always reply, "Whom did you ask?" Invariably, they say they never asked anyone. They can only recall that someone said the magic words and made it all legal.

I am reminded of Sue Ellen and Tony, a couple in their early twenties, who invited my wife and me to their wedding. Both bright, attractive, but headstrong young people, their courtship had been filled with bickering and major disagreements. Their families were incompatible and they themselves were intolerant of each other's friends and hobbies.

In spite of these forewarnings, however, they wanted desperately to get married—and so proceeded to be, on the premise that time would solve all problems. Unfortunately, they neglected to discuss or even read the marriage contract until they were reciting it at the ceremony—and thus setting themselves up for a long series of conflicts and miseries.

At the wedding reception, I overheard Tony telling a group of his friends, "If she thinks I'm going to sell my motorcycle, she is in for a big surprise; and I intend to use my season ticket to the football games whether she likes it or not!" As I later danced with the bride, she spent a full ten minutes elaborating on the major points upon which she and her new husband disagreed. Even the honeymoon plans were among the subjects of disagreement. I told her to come to see me at the office after the honeymoon and we would see if we could provide them with a marriage contract that might assure some happiness.

It was not until three months after the wedding that they came to see me. As I expected, a stormy course had followed the honeymoon. My analysis of their problem was that they were trying to function in a marriage without an agreed-upon contract. I thereupon gave each of them a piece of paper and asked them to list on one side what they wanted from marriage, and on the other side what they were willing to give in return.

Fortunately, they loved each other and wanted the marriage to work, and their lists reflected this. After I examined what each had written, I asked them to exchange lists and discuss the discrepancies. One by one, they were able to reach an agreement on each point and finally I suggested that this would represent a renegotiation of the marriage contract—one that they understood and agreed upon. They both signed the new contract and I signed as a witness and made a photocopy for their charts.

It would be incorrect to say that the marriage from then on was completely free of problems. It was not. But at least they now had a contract to use as a set of rules to help solve problems. They understood what was expected and could adjust accordingly.

As a result, a marriage that was on the brink of disaster became a stable and permanent one. There are now two well-adjusted daughters and a happy marriage where there could have been misery and divorce.

The obvious moral to this true story is that it is imperative that each person understand and agree to abide by the particular marriage contract that is proposed. If it is not appropriate for you, then change it to suit your agreed-upon needs; or even write a completely original one addressed to your own specific needs. But understand it and agree upon it; otherwise, it will be impossible to live by it.

For background purposes, it would be wise to review a traditional marriage ceremony and analyze it. Here is one:

> The officiating person asks, "Do you take (name), here present, for your lawful wife?"
> The response is, "I do."
> Then the officiating person asks the bride, "Do you take (name), here present, to be your lawful husband?"
> The response is, "I do."
> (The verbal consent itself is not sufficient; it must be expressed in some nonlingual, tangible sign by both.) After obtaining mutual consent, the

officiating person bids the bridegroom and the bride to join their right hands.

Then the bridegroom says after the officiating person, "I (name) take you (name) for my lawful wife to have and to hold from this day forward, for better, for worse, for richer or poorer, in sickness and in health, until death do us part."

The bride then says after the officiating person, "I, (name), take you (name) for my lawful husband, to have and to hold from this day forward, for better, for worse, for richer or poorer, in sickness and in health, until death do us part." With their hands still joined, the officiating person says, "I join you in matrimony."

Yes, that is one traditional ceremony, experienced by untold millions. But even a traditional ceremony is too often misunderstood. What does it all mean? Before you proceed any further in this text, I urge you to reread the words of that ceremony. Language is largely a subjective means of communication, and so each person has his own interpretation of the words *husband* and *wife*. Just what is your own interpretation of the two words? If your definition is significantly different, make note of it.

Now that you have defined *husband* and *wife*, let us look at a lexicographer's definition. *Webster's New Twentieth Century Unabridged Dictionary* defines the two words as follows:

> husband. 1. to become or act as husband of, to direct and manage with frugality, to use with economy; the male head of a household; one who directs the economy of a family. 2. a man joined to a woman by marriage. 3. a married man. 4. a manager of a household. 5. a male animal kept for breeding purposes (rare); ship's husband.
>
> wife. (woman) 1. a woman. 2. a married woman specifically a woman in relationship to her husband; the state, character, or condition of being a wife.

As you can see, the definitions are general, and your own interpretation is therefore very important. Every effort should be made for you and your mate to agree on just what a *husband* and *wife* are so that you will better be able to live up to your bargain. Until recently the wife's place was in the home. The husband worked while the wife's activities centered on raising children and making home life, as well as the home itself, into a work of art. In this respect, her role had not changed since Anglo-Saxon times. And in most countries her role still has not changed.

But now, in the United States, the wife, although bound by the same marriage contract as her ancestors signed, is nevertheless interpreting that document in a very different way. How many women forty years ago were expected to contribute to the family income? How many women participated in politics? The world of business was a man's world until recently.

It may be argued that a woman who spends four years in college and even several more in graduate school may not be content to be a homemaker exclusively. Her career might constitute her main interest in life. She may still choose to marry, and if she does, then her marriage would necessarily be different from that of a woman who merely works until she has a husband to support her. I myself maintain that not all wives should be expected to be the same. As long as each partner follows the marriage vows, then the actual interpretation of the words *husband* and *wife* has a range of definitions. One might argue that such words are like the "elastic clause" in the U.S. Constitution that allows congressmen to apply the meaning of the great document to modern times.

The word *husband* is hard to define. Only a few generations ago, the husband was *the* boss. Everyone expected him to rule with an iron hand and to have all of the respect, rights, and immunities that accrued to his rank. He routinely made the major decisions for the family without consulting his wife. He was, in most cases, expected to build his own home. He taught his sons their trade. He was a soldier also, ready to defend his family day and night.

That life-style significantly contrasts with today's prospective husband. Today's husband was probably raised by parents who had read a book on childcare that concentrated more on understanding children than on disciplining them. He went to a school where boys and girls were treated essentially as equals, and possibly was even embarrassed through much of his early life by having girls excel him academically.

Today's young man has been taught that he must rule the home with a helping hand rather than with an iron hand. He also knows that women have achieved political equality, and that the new interpretation of antidiscrimination laws is such that women are given equal opportunity in the world of business. Women's equality has obviously extended into marriage as well. In short, the power that his forefathers enjoyed by virtue of being born male is no more.

Furthermore, some generations ago, when a wife pledged to love, honor, and obey, both she and her husband knew that if she did not, it would be his privilege, even his duty, to beat her into recalling that pledge. Today's really good marriages are closer to being an equal partnership. Special equality means that there is a considerable overlapping of the roles of men and women. A husband is no longer considered the sole breadwinner; a woman is no longer considered the sole homemaker. The overlapping of roles is both typical and confusing. It is for these reasons that they should be understood and agreed upon as part of the marriage contract.

To Have and To Hold
I maintain that this expression means to stay together and to keep working at it. If, on the other hand, it means something else to you, please make note of it.

For Richer, for Poorer
At first glance, this would seem to mean that it is your duty to stick by your mate in times of economic adversity. However, experience has shown me that economic well-being is a two-edged sword. Economic prosperity is as great a threat to a happy union as is dire poverty. This is an obvious fact since the divorce rate has traditionally been higher among the more affluent than among those less privileged financially.

In Sickness and in Health
No one will question the morality of devoting oneself to a sick mate as long as the sickness is a physical one; however, people are not so loyal to a spouse who is emotionally ill. The reason is not so much that the healthy partner is unwilling to stick by the sick mate but that most people do not perceive emotional illness as a sickness.

Instead, many people misinterpret the symptoms to be basic personality traits, such as meanness, jealousy, irritability, paranoia, emotional instability, pessimism, irresponsibility, impatience, and countless others. (Sometimes it *is* just a personality trait and not illness at all. This is a different matter.) Since many mental illnesses are both treatable and usually curable if they are properly diagnosed, anyone who abandons an emotionally ill partner —ignorant of the true nature of the sickness or not—is as guilty of breaking the marriage contract as if abandoning a mate who was stricken with tuberculosis. Granted, some mental problems are overwhelming, and few people can cope with them gracefully. Nevertheless, it is the healthy mate's responsibility to seek help for the sick mate and to personally help in every way possible. Some realistic exceptions to this are conditions in which a couple are just not meant to be married. In such conditions, marriage simply contributes to the illness. Certain emotional disorders that cause a person to be decompensated when challenged with responsibility are examples of this.

For Better, for Worse

We all have our good and our bad days, and sometimes many of us have a long run of bad days—bad in disposition, bad in personal performance, bad in judgment, bad in luck; just plain bad, bad, bad, bad. Sometimes the bad days grow into bad weeks, bad months, or even bad years. For most of us, the pendulum will swing the other way, and life will indeed get better if we work on it with determination and good planning. It usually takes more than good luck to make them better. It takes hard work, a good plan, and patience, and an abundance of love. The most helpful asset in coping with bad times is a devoted faithful mate, one willing to forgive and tolerate mistakes. Understanding, forgiveness, and encouragement *better* a marriage. Ignorance, accusation, and mockery *worsen* a marriage. Introspection and faithful cooperation are the servants of marital success.

> *Let me not to the marriage of true minds*
> *Admit impediments; love is not love*
> *Which alters when it alteration finds.*
>
> —Shakespeare

Until Death Do Us Part

The implication of this commitment is obvious—it means until the couple is separated by the death of one partner. By current standards, however, many people have learned to interpret it as meaning until it is no longer convenient. This is probably the most important item of all for couples to agree upon when committing themselves to the marriage contract. If indeed they really mean "till death do us part," then the motivation to rectify problems as they arise is actually stronger than it would be if the contract were interpreted to mean that the commitment was valid only until it seems to be (temporarily) intolerable.

Marriage contracts are as different from one another as are a lease and a purchase agreement. It is not my purpose here to dictate to any couple as to what they must do with their lives and therefore to what type of marriage contract they must agree. I do, however, feel obliged to acknowledge that temporary contracts as outlined above are rarely successful since their permanence is constantly in question. The important thing is to understand the specific contract which you and your partner are agreeing to and live by it. If indeed it is predicated on a more temporary nature and seems not to be working out, it may be worth reconsidering and perhaps negotiating a new contract which may commit you to your marriage for life. Please comment on your own understanding on this matter and ask your mate to do the same.

I Now Pronounce You Man and Wife

The interpretation of this pronouncement depends on the interpretations of the vows already discussed. According to my traditional view, therefore, it means the surrender of individuality and privacy and the initiation of being half of one new entity. (On the abstract level, this new entity, marriage, is a whole that is greater than the sum of its parts, its partners.) It means that the two partners dedicate their minds and bodies to the pursuit of marital happiness. It also means complete sexual surrender; and overthrowing all sexual inhibitions for the sake of the partner. Each partner must become the foremost interest and responsibility of the other partner.

Once married, the order of responsibility in life changes. After ensuring one's own physical and mental well-being, *the mate comes before everyone else.* The reason is that if the marital partnership itself is in trouble, it is impossible, and out of order, to be a good parent or a good son or daughter.

Next, one's loyalty is to his or her children, for they are the flesh-and-blood result of the spiritual union of marriage. And even if every offspring could not be described so poetically, they nevertheless deserve no less than second place in the parents' order of responsibility. Should there be time and resources beyond what the partners themselves and their children require, then and only then can the couple think about helping their parents and other family members.

Please note what I have said: each partner must first ensure his own physical and mental well-being. Then he must direct his responsibility to the mate. After that, the responsibility is to the children. And after that, to parents, to other family members, and to friends. If, at any time, there is a conflict over where responsibility lies, one must recognize that it lies with that person who holds the higher rank in the order of responsibility.

I have acknowledged that every marriage is different, and each marital contract is different. People agree to different things as they accept the responsibilities of marriage; however, unless a prior understanding has been reached, the chain of responsibilities should be as outlined above. In evaluating one's own marital problems, it would be well to think about this point and realize that the contract calls for becoming man and wife; nothing is said about becoming son-in-law, daughter-in-law, brother-in-law, sister-in-law, or such.

Before continuing I would strongly advise you to discuss this chapter with your mate and possibly with one or two other couples. Comparing interpretations of the marriage contract could be very enlightening. It may also serve to answer any questions about the shortcomings of your own marriage, as well as give you insight into the shortcomings of other marriages. You might also make note of any special-agreement clauses, both spoken and unspoken, of your own marital contract—any that make your marriage different from the ones I have been discussing.

Be mindful of special situations, such as having agreed to have a sick parent live with you and become an integral part of your family; or possibly having realized in advance that one of you has an extremely demanding job and that your mate has been willing to settle for limited companionship. As a wife, you may possibly have a career that you intend to pursue, so there is an agreement to make some of the responsibilities of marriage secondary to your work. Children from a previous marriage could also be a factor.

These are just a few suggestions. I am sure that each of you has a list of provisions that were intended to be part of the marriage contract. It would be well to put them down now, so that you can consider them in evaluating your own situation. If your marriage is not working, it might be a good idea to analyze the rules by which you are functioning. If they are not currently satisfactory, consider renegotiating your contract and laying out a set of rules that might be mutually more satisfactory.

In summary, understand your own specific marital agreement and do your best to live by it!

·4·

The Wedding Day

Unquestionably, one of the most important days in anyone's life is the wedding day—the day when the magic transformation finally comes; the day when a person ceases to be an independent individual and becomes half of a marriage. Whether elaborate or modest, whether civil or religious, the wedding ceremony heralds the commencement of a new status in life for the bride and groom. It is a day, therefore, of great symbolic value. It is a day of significant transition for the parents as well. The wedding day traditionally is a day of jubilance and celebration; a holy day when the partners, in the presence of their family and friends, profess their love to each other and pledge the rest of their lives to each other. It is a day when family and friends have the opportunity to wish the new couple well and to get to know one another. It sounds as if it should be the happiest day in a person's life, and frequently it is.

When problems arise concerning the wedding day however they can be many, and their effects can be lifelong. Difficulties are usually centered on a few fundamental factors,

1. Acute anxieties that manifest themselves in all parties involved because of the personal, social, and financial magnitude of the event.

2. Ambivalence toward the event—sometimes on the part of the couple too. Habit makes most people very reluctant to undergo any sort of change.

3. The obvious pressures brought about by the changes that will affect the lives of everyone concerned from this day forth.

It is very easy for all parties to be so caught up with the problems of their own particular role that they lose sight of the problems of the other members involved.

The bride, for instance, is usually completely consumed by the pressures that have come from preparing herself for the day, as well as experiencing genuine stage fright over her part in the imminent ceremony. She is also pressured by the responsibility of seeing that family and friends are well attended to, taking care not to offend anyone. She is also obviously concerned with her honeymoon plans and ultimately plagued with concern over whether or not she has made the right choice for the rest of her life. The bride is also frequently troubled with the economic realities that come with preparing for the wedding, the honeymoon, and her future home. A great deal is expected of her; sometimes more than she can handle.

The groom's responsibilities and anxieties over the wedding day are basically the same as the bride's, with the additional problem that he is probably seeing his bride in a nervous state that exceeds what he ever thought she was capable of. She may very well be having difficulties in coping with her anxieties and preoccupations over minute details—all of which may seem insignificant to him.

The parents probably have the greatest number of problems on the wedding day. They are forced to accept the problems of their son or daughter along with the problems of the new son-in-law or daughter-in-law who may not have been their choice. They are usually put into the position of economic duress by the wedding itself, and they also may have the problem of coping with the cultural differences between themselves and their offspring's new in-laws. In addition, they can also be anxious over personal hardships that may ensue from the marriage, such as loss of their son's or daughter's income from their family budget, the loss of general help from the son or daughter, feelings of anxiety about the success of the marriage, and worry about the economic stability of the new young couple.

Not all wedding days are beset with all of these troubles; however, it is the exceptional wedding in which some of them are not present in one form or another. My purpose in outlining them is to bring them out into the open, so that each person can understand what the rest of the cast was going through during the scenario. With such understanding, it may make it ever so much easier to accept and forgive the behavior of everyone concerned on the wedding day. Unfortunately, most people are so blinded by their own concerns on that day that they never really do quite understand the feelings of the other people and often spend a lifetime resenting behavior and indiscretions that occurred. This may sound like an exaggeration, but I have seen it over and over again. A daughter-in-law, for instance, will develop a lifelong resentment toward her mother-in-law because of an indiscretion that occurred on the wedding day. And the daughter-in-law may never take the time to appreciate the hardships that the mother-in-law herself was enduring on that same day.

If your own wedding day was less than perfect, this is obviously not abnormal. If it has marred your marriage in any way, I urge you to reconsider the day and attempt to look at it through the eyes of everyone concerned to determine if you might not be able to resolve the differences. You might also consider writing some comments about your own wedding experiences and adding them to the text. If you do so, you may find that the next time you read it, it will be far more meaningful to you. It may also help when it comes your turn to be a parent on your own child's wedding day.

·5·

Honeymoon, Sexual Adjustment, and Family Planning

One of the most joyous times of a married couple's life should certainly be their honeymoon. This is the time when lovers are finally alone together, and all of the barriers that separated them before are removed forever. They have saved their money and vacation time, gathered their very best things, and have hastened off together to devote all their time and attention to each other. There are no more "no-no's," no more deadlines, no more explanations to anyone. Even all the anxieties and concerns of the wedding day are behind them. What indeed could be more Eden-like? And by and large, honeymoons are just that.

Most couples find that even their greatest expectations about honeymoon happiness and marriage have been transcended. They find in each other a fun-loving closeness, crowned by their sexual freedom, which excels even their wildest dreams. Early sexual adjustment too, if they are lucky enough to have it work out from the beginning, brings with it a form of peace and satisfaction; a release of pent-up tension that too many people have never experienced. (As a matter of fact, most of us who have had substantial training in interpersonal relations, and can judge people's feelings by their expressions, can pick out a happy honeymooning couple in any crowded resort. They virtually seem to glow with happiness and a look of peaceful contentment.)

When honeymoon problems do arise, however, they are extremely sad. Frequently, they are the result of neglect and poor preparation. Most problems fall into the following categories:

1. It is frequently the first full-time exposure to the habits and

shortcomings of each other, and it becomes obvious that these shortcomings are more difficult to tolerate on a twenty-four-hour a day basis than they were on intermittent dates.

2. It is frequently the first time one or both partners are required to surrender all privacy. Most people enjoy some degree of privacy and may soon resent the constant presence of another person regardless of how strong the love attraction may be.

3. Homesickness is a problem with many people of all ages. The insecurity and challenges of the honeymoon are panic producing and can ruin what should be an ecstatic time of life.

4. Disappointment in the reliability, attention, and compassion of the new mate. For many couples, this is the first time that they are completely dependent on each other, and the assumption of this responsibility is not always gracefully handled.

Sexual Adjustment

Obviously, proper sexual adjustment is a prerequisite to a happy honeymoon. Proper sexual preparation, preferably under the guidance of a family doctor, is extremely helpful in guiding the young couple to a successful adjustment.

I should like to review briefly the preparation that I offer young couples in my particular family practice. The first thing that must be realized by a couple approaching the time of their honeymoon is that any sexual act which brings *mutual* satisfaction is morally and socially acceptable. Mind you, I said anything that is acceptable to *both* partners. If any act of one partner is distasteful to the other partner, it is obviously not to be forced. Whenever such problems arise, the couple must discuss them until they achieve a mutual agreement. If they cannot agree, a discussion with a third party, preferably the family physician, would certainly be in order.

It is natural, socially acceptable, and, as a matter of fact, advisable for the husband to have complete freedom of his wife's body and for a wife to have complete freedom of her husband's body. The husband should feel comfortable in stroking and fondling his wife's breasts and clitoris, and in making love to her in any way that she finds stimulating. For her part, the wife should feel completely free to assume the initiative and pet anytime she sees fit to do so. Her husband's body is hers as much as her body is his. Both partners, though, should realize that the male and female receive sexual stimulation in different ways.

The feeling of being loved and coveted by the mate is the primary stimulus for both partners. The male, however, is driven very strongly by the physical experience of orgasm, which becomes, after a certain point of stimulation, a nearly uncontrollable desire. And this desire will go to completion (in many) regardless of his personal wishes for self-control at that time. This is predictable because most males, even in early puberty, have sexually stimulating dreams, dreams that precipitate ejaculation and, for all intents and purposes, the physical satisfactions of the entire sex act. Note that this occurs with no sensual stimulation nor even physical presence of a female. It is a sex act contained and completed only in the mind of the male.

For the woman, though, it is usually quite different. The woman has physical desires for her husband, but she most often associates these desires with her overall desires for security, affection, protection, passion, warmth, and safety—all in her husband's arms. The woman also yearns for the ultimate feeling of femininity, namely the feeling of being able to give satisfaction to her husband and to herself; moreover, the man's identification of virility with masculinity begins during the honeymoon and usually becomes stronger later.

It is obvious from even the short discussion above that sexual stimulation is far more complicated for the female than it is for the male, and so it takes her a little more time to adjust, at least in the beginning. The male's readiness for the sex act is obvious. The penis becomes erect, enlarged, and firm. And the male's behavior indicates he is completely on edge and overcome by the stimulation. The female, however, does not always display her readiness in so obvious a manner. Her stimulation is manifested by a feeling of warmth and thrilling chills as her nerve centers and nipples and clitoris are stimulated by her husband's love play. Then she has a craving for her husband to commence the sex act.

A very important sign of her readiness is when the lubricating glands about the vagina begin to secrete, and the vagina becomes moist and well-lubricated. This is nature's way of assuring that the entrance of the penis into the vagina is a smooth and slippery one. Without adequate lubrication, the entry of the penis into the vagina and the friction from the in-and-out excursions of the penis through the vulva can actually be very painful. As a result, the female finds herself pushing her husband away, out of a natural protective instinct. This is extremely distressing because the husband himself is in the phase of uncontrollable stimulation at the time. If he does not understand what is happening, he feels rejected. Simultaneously, the wife feels guilty and loses self-confidence and is inclined to consider herself frigid. And here indeed is a couple in a great deal of trouble at the very beginning of their marriage.

Along with the understanding of these aspects of the sex act, it is equally important to know that the virginal female on occasion has a very small hymenal opening through which the penis must pass. This opening will gradually stretch and enlarge as she becomes accustomed to a full marital life. In the beginning, however, this stretching often hurts, and the first sexual experience for a virgin bride is frequently unpleasant. (The first sexual experience for many women, however, is perfect.) The sexual urge in the female, regardless of how strong it is, cannot neutralize the pain experienced by the forceful stretching of the hymenal ring. What a horrible experience it is for both members of the partnership to finally reach the promised land of happiness, only to find pain and disappointment.

Actually, there is little excuse for this. The premarital physical examination by the family physician, if the bride-to-be has the good judgment to submit to one, would reveal such a stricture, and the physical examination in itself should suffice to stretch the hymenal ring enough so that a pleasant sexual experience would result on the first honeymoon night. If not, a simple incision under local anaesthesia would solve the problem in an easy, painless way.

Another common cause of sexual disappointment on the honeymoon is that the male frequently becomes stimulated to the point of uncontrollable ejaculation (premature ejaculation) long before the female is ready. One must remember that the male by instinct is a sexually ready individual at most times whereas the virgin female is trained from early childhood to protect her chastity and have sexual inhibitions. In many cases, in the past girls were taught that sexual relations, although a necessary marital duty, fall into the category of being dirty or somewhat disgraceful. Compound this, if you will, with the scientific fact that the duration of time required to sexually stimulate a male to the point of ejaculation is inversely proportionate to the frequency with which he has ejaculation. This simply means that the more often a man has relations, the more time it will take him to reach the point of readiness. For instance, any male who has gone a long, long time between ejaculations will have an extremely difficult time holding back during the sexual foreplay his partner requires.

The situation with the female is precisely the opposite. The first time she ever copulates is the most difficult for her because she must train herself to let go although she has all the problems of readiness that have been discussed above. Once she has overcome these barriers, however, and has had several satisfactory sexual experiences, she is far more ready and far more easily stimulated. At this point, the marital partnership tends to gravitate to some sort of equilibrium. But unless a couple understands all of this well in advance, it is predictable that they would be vulnerable to many frustrating disappointments—some of which could damage the marriage for a lifetime.

A young couple came into my office several years ago and related a very sad story. They had been married for six weeks, but the wife had been completely unable to receive her husband because of the excrutiating pain which resulted every time they attempted intercourse. From the onset of the marriage until their visit with me, they had submitted themselves to a great deal of introspection. The wife was convinced that the problem resulted from her strict upbringing, wherein all mention of sex was completely forbidden. She had been told that premarital sex was sinful, that extreme modesty was the order of the day, and that any deviation from that way of thinking was an absolute disgrace. As she reflected on her current plight, she was sure that she had a mental block against readjusting her thinking to that of a married woman. She added, in support of her theory, that she had had endless preparations as a young girl on how to avoid sexual stimulation but that no one had ever uttered a single word of reassurance to her that sexual stimulation after marriage was both a beautiful thing and part of the very foundation of a good marriage. She went on to say that at one time she had regarded sexual contact as being extremely distasteful, and, as one of her elders had told her, that "nice girls don't enjoy it."

Fortunately, she had done enough reading to be assured that nice girls do enjoy it and that nice girls should enjoy it. They could conceivably enjoy it even more because they are capable of expressing more meaningful love and receiving more meaningful expressions of love from their true mates than are their promiscuous female counterparts.

The husband had a reasonably good attitude toward the situation. He was patient and tolerant, and said that he had read that some women are basically frigid and incapable of sex (incidentally, this is completely erroneous), but he loved his wife so much that if they could *never* have relations, he would be willing to remain married to her and to love her for her many other fine attributes. He made a very sincere statement for which one could not help but have great respect, namely, that in their marriage contract he had agreed to take his wife, to have and to hold, in sickness and in health; and if this problem proved to be everlasting, it was a form of sickness that he was willing to accept and adjust to.

Both of these young people were college graduates, extremely intelligent, and very much in love. They had assessed their problems very realistically and commendably. The happy outcome was that my simple physical examination revealed the young lady to have a marked stricture of her vaginal opening, which was firm and rigid to the point where the diameter was too small to admit the thickness of a pencil let alone the thickness of a rigid penis. It was much too tight to ever be stretched by natural sexual activity. A very simple incision under local anaesthesia in the office solved the problem and permitted them to carry on a normal sexual life thereafter.

It is worthwhile to note, however, that all of the other factors that they had considered could have caused the same problem they were experiencing. Their resolution of these many hang-ups was also quite necessary for them to be able to establish good sexual adjustment, which fortunately they did.

A simple examination prior to marriage could have saved them a great deal of grief. A visit to the family doctor's office could have also given them information on solving other, less serious problems. For instance, the doctor should advise a young couple that in their first several attempts at intercourse they could expect the wife to lack adequate vaginal lubrication and that a good water-soluble jelly, such as KY Jelly or Lubritene would be a very handy item to take along on the honeymoon.

Much has been written, especially in the Orient, about the various positions in which the sex act is performed. I really do not intend to get into an extended description of these at this time because I really don't think that a description of exact positions is of any value to anyone. Suffice to say that *any* position that permits the entry of the penis into the vagina without discomfort to either partner is acceptable as long as the penis strokes over the clitoris or the clitoral area during the sex act. The stroking of the penis over the clitoral area is extremely important because most of the actual sensual stimulation to the female arises from the manipulation of the clitoris, not by the vagina being occupied by the penis. An attempt at establishing variations in technique is wise but not essential.

Women who have been married for as long as forty years, and who have given birth to as many as six children, have told me that they have never known of the presence of the clitoris at all. And so they have gone through an entire married lifetime without ever having experienced a real orgasm. This is indeed sad. The clitoris is a small, pea-sized prominence situated where the small lips of the vulva meet in the front. It is not a markedly prominent organ; however, the nerve centers in it are anatomically similar to those of the head of the male's penis. Any woman who doubts that she is getting adequate stimulation in the sexual foreplay would do well to explore her own anatomy and ascertain that she knows the place of the clitoris; then she can guide her husband to it. A husband should make himself aware of the location of his wife's clitoris and stimulate it during the foreplay.

The coital position that puts the woman above the man is of value during pregnancy and also helpful in cases where the wife suffers from claustrophobia. It also serves to reassure the husband that love-making is not 100 percent his idea. An expression of aggressiveness on the part of the wife frequently does a great deal to reassure him that she also gets satisfaction and pleasure. Any position, as I have said, is satisfactory as long as it brings mutual satisfaction.

One of the most commonly asked questions, without common answers, is how often do married people have intercourse? This varies with the age of the couple, the length of time they have been married, how much privacy they have, what their habits and work schedules are, and their general physical and mental health. Newlyweds frequently tell of having intercourse daily, and some have it more than once a day. However, once the initial honeymoon is over, an authoritative survey of the question shows that couples in their twenties have intercourse an average of three times weekly, twice weekly in their thirties, and once weekly in their forties. There are no accurate statistics on those who are fifty and over. Some people say, though, that they have relations twice weekly for the balance of their marital life. Most, however, are not able to perform that often and reduce their frequency to approximately once every other week or less. Many factors play a part in this, and it can truly be said that no two couples are alike, nor should they be expected to be.

There is no such thing as having intercourse too often. The only physically limiting factor is the ability of the male to perform, which brings us to the subject of male impotence. *Male impotence* is a situation in which the male has difficulty in developing and maintaining erection and performing the sex act with his wife. The common reasons for this are

1. Excessive use of alcohol. (The older the man, the less alcohol he can consume and still perform sexually.)

2. Physical illness—many are capable of producing this symptom.

3. Fatigue.

4. Medications—many are capable of causing impotence.

5. Commonly used street drugs, such as marijuana and other narcotics.

6. Emotional upset, depression, anxiety, and fear of impregnating his wife.

7. Excessive sexual performance. (Capacity decreases as age increases.)

8. Obesity.

9. Lack of interest in one's mate. Lack of attractiveness, hostility, guilt, and lack of respect can all be contributing factors.

Regardless of the apparent cause, the symptom of impotence warrants a visit to the family physician and a complete checkup to rule out significant illness.

Family Planning and Birth Control

A mutual agreement on family planning is also an absolute essential in preparation for the honeymoon. It would be impossible to overemphasize the importance of mutual agreement on the size and timing of a family. Religious, personal, and socioeconomic variations, of course, will determine each particular couple's preference. It is not my purpose to tell couples how many children they should have or when they should have them; however, it is my express purpose to review the various forms of contraception, so that they can approach family planning with a full awareness of the facts.

There are ten basic methods of birth control:

1. Withdrawal of the penis prior to ejaculation.

2. Douching after intercourse.

3. Rhythm.

4. Rubber condoms.

5. Diaphragms.

6. Jellies, creams, foams, and capsule or tablet inserts.

7. Intrauterine devices (IUD's).

8. Hormonal prevention of ovulation by so-called birth-control pills.

9. Vasectomy of the male.

10. Surgical sterilization of the female.

Withdrawal prior to ejaculation (called *onanism* and practiced even today by certain religious groups) is the worst method of all. It is completely unreliable and is frustrating to both partners. It is absolutely not recommended.

One of the earliest forms of birth control, and one that is fairly successful, is *postcoital douching* with vinegar and water, or plain water, or one of the many commercial solutions. The method is quite simple, inasmuch as the woman merely floods her vagina to wash out the semen. If it is performed immediately following coitus, one could be approximately 90 percent sure that enough of the sperm would have been washed away to sufficiently protect against pregnancy. Studies have shown that the number of sperm necessary to make a seminal fluid strong enough to reliably produce pregnancy is approximately 60 million sperm per cc. The average volume of seminal fluid ejaculated with each orgasm is 5 cc. This means that approximately 300 million sperm are present with each ejaculation. Nature's purpose in producing such high numbers is to have them run interference, as it were, for the one single sperm that is destined to fertilize the ovum (egg). It is easily understandable that if a total of 300 million sperm in an ejaculation are required to reliably fertilize an egg, that if you were to wash out a substantial number of them, pregnancy would be prevented. The vagina is a closed pouch, however, and it really takes only one sperm to reach its target and cause conception; therefore, douching is far from being a completely reliable method. This, coupled with the fact that it is both unromantic and unfeeling to jump out of bed and into the bathroom, makes postcoital douching somewhat distasteful.

The so-called *rhythm method* of birth control is a time-honored one accepted by most religious groups that object to all artificial methods of contraception. Volumes have been written in an effort to explain the rhythm method; however, it is really quite simple to understand. It is based entirely on avoiding coitus at the time of ovulation. This is the time when the ovum is produced by the ovary and popped off into the fallopian tubes. From this moment, the woman is fertile for approximately twenty-four hours. This date is most reliably predicted by subtracting fourteen days from the next expected menstrual period; in other words, fourteen days prior to the onset of the next expected menstrual period. For example, if a woman is due to commence menstruation on the twenty-eighth of the month, she would be reasonable in guessing that her date of ovulation would be the fourteenth of the same month. There are, however, three major pitfalls in this system. First, the date of the next expected menstrual period is not always reliably predictable because most women are irregular at one time or another in their menstrual history. So, if it were an irregular time, the calculated date of ovulation would be wrong. For this reason, it would be wise to abstain for three days *both before and after* the predicted date. The second pitfall of the rhythm system is that sperm life is unpredictable. It is generally accepted that a sperm remains viable for an approximate period of forty-eight hours after being deposited in the vagina; however, there are exceptions to that rule, for records show that some sperm have lived considerably beyond that length of time. Therefore, one should abstain from sexual relations at least three or four days prior to ovulation to compensate for this possibility.

In summary, this means that to be safe, a couple should refrain from having intercourse three days prior to ovulation and three or four days after ovulation. Now when we tabulate all of that we come to the conclusion that the conception period, if there is one, would be approximately eleven to seventeen days prior to the next expected menstrual period. Abstinence from relations, therefore, is recommended for those six or seven days if pregnancy is to be prevented.

Actually there are some more specific methods for determining the exact day of ovulation. For instance, the keeping of a basal temperature chart as well as some tapes that measure reducing substances (sugarlike substances) in the vaginal lining will denote the exact time of ovulation. These tests, however, are of more help in fertility problems, that is to say, in determining the date of ovulation for the purpose of causing a pregnancy. Once the date of ovulation has been established, it is already two to three days too late to avoid pregnancy.

The third disadvantage to the rhythm method is that when husband and wife are engaged in love-making, it is quite inopportune—and almost laughable—to pause and refer to accounting and tabulation of dates and the status of fertility. Actually, one of the main causes of failure of this method is that people are quite unreliable in keeping records and even more unreliable in paying attention to them. Shakespeare said, "Nature must obey necessity," and couples seem to eagerly agree.

A simple and fairly reliable method of contraception is the *condom,* which is simply a sheath, most commonly made of thin balloonlike rubber. This sheath fits over the penis, receives the semen, and prevents its entry into the vagina. Condoms come in various degrees of sophistication. Some are completely plain and fit tightly over the penis; others are similar but are packed in a lubrication; and still others have a pouch to receive the seminal fluid without causing a spillback onto the head of the penis.

Although its effectiveness is fairly reliable, there are certain disadvantages to the use of a condom. Some couples find it romantically repugnant because foreplay must be interrupted to apply it. The male experiences reduced sensory effect because of the rubber barrier. The reliability of the condom may be lessened by being defective: that is, it already may have a perforation prior to use, or, it may accidentally be perforated while applying it or using it. Finally, the condom may actually in some cases slip off the penis and spill the seminal fluid into the vagina. Fears about such problems are common; however, the occurrence of accidents is quite rare.

The *diaphragm* is an intravaginal device that incorporates a springlike ring upon which a flat piece of rubber is suspended. The diaphragm is inserted into the vagina and serves to cap the cervix (mouth of the womb or the channel through which sperm must enter on their pathway to the uterus and fallopian tubes). This is a somewhat unreliable method with a failure rate of approximately 7 percent. It has, however, been accepted by many women over the years in spite of its disadvantages. In addition to its high failure rate, there is a basic objection to having the foreign body in the vagina, which in some instances causes discomfort as well as hygienic difficulties. The diaphragm is not as popular now as it used to be because of the availability of other more reliable and less cumbersome devices.

There are currently a wide variety of *creams, jellies, tablets, suppositories, capsules,* and *foams* with contraceptive properties; they chemically immobilize the sperm. Their packaging varies although their principle is basically the same. They usually come with insert tubes with a plunger, so that the material is deposited directly into the vaginal vault; this is done just before intercourse. The rate of effectiveness of these items is reported to be higher than 95 percent. They have been used for many years with a fair bit of satisfaction.

Their disadvantages include, like in the use of the condom, interrupting love play to go through the fairly complicated procedure of inserting the material. Unless, of course, the female anticipates that coitus will subsequently take place and uses the device in advance—although the material should be inserted no longer than one hour prior to intercourse. Also, some females find these items irritating to the vulva and vagina; and they should not be washed out of the vagina for at least ten hours after coitus. This means that if the woman attempts to carry on her usual chores before douching, she will find that she has a rather heavy discharge of seminal fluid and cream or jelly running from her vagina, for which she will probably be forced to wear a pad.

Intrauterine devices (IUD's) are simply plastic or metal coil inserts which the physician places into the uterus through the cervix. This is done in the physician's office in a routine visit. It is rather easily done and would seem to be an ideal method of contraception since there is no need to take systemic medication, no interruption of foreplay, and no record keeping.

The disadvantages of the IUD are: (1.) Sometimes the female spontaneously expels the device. (2.) There is a failure rate of approximately 5 percent, even with the intrauterine device in place. (3.) Bleeding can occur between periods as a result of the IUD. (4.) The device represents a threat to an established pregnancy. (5.) The device cannot be used by women who have never borne a child. (6.) There is some genuine uncertainty about the way the device achieves contraception. One suggestion is that it works by creating a spontaneous abortion of an otherwise viable pregnancy at the time of the anticipated menstrual period. If indeed this is so, it raises the moral questions about abortion.

The most common method of contraception now in use is the *birth control pill*, which uses hormones to suppress ovulation. Of all the methods currently used, the "pill" is by far the most reliable. It has been said that if the woman is faithful in taking her medicine as prescribed, its effectiveness against pregnancy is 100 percent. And "the pill" has the advantage of not interrupting love play.

Aside from the expense of the medication, about $5.00 per month, the only real disadvantages are potential side effects, which occur in approximately 15 percent of women. Fortunately, the other 85 percent take the pills without any recognizable discomfort or hardship. The potential side effects are as follows: (1.) Nausea, particularly if taken on an empty stomach. (2.) Weight gain, as a result of fluid retention; much the same type that a woman experiences prior to menstruation. (3.) Nervousness, irritability, and depression. (4.) A slightly increased statistical chance of contracting certain types of malignant diseases (of the uterus and breasts). (5.) A predisposition to phlebitis in women who are already prone to this condition. Women with varicose veins are usually advised against taking this type of medication. (6.) Recent statistics have strongly suggested an increase in coronary heart disease in women over forty who take the "pill." There has also been a suggestion of increased tendency toward strokes in women who have taken birth control pills for a long time. Under the guidance of a conscientious physician, the side effects, even subtle side effects, usually can be prevented or controlled to some degree.

Tubal ligation is a surgical procedure, in which the female is made permanently sterile by cutting and tying the fallopian tubes (the tubes through which the egg must pass to get from the ovary to the uterus). The procedure, which is relatively safe, usually requires one to three days in the hospital. The great disadvantage is that it carries the risk of anesthesia and abdominal surgery, and it is not a reversible procedure. Once it is done, it cannot later be corrected. The woman is sterile for life—if she were to lose her children or have occasion later in life to remarry and crave children with a new husband, she may be very sorry she ever underwent the procedure. This is rare, but it does happen. Other surgical procedures, such as removal of the uterus or ovaries also render a woman permanently sterile.

Vasectomy for the male is a surgical procedure (usually performed in the physician's office), which renders the male sterile by cutting and obstructing the vas—a tube responsible for the delivery of the sperm. This is simple surgery with few side effects. The disadvantages are occasional residual tenderness that can persist for a long time, and that it too is an irreversible procedure. Also, it is sometimes ineffective and pregnancy can still take place.

I have discussed sexual adjustment and family planning at some length, and have endeavored, moreover, to present the matter in such a way as to give newlyweds a foundation for making the necessary adjustments and decisions of early marriage. It has always seemed ironic to me that sex has become the paramount topic of discussion in the lay press, magazines, television, and movies; yet despite all that is written about it, the American society as a whole is grossly misinformed about sex. In its factual aspects, it is a sadly neglected subject. If, after reading this chapter, you still have questions, I would heartily urge you to consult your family physician. In most cases questions about sexuality have exact answers. Do not attempt to participate in one of the most important aspects of life without really knowing what it is all about. If you have problems, admit them and work toward resolving them. Because the sexual satisfaction of mature individuals is an essential, a person who is denied adequate satisfaction is going to resent that denial, sometimes bitterly. This is so with males and females alike. Sexual satisfaction is not merely one of the building blocks of marriage, but rather the mortar which holds those blocks together and fills in for some of the missing ones.

I am put in mind of one troubled woman who loved her husband very much and was convinced that he also loved her very much. They had a problem of sexual incompatibility, however, based on her own unresolved sexual inhibitions, ones that she was extremely reluctant to correct. When I advised her that she could not hide from the obligation of solving her problem, she resisted and asked in a pathetic tone, "But, Doctor, isn't there some other way that I can express my love to him equally?" And she went on to say, "I try to bake his favorite cakes, keep his house in the best way I know how, and flatter him at every turn, and I have a job to help with expenses. Is this not enough? What's so important about sexual satisfaction that makes it such a basic essential?" She posed a good question and was totally sincere about it. My answer was that sex is a basic human urge, one that is in the same category as are hunger, thirst, and sleep.

Her husband, when I saw him privately, was to confirm my explanation. He said, "Yes, I know her problem, and I can fully appreciate how hard she tries to overcome it by offering me all these substitutes. But when you look at it realistically, I can buy my favorite cake for $5.00; I can hire someone to clean the house for $3.00 an hour, and I receive flattery from everyone I meet who is trying to sell me something or impress me. If that is all there would be to marriage, I would have spared myself the aggravation of all the other responsibilities attached to it." He was right. A mate, after all, is quite different from a housekeeper and also different from a best friend. For that matter a mate is different from a mistress, who is a sexual companion *only*. The mutual sexual surrender in marriage is based on love and is the main factor that makes marital sexuality different. Fortunately, this couple was understanding and worked toward a solution to their problem and enriched their lives manifoldly.

Be honest with your physician when you go for premarital counseling and admit your concerns and inadequacies. There is no way that a doctor can be sure of what you know and what you do not know unless your approach with him is candid and even somewhat aggressive. You might even consider writing out a list of questions prior to your visit, so that all of your concerns might be clarified.

Several years ago a young couple came to me for premarital counseling three weeks before their wedding. I spent a good half hour with them, covering what I thought to be every necessary aspect of sex education. At the end of the session they graciously thanked me for my time and interest and I wished them well with their wedding and marriage.

The day before the scheduled wedding I received a frantic telephone call from the young bride-to-be, asking if I could see her immediately because she had some serious problems that required my help. I agreed of course, and she presented herself at the office thirty minutes later. Full of anxiety, she entered my consultation room. "Whatever is the matter?" I asked. "Has something gone wrong?" "Oh, no, not at all," she replied, "except that I was too embarrassed to ask you when I was here with my fiancé. But I just must know—where do you put it, and what do you do with it when you get it there?"

I'll not pretend that I was able to hide my amusement, but the young lady was dead serious. "Did you not really understand my explanations of the anatomy and physiology?" I asked. "I guess I did to an extent," she replied, "but all those pictures and diagrams somehow just didn't seem to answer the question." To say the least, my answer to her this time was put in very simplistic terms; and it must have served the purpose well because it is now five years later, and they are enjoying their three beautiful children.

Again, I beg of you, please do not hesitate to ask your physician specific questions about sexual matters regardless of how simple or embarrassing they might be. It is even more simple and more embarrassing not to know the answers.

At this point, I suggest that you supplement my own discussions about the honeymoon, sexual adjustment, and family planning by adding your own experiences. Note any major unresolved problems that persist in your own marriage. Your notes, added to mine, might well serve as a basis for the diagnosis and solution of any marital problems of your own.

By the way, if your honeymoon was a disappointment, don't be discouraged. There is always time for another, and another, and another. . . .

·6·
Early Marriage Until the First Pregnancy

Early marriage, from the end of the honeymoon until the commencement of the first pregnancy, is a very, very special time of life. Obviously, the time period varies a great deal from couple to couple because of specific situations. (For couples who remain childless, this phase will exist for the remainder of the marriage.) However long or short it may be, it is a time when the couple can enjoy a degree of freedom that they will not experience again for many years to come. It is a time when they come to share household responsibilities; and develop new adult skills, such as cooking, and homemaking, and decorating. It is a time when—if they choose to—they can simply drop everything and go out to play together. For most, it is a happy, trouble-free time of life, which is for all intents and purposes a delightful extension of the honeymoon. Everything is new; everything is easy. Ideally, the bonds of marriage solidify and strengthen, and interdependence increases.

There are some pitfalls however. And these are usually caused by changing one's image from that of a separate individual to that of one half of a team. In early marriage, people have difficulties giving up some of their premarital social activities. Young men only gradually learn to give up their nights of athletic activities, club activities, and social drinking with their buddies, without resentment. Women only gradually learn to give up their relationships with single girl friends, whose interests are conspicuously different from those of married women. Resolving these differences is usually not too terribly difficult because people soon find that they cannot cling to the things of the past. They become more future-oriented.

Moreover, their single friends usually become married themselves, and they are no longer the same people they were either. Even though many will sing choruses of "That Old Gang of Mine," the truth of the matter is that when that old gang gets together, things are really quite different. If indeed the marriage has the fascination that most young marriages do, single activities become less and less attractive.

The primary exception to this predictable change is the marriage in which one partner was reluctant to marry in the first place and only did so after the enthusiastic partner promised that there would be many concessions, and that it was not really expected that they would be 100 percent devoted. A similar case would be that of, say, a reluctant girl who may be willing to accept her boyfriend for a husband although she sees many faults in him. She secretly, of course, plans to train him to suit herself after the magic words are said at the altar. Such a new wife frequently finds that the young man does not respond so easily to training, and on his part feels that he has been sold a bill of goods, which he does not accept gracefully.

When problems of this nature arise, it is well to look back at your own particular marriage contract and ask yourself just what promises were expressed or implied in this area. It is true that if less was pledged than what is now expected, problems will arise that may require renegotiating some parts of the contract.

The other major problem of early marriage is that the young mates frequently find themselves disappointed with each other. They have a tendency to compare the new mate to their parent of the opposite sex and be somewhat disappointed at the results. For instance, many a young man assumes that it is natural for a woman to know how to cook, to keep house, and to be organized at every domestic task. After all, his mother was. He might, on occasion, have the poor judgment to remind his wife of this fact. The wife, on the other hand, might find herself taken aback and disappointed to learn that her husband, who had always seemed so masculine, is not able to do some of the things that were second nature to her father—for example, replacing broken windows, fixing leaky faucets, repairing electrical appliances, or seeing to it that all the bills are paid. If she voices her disappointment to her husband, it can often cause resentment—resentment that can leave deep and permanent scars.

This is a potentially explosive area. It should be acknowledged as such and handled very carefully. If there are disappointments, they should be discussed openly before such odious comparisons are made. It is a time when mates need each other's help and understanding, not criticism. Otherwise, the situation can grow so bad that out of embarrassment and frustration, the mates can have a strong urge to just give up on the marriage.

This is also the very time when people come to the shocking reality that marriage is really for better or for worse, that many of the exasperating shortcomings of their mates are for keeps. Indeed, many basic character and personality traits are virtually impossible to change, and one must reconcile oneself to this fact. This is not always easy. It is infinitely easier to tolerate someone's bothersome habit for a three- or four-hour date than it is for twenty-four hours a day, seven days a week.

When couples realize that certain habits are forever, it seems to be their natural inclination to go to their parents and complain about their new mates. At this point, it is frequently very tempting for the parents to take the part of their own son or daughter and become hostile toward the mate. This action, though, simply serves to throw fuel on the fire rather than to offer any real constructive solution to the problem. Moreover, opening a discourse with the parents brings in-laws into the fight as well—all of which makes it harder and harder for the couple to concentrate on the real problem and set about resolving it. Also, it is typical for parents to take the problems of their newlywed offspring more seriously than does the couple itself. Often the couple must reject the parents in order to make up.

The golden rule in solving problems of this type is that if you cannot resolve them on your own, do not solicit help from a friend or a relative, but from a qualified third party. The family physician is the first one to consult. You must be willing to follow his advice with the same trust that you would have in taking any of his prescribed medicines. It has been observed many times that lovers forgive and forget, and go home to live happily ever after, yet the family member to whom they told their problems may carry the memory of the injustices in his mind forever.

An unbreakable rule for newlyweds is that they must *never speak derogatorily about the mate to any outside person* unless of course it is to a professional helper.

With the sophisticated birth-control methods available today, most couples attempt to resolve their early problems and develop some degree of maturity together before attempting to have children. All too often, however, they procrastinate so long that they become too old to have children.

In my opinion, it is nearly impossible to progress to a point of complete unselfish maturity until one experiences the challenges and satisfactions of parenthood. The present socioeconomic climate is indeed a difficult one in which to consider having children; particularly when one considers the necessity for two incomes for the maintenance of the standard of life to which most people are accustomed. Even the community planning for many urban communities seems to be planned with the assumption that there will be no children in many apartment and condominium complexes.

I urge you, however, to plan to have children as soon as it is in any way practical—if you plan to have them at all. The sooner you have them, the more you will be able to enjoy them with your youthful enthusiasm. It is certainly worth the sacrifice, both for the pleasure of having them and the security of having them to help you in the years to come. Likewise, the couple who has their children early enough will not be saddled with the economic responsibilities of children in their advancing years.

This is not always controllable, however, and things have a way of working out well whenever children come if you approach the challenge with a good plan and a positive attitude.

·7·
The Subject of Children

No text on marriage could be complete without mention of children and their rearing. Children, after all, are the foremost project upon which the partners of marriage collaborate. Since this is, however, a text on marriage, and the subject of child rearing is a subject that requires a full-length text of its own, I shall limit my comments to a few handy tips that I hope will serve you well.

Children are children—not miniature adults, and as such, they thrive on love, attention, teaching, discipline, respect, and understanding. For parents to be able to impart all of these, they must have a mature approach to parenthood, one in which the magnitude of the task is understood and accepted with enthusiasm. It requires time and selflessness. It requires love and willingness to express it without reservation. Parents who possess these qualities and are willing to give of themselves without reservation will be rewarded with children who love and respect them and make their sacrifices worthwhile. The following list of rules should make the job easier:

1. *Always make your child feel loved.* It is true that you may not always like him, for children indeed are not always likable, but never give your child the insecurity of not knowing that he is always loved no matter what he does.

2. *Be consistent.* Consistency with regard to the rules that a child must follow is an absolute must. Both parents, and for that matter, all adults in authority over children, should maintain the same rules by which a child is expected to behave. If the parents disagree on what those rules should be, it is impossible for the child to conform to them without a great deal of confusion.

3. *Insist on respect and performance.* Parents who attempt to buy their

children's affection by compromising the necessity for them to demonstrate respect or to perform as they are expected to will invariably end up with uncontrollable and confused offspring. Even though children will resist conformity, it has been my experience that those who are forced to obey the rules and forced to extend respect to authority end up as the best achievers and, ultimately, the happier people. Likewise, their parents are rewarded with respectful, successful children who make the whole project worthwhile.

4. *Establish a code of firmness with understanding.* Firmness has been discussed above. Understanding speaks for itself. Whenever the children have difficulty performing whatever the task may be, try to understand why they are having difficulty and help them with it toward a successful end. I am sure you will find that this is a much better approach than its two alternatives, which are, (A.) Forcing them to feel like failures, and (B.) Excusing all indiscretions with automatic forgiveness.

5. *Never yield to your children's peer pressure.* Each family must have its own set of rules and stick by them. The fact that everyone else is doing it does not make it right. The sooner children understand that, the happier the entire family will be. If you yield to the form of reasoning that is based on "If the neighbors can do it, why can't I?" you will find that the initiative of child rearing is lost and likewise so will be any hope of maintaining control over the children.

6. *Talk to your children and listen to them* on a one-to-one basis regularly. Set aside at least one hour a week for each parent to be alone with each child for the purposes of sharing ideas and experience. If you are able to do this, you will cultivate a mood of closeness between parent and child that should last a lifetime.

7. *Accept your child for what he is, and love him for what he is.* Children come into the world with a predisposition for specific talents and interests. They all have different intellects and therefore perform in school on different planes. They all have different physical prowess and therefore some excel in sports and crafts while others do not. It is a great mistake to force a child into a vocation in which he does not fit. It is an equally great mistake to expect the child to perform beyond his abilities. This is not to say that every child should not be encouraged and prodded to reach his maximum potential in every field of endeavor, but it is to say that he should not be made to feel guilty for not being able to achieve what is beyond his reach.

8. *Read to your preschool children.* Reading to your children brings about a form of child-parent communication that is not only pleasurable but is an excellent springboard toward future learning. It also is an excellent way for parents and children to spend their idle moments. Certainly it is preferable to offer this form of attention to your child before he demands it by misbehavior. Always read to your preschool children!

9. *Include your children in all social activities in which they can participate fruitfully,* but do not force them into activities that are impossible for them to enjoy or endure. Such an undertaking is guaranteed to end in disaster.

10. *Never nag or scream* at your children. Repetition which is constantly ignored is much worse for the child than never correcting him in the first place. If indeed the child needs correction, take him aside, speak to him on a one-to-one basis; or if the child is too young to converse with, issue a firm reprimand—whether it be a harsh word or a physical enforcement. But make the one correction firm enough so that it is understood and need not be repeated. A mother who constantly nibbles away at her child saying, "Johnny, don't, Johnny don't, Johnny don't" soon has trouble understanding if Johnny ever understands anything she is saying. Constant nagging is useless! If you find yourself falling into that trap, rethink your approach and ask for help from a knowledgeable source!

11. *Parents should take private time to themselves* individually and as a couple regardless of how many children they have. Without some degree of freedom and individuality, and without some time when parents can express their love for and interest in each other privately, it would be impossible for them to act effectively as parents. After an evening or a weekend away from the children, you will all be happier to see each other again. A weekly Saturday night date can be the ideal plan.

12. *Try to see the world through your child's eyes.* One must remember that young children possess an air of innocence, a lack of inhibition that at times can strip the entire family of all semblance of dignity and sophistication. At such times, it is often difficult for us to respond by seeing the world through the child's eyes; but we must certainly try.

An amusing incident once occurred in my waiting room that makes this point very well. A very conservative thirty-six-year-old father brought his lovable and enthusiastic three-year-old son into the office for a periodic check-up. On that particular spring evening, my waiting room was extremely crowded; the father arrived in his three-piece business suit, followed by young George. As George saw me go by, he shouted, "Doctor, Doctor, guess what?" I went to the waiting-room door and replied, "What, George?" George answered, "We're late for our appointment. And guess why we're late?" Without giving me a chance to reply, George continued, "We're late because Daddy got his do-do caught in his zipper and couldn't get it out." Needless to say, the father was embarrassed, horrified, furious, and humiliated, all at the same time. The fact that I and the twelve people in the waiting room were all roaring with laughter made the situation even worse. George was completely confused. He did not realize that there was any humor associated with the statement at all. I sensed the situation and invited them promptly into the office to rescue them.

Fortunately, the father was mature enough to be able to respond appropriately (in my presence at least), but if he were to have responded with reprimand and punishment for something that the young fellow had no comprehension of, it would have indeed been a shame.

The moral of the story, therefore, is: try to judge your child's actions on the basis of what it means to him. If it is socially unacceptable, explain to him why it is—with patience and understanding.

The above list was only a brief outline of my favorite suggestions to parents and probably the ones that I have offered and seen used most successfully. I am sure, however, that you all have your own favorite rules on child raising, which are perhaps more important to you than the ones I have listed. Enumerate them. You will be surprised at how much you will appreciate reading your own suggestions when you get into trouble raising your own children. You will also be able to keep them as gems of wisdom to pass on to your children when they are raising your grandchildren.

·8·
Life with Children

The childbearing years are years of dedication, sacrifice, maturity, and, ideally, the time when most people realize the greatest satisfactions of life. The realization of the first pregnancy is a very exciting time. It is the time when the marriage truly becomes reconsummated, blessed once again by God. When the pregnancy is desired, it is the absolute culmination of the true meaning of marriage. Up until that time, marriage is a union of two people who still retain a great deal of their personal, premarital identity. Up until that time, the severance of a marital relationship would merely be the parting of two independent individuals. But with the onset of the first pregnancy, all of this changes. Husband and wife have yet a higher role; they now think of themselves as father and mother. And the new baby ordinarily awakens in both mates a responsibility that far surpasses anything that either has ever known.

Even many of my colleagues, who are trained to handle responsibility, have told me that no responsibility they ever experienced up until fatherhood or motherhood ever demanded so much of them. It is true! There is nothing else that is so demanding as fatherhood and motherhood. It is a twenty-four-hour-a-day, seven-day-a-week-job from the day of birth until the day, many, many years later, when the children become self-sufficient. It is perhaps the only job that a person cannot resign from nor divorce himself from forever and ever.

Pregnancy
Pregnancy is the wonderful mystical experience that begins with the conception of the child. Ideally, the wife has a new-found respect for her husband because she now fully understands the potential of his masculini-

ty. He has created in her what will be the full expression of her womanhood. The husband, too, is usually overwhelmed with fascination and respect for his wife; he is quite proud of himself as well. With a desired pregnancy, these are unrivaled expressions of fulfillment, and the anticipation of the unborn child is a bigger thrill than any other I know.

The problems of early pregnancy, however, are many. Frequently, both parents-to-be are frightened by the responsibilities that loom before them, and anxiety about the well-being of the child to come. It is typical for the pregnant woman to frequently not feel well. Many women have described morning sickness, a miserable nausea that occurs very often in the first three months of pregnancy, as the most intolerable experience they have ever endured. Frequently, there is also present a normal degree of depression during the first three months and the last three months of pregnancy. The temporary effect is that there is some degree of personality change. If this is not understood by both expectant parents, it can cause a multitude of problems. The depression of the first three months has several underlying causes. First, the fact that the mother-to-be frequently does not feel well is in itself extremely depressing. Second, the realization that her appearance is changing also can be upsetting to many young expectant mothers. And third, the restrictions that come with early pregnancy can be very disturbing. For instance, the mother-to-be must often curtail some physical activities, sexual relations are sometimes uncomfortable, and she has a restricting feeling of fatigue.

The middle three months of pregnancy are neither so remarkable nor so troublesome, for the newness has worn off, yet it is too early to be anxious over the birth of the child.

The physical discomfort of the mother-to-be increases weekly in the last three months of pregnancy, and depression is commonly related to this discomfort. The woman is awkward, markedly restricted, and feels generally indisposed. Her fears of the oncoming responsibilities are also dominant concerns.

The husband has many, many problems at this time too. It may be the first time that he is forced to share his wife, and she routinely needs a great deal of companionship, reassurance, and consolation. He is often left out of the preparations for the new child as well, since it is so often considered to be a feminine activity only. (But, fortunately, men are now participating more.) Moreover, sexual contact with the wife is increasingly difficult and often unsatisfactory. All too often, this drives the husband away from the wife rather than closer to her, and it is at this time that he is frequently driven to seek out other recreation and interests.

The best advice that can be given to any young couple expecting a baby is that the term of pregnancy should be, as much as it can, a partnership. The father should be included in all phases of the preparation and encouraged to help select the baby clothes and furniture. Participation in prenatal classes helps a great deal. The popularity of these classes has done much to rectify the husband's isolated circumstances, even to the point of assisting and observing in the delivery room. I heartily endorse this practice.

Each pregnancy should be looked upon as an exciting, mystical, wonderful experience shared by both mates. I would advise each wife not to exclude her husband from any phase of the preparations and to do her best to make him feel as important as possible. I would urge husbands to make as big a fuss over their pregnant wives as they can. Many women during pregnancy have a feeling of being unattractive, and only a husband's reassurance can offset this. Whenever possible, a husband should tell his wife of his enthusiasm for the pregnancy and make her feel extra special because of it. Personally, I have always found the blush of vitality in a pregnant woman to be a beautiful thing. After all, it is a true miracle unrivaled by anything else I know.

This cannot be overemphasized because many of the *lifelong* problems of frigidity and lack of communication are started by the problems of mismanaged pregnancies. An unpleasant pregnancy breeds fear of future pregnancies, which is the most common cause of female, as well as male, frigidity. It is a fact that husband or wife, or both, are not going to be happy about every pregnancy, but since there is nothing that can be done about it, it is unrealistic and unreasonable not to exude enthusiasm over what is, by common consensus, a blessed event. If ever mates need each other, it is truly at this time. It is not a time for blaming or criticizing each other for the pregnancy. This is the time to make love, not war.

I have so often seen cases in which women will intentionally test their husband's devotion by questioning his attitude toward the forthcoming blessed event. Heaven help the husband who unwittingly admits that it is not a good idea or is not a good time, for this is an outward expression of rejection—not only of the pregnancy but of the love that created it.

Legalized abortion is now an option available to couples faced with an unwanted pregnancy. My own feelings, however, are that I have difficulty justifying it. However, this is a very private matter that must be decided by both partners on an individualized basis. My experience has been that children always bring love with them into the world, and this love is adequate to stimulate the strength parents need to cope with the challenges.

Pregnancy is such a wonderful experience when it is properly managed. Enjoy it together!

The Infant and the Preschool Child

Being a parent of an infant to school-aged child is unparalleled in its rewards. Never before nor afterward does a parent have the feeling of being so all-important to another person. Children of this age thrive on being played with, and most of us as parents thrive on playing with them. Every day is a new and exciting experience for parents and child.

Problems, when they arise, are usually problems created by disagreement between husband and wife over the methods of raising children, or created by the father or mother not taking an active enough interest in participating. Parental immaturity, manifesting itself in intolerance of the child, can also cause problems. No one partner should dictate what is right or wrong about raising children. The only advice that can be given is that problems should be discussed openly and decided upon with mutual agreement. Every question is answerable as long as people are willing to reason. Once a decision has been made, it should be put into practice without resentment.

Many fathers who lack interest in their young children have become frustrated in their efforts to participate in rearing them and have, therefore, withdrawn. Since this phase is so completely demanding, it is common for couples to neglect their privacy. All too often, devotion to children will cause partners to deprive themselves of the good times that they enjoyed earlier in the marriage. Though most parents sacrifice willingly for their children, it is important that people retain enough of their own identities to make themselves interesting to each other. It is equally important that they have satisfactions in life other than their children.

Mothers who have been devoted to their careers sometimes have difficulty adjusting to life at home with a new baby and are eager to resume work as soon as possible. If it is in any way feasible, however, I would urge all mothers to plan to stay at home with the children as long as possible.

There is no realistic substitute for a mother-child relationship to produce secure and well-adjusted mothers and children.

Unless couples get out and play together, they become so starved for fun and recreation that they tend to seek it elsewhere. How often have you heard a man say that he loves his wife and children but that there is not enough in the home to make life interesting? This is the point when most men complain that their wives will no longer join them to go out and do the many things that made life fun earlier in their marriage. This type of dissatisfaction is dangerous. Beware of it and take the time to be lovers and playmates regardless of the sacrifice. Otherwise, the frustrations could be disasterous. Babies are the world's most lovable creatures. Enjoy them to the fullest while they are young. Teach them, love them, and guide them. The rewards are boundless.

Years from the Beginning of School to Puberty

From the time they start school until they reach puberty, children go through what is known as the latent period of development. This is a period when they become progressively more self-sufficient, and they are really quite a joy to watch. They usually play with other children of the same sex; they copy the parent of the same sex; and they do their best to identify themselves with the parent of the same sex. It is the time when, by example, parents are teaching their children to become adults. At this time, the children's behavior strengthens the parents' ego, for the children are full of questions and are usually willing to accept the answers given by their parents as being the definitive truth. The mother who wants to teach her daughter to bake a cake or sew a dress should find a student with boundless enthusiasm. The father who wants to teach his son to bat a ball, or catch a fish, or hammer a nail has usually only to offer a token interest in his son, and he will invariably get all the response he could ever hope for.

These are the years when most parents are also growing. The husband has typically advanced his career to a point where he is no longer low man on the totem pole. The family income is such that the mates can afford to spread their wings a bit and buy a permanent home. Even an occasional vacation with the children is possible because they are old enough now to take along, and they can enrich themselves on the experiences offered to them.

Marital problems, when they arise in this phase, are usually based on lack of communication between the mates. The husband is usually more involved with his work in these years than at any other time of his career, and he can easily be distracted from his wife and family. The wife must be willing to demonstrate a keen interest in her husband's work, and also include him in home projects of any magnitude. The wife, on the other hand, frequently gets caught up in her responsibilities and involvements with her children and with other women to the extent that she may often fail to leave enough time for her husband. For the working mother, it is even more demanding. Parents at this phase are getting a bit older too and must develop new methods of recreation. Young couples find pleasure in participating in athletic activities, going to games, and pursuing their hobbies the same as they did prior to marriage. As couples get older, however, they usually develop interests in the theater, the arts, and in more formal social activities, such as civic affairs. All too often, this transition is embraced by one member before the other, and lack of communication can result. Please always try to be mindful of these differences in growth and development, and try to reach out to each other to keep from drifting apart.

Adolescence to Maturity

When the children reach adolescence, they are quite independent. They no longer need baby-sitters. They no longer need, nor will they accept, constant surveillance. And bit by bit, they fly farther and farther from the protective wings of their parents. As the parents watch the young ones fly with their own wings and strike out for achievements in their own right, it is extremely difficult to let them go unprotected and hard to give up the position of feeling indispensable. And yet, it is also quite a relief for parents to feel that they are no longer so completely needed.

The adjustment to not being needed so much is practically an exact reversal of the adjustment that comes at the birth of the first child. The firm binding that babies give to a marriage is removed, and the mates are again left alone. The feeling of importance that they derived from the young children is gone, and now they must get their sense of importance from their own accomplishments and from each other. The delightful young children who just a few years ago made their parents feel that they knew everything will, at this stage of the game, frequently accuse their parents of not knowing anything at all about today's world. Again and again they will say "But, Mother, you don't know how things are these days," or "Dad, how could you have so little understanding?"

It seems sometimes that everything the children ever did to bolster their parents' egos is now quickly undone. The same couple who looked at each other with adoration as they gazed upon the beautiful baby that they created will at this time often look at each other with bewilderment when they realize what is happening. The same father and mother whose seven-year-old child had flattered them with the feeling that they were all-knowing now have their self-confidence challenged. The only key to survival is to try to keep a sense of humor about it and not permit predictable child rebellion to cause you to lower your family standards and traditions. Parents are and must still be in charge, and insist on achievement and abiding by the rules of the family.

The adolescent child also challenges the self-confidence of the parents by his physical appearance and performance. For example, at some time during adolescence, a son will demonstrate that he now can hit a baseball as far as his dad and can run even faster.

Adolescent daughters as they blossom become very lovely, which often brings them into competition with their mothers. Mother might feel resentment from her friends who say, "My, isn't your daughter pretty, just as you used to be when you were young" or "Your daughter has the same kind of figure you used to have before you had children and got fat." Amusing as it may sound, these are very challenging and very stressful situations, ones most people do not adapt to very easily. Such problems culminate in parents wondering about their own youth and vitality. Asked when they first had the feeling of getting old, eight out of ten people said that they had the feeling of getting old when they compared themselves to their teenaged son or daughter. Some people accept this gracefully, but others find it to be such a challenge to their security that they are driven to do very foolish things. Only reassurance from the mate that whatever is happening to one of them is happening to both, and evidence that they are still indeed satisfied with each other, can ease the distress that arises at this time. Try to be understanding and demonstrate your love and devotion for each other at this time, for it is desperately needed.

When the Children Leave Home

When the children leave home, the job of parenthood for all practical purposes is complete. This is so whether they leave home to go away to a job, to go away to college, or into the service, or get married. When they leave, they are gone—and parents must let go. From this point on it is an adult-to-adult relationship between parents and offspring. And parents are forced to accept the persistent immaturity and inadequacies of their offspring with the hopeful reassurance that time and responsibility will make the man or the woman mature. Parents who attempt to cling and rule beyond this point end up spoiling their children's opportunities to develop on their own. They also present themselves with the impossible task of trying to live another adult's life. Such interference can bring nothing but endless grief to all concerned.

After the sons and daughters leave, the only help that parents should offer them is to answer with discretion when they are called upon for help. There are even times when parents must turn their backs on an appeal for help, particularly if it involves criticism of mates or new environments —that is, factors that cannot be changed. Children will come home and relate horror stories to their parents about the inequities that they live with. The parents, in turn, necessarily sympathize with them over their apparently insurmountable problems. Then, the offspring usually go home and adjust well to their problems while their parents remain with the worry. Obviously, one must listen to an adult offspring's problems, but a firm rule to follow is that you may listen, but you must not attempt to solve the problem. You may share your experience and wisdom, but never attempt to make their decisions for them. ("Give every man thy ear, but few thy voice," Shakespeare said.) The only help you can be is in encouraging your children to solve their own problems themselves—and be willing to accept their decisions.

After parents and grown children adjust to being apart, things usually smooth out very well. And, by the way, after living apart for some years, grown children usually have a renewed respect for their parents. Mark Twain summarized it beautifully by saying that as a boy of eighteen he could not understand how his father had lived so long and learned so little. And by the time Twain was twenty-one, he could not understand how his father could have learned so much in only three years.

·9·

From the Time Children
Leave Home Until Retirement

Couples who still have a significant number of years from the time the children leave home until retirement usually experience a delightful second honeymoon. They still have a good bit of youthful vitality left, and they usually have a solid economic foundation since the economic weight of the children has been removed. The mortgage is usually just about paid, and the husband's career (and the wife's too if she is employed) has reached a level where he enjoys substantial security and a high degree of satisfaction from his work.

The couple have now regained their privacy. Usually, people at this stage of life have achieved a degree of maturity that has helped them to overcome most of their past intolerances toward each other. There are many new pleasures to enjoy, and moreover, there is the anticipated role of grandparent—a delightful avocation in itself.

Problems, when they exist at all in this period, are generally one of two types. Mates who have drifted apart during the long period of child rearing, may find it difficult to rekindle the romance of years gone by. Or they may be so panicked by the adjustment to later life that they are obsessed with trying to recapture their youth individually.

For those who find that they have grown apart and have become a bit strange to each other, a new courtship is usually in order. This means, to begin with, that the couple must find current interests that they both enjoy. It means renewing old (but pleasant) habits of flattering each other, giving gifts, surprising each other, and indulging in frequent datelike activities. A new husband-and-wife recreation would also be a good idea.

Travel, adult-education courses, home-improvement projects, cultivation of new friends, theater, movies, adult sports participation, and involvement in clubs or community activities are a few suggestions.

All in all, this can be a very exciting time, but many people never get around to approaching it quite that way. Unfortunately, they look on this rediscovered privacy as boredom, and become testy toward each other. It is a psychological fact that if the importance a person once found in his relationship with his children is to be taken from him, he or she must have a replacement. (Love, like nature, abhors a vacuum.) If this replacement does not come from the mate, he or she will very often have a feeling of emptiness and lack of fulfillment. If there is, as Robert Frost said, "Nothing to look forward to with hope," trouble can ensue. For people who feel this way are natural potential victims for romantic entanglements. The impulse to do this comes from a desire to feel needed as well as from a desire to still feel sexually attractive. If people are mature enough to realize that the best proof of sexual identity comes from the marital partner; and if they would allow this to happen by resuming the courtship referred to above, most of these heartaches would be prevented long before they ever started.

·10·

After Retirement

If everything were to go perfectly, married life after retirement would be the blissful reward for which a couple has worked a lifetime. At last, they have their entire time to devote to each other and to do all the things they have always wanted to do. Routine pressures, for the better part, disappear. There is no worrying about getting to work on time, pleasing the boss, or having to meet deadlines in assigned jobs.

Many couples find a life of incomparable peace and contentment in this phase. Their maturity, moreover, assists them in forgiving most of each other's shortcomings, and they are delighted to enjoy each other's companionship and security.

The illnesses that come at this time of life frequently offer the mates a chance to care for each other and to outwardly demonstrate their devotion to each other; thereby, they grow closer together than ever before. At this time, the children have usually established their own pattern of life, and grandchildren offer the retired couple the satisfaction that their own children once did.

In most companies retirement at a specified age, usually sixty-five, is mandatory. Retirement programs are economically more comprehensive than formerly, but even so retirement checks will usually not allow a couple to retain their preretirement standard of living.

For some strange reason, which I have never been able to understand, people over sixty-five who still work productively must forfeit their social security benefits if they have earnings above a specified amount. Advances in modern medicine have extended the productive as well as the chronological lives of most people, but this has apparently developed into a double-edged sword. It could be argued that extended productivity provides a retired person with a much longer period to enjoy his privacy and independence. But it could also be argued that it is unfair to deprive men and women of work after they have dedicated a lifetime to mastering their chosen careers.

Many people find themselves immediately bored with retirement. They frequently consider it humiliating to be deprived of the privilege and dignity of working. This breeds bitter resentment and makes them extremely difficult to live with. It is, after all, quite a comedown for a person who may have supervised other people and been empowered to give orders, to now be reduced to a nonproductive role in life.

For the nonemployed wife, though, retirement should be that happy day when she can have her beloved husband at her side any time she chooses. But it also represents an end to much of her cherished privacy. For years, she has been able to do as she pleased while her husband was away working. And yet, for many people this is not a problem at all because, typically, the husband will have hobbies and interests that take him out of the house as often (if not more) than his job once did. In other cases, the couple will have such a long backlog of things that they have been looking forward to doing together that they just never seem to have enough time to do them.

Problems arise when the mates both feel a lack of satisfaction from any given day and, unreasonably, blame each other for the predicament.

Each case is different, of course, and it would therefore be impossible to offer a rule that addresses itself to every problem in this age group. In general, however, if the couple is open-minded enough to survey a problem, and if they find it to be boredom, which is typical, they can usually solve it by generating new interests that get them out of the house and out of each other's hair.

A good plan is a must in order to cope with this transition (and all transitions) in life. It is extremely important that retirement be looked on as a beginning, not an end.

Not too many years ago, there were major differences in the social structure of our country that made this much less of a problem. Families were close together, and retired people had many obligations to their loved ones (and their loved ones reciprocated). They still had an active family role to perform. It seemed, for example, as though some younger family member or other was always sick and required errands to be run that the older people could do. Retired men could always busy themselves doing odd jobs in the homes of their children and were indeed welcomed to do so. Many people tell of the closeness that they had with grandparents who had the time to listen to their problems as children and the wisdom to offer their guidance and understanding.

Unfortunately, our modern socioeconomic system has deprived many people of this family closeness. Unlike before, sons or daughters rarely live on the same block as their parents. Typically, offspring live in a different town or a different section of the country. Since many people are employed by national and international corporations, they often are forced to relocate; and it is not at all uncommon for grandchildren and grandparents to see one another so infrequently that they are practically strangers.

Modern society, however, has many advantages that were not available in years gone by. Rapid transportation has helped people stay active, as well as allowed them experiences that our forefathers never knew. Modern conveniences have made housework infinitely easier, so older people can accomplish much with a minimum of effort and thereby retain their independence. There are also many senior citizens' organizations that offer a great deal of stimulating companionship. The one important thing, however, is that people must feel assertive enough to take advantage of these worthwhile services.

Happiness comes in different forms for each retired couple, and there is no one formula for happiness. Each couple must find its own formula, and they will stand a much better chance of finding it by working together and discussing it openly. There is always interest, opportunity, and pleasure available for those willing to assess their needs and pursue them.

·11·
The Elderly Retired Couple

"In sickness and in health, till death do us part"—this is the phase of life when nature invokes that clause of the marriage contract. Unfortunately, the aging process is not always equal, and there comes a time when one mate will become sickly and incapacitated before the other. This, of course, means that the major occupation of the healthy mate is the care of the debilitated partner.

Sad as it is to see one's mate suffer and eventually succumb, it is equally heartwarming to see the true meaning of marital devotion flourish in these hours of need. The willing sacrifices in this phase compensate for any selfish conflicts that might have existed earlier in life. For most, no task is too formidable if it gives any consolation to the suffering partner.

Children usually help out when they can, but the relationship of the elderly couple is most often a very private affair, so private that although they are frequently troubled, they usually insist on the dignity of making their own decisions. Were they to relinguish this right, they would lose their self-respect and end up with insurmountable problems.

The problems of couples in this phase of life usually are those of genuine nature and reduced circumstance rather than the self-inflicted problems of earlier phases. Obviously, most of the health problems of the very elderly can be easily understood but are frequently impossible to cure. And they get worse, not better. Fortunately, most people who have reached this phase of life have a mature and realistic attitude toward old age and are able to face up to it reasonably well. But please never settle for suffering without pursuing every effort to restore or at least maintain good health with the guidance of your family physician. Problems with vision and hearing are particularly important to check regularly.

Several abnormal conditions that may cause behavioral problems are deserving of mention. Probably the most common of these is the situation that arises when the more dominant mate is the first to become incapacitated. Often the more dependent mate is able to rise to the occasion heroically and shoulder the heavy responsibilities. But just as often, the sad happening is that the dependent mate, after a lifetime subordinate role, cannot adjust himself or herself to the demands of the other. Both partners are certainly too old to learn to manage finances or to negotiate business transactions, and the only salvation is to turn matters over to a more capable person. The aged person who does this should not feel guilty. After all, it is harder and harder to learn new skills as one grows older. If there are no responsible family members who can help, a physician or clergyman will gladly assist in guiding you toward someone who can. Unfortunately, many couples seek no such help because they are too shy to ask for it. It is silly for them to be shy; people want to help. When there is a death in the family, scores of friends and neighbors come from all over and offer to do anything they can. Many of these same people are more than willing to help as a matter of course. They should not require a family tragedy to goad them into action.

Sometimes family and friends can be officious and try to do too much. I have seen many overindulgent sons and daughters be so protective of their elderly parents that they rob them of their self-confidence. The elderly obviously move slower; their hearing isn't quite so good, and they often have difficulty acclimating themselves to new environments. All of this, however, does not mean that they are incompetent. So if a son or daughter assumes the right to answer questions that are directed toward the parents without giving the parents a chance to answer for themselves, the parents after a while get out of the habit of trying to be self-reliant. And once an elderly person loses self-confidence, it is only the rare exception who regains it.

The other problems of the elderly couple are in relating to their children, the management of illness, and the personal adjustment to old age in general. I would urge you to make notes on any experiences on old age that I might have overlooked. Your notes may record problems that the older reader has himself experienced or problems that the younger reader has experienced with elderly parents. If any problem seems insurmountable, it would certainly be wise to discuss it with an interested family physician.

Grow old along with me!
The best is yet to be,
The last of life, for which the first was made.
                              —Browning

Part II

The Problems of Marriage

The course of true love never did run smooth.
—*Shakespeare*

Introduction

As you read Part One, you probably were able to project yourself into many of the situations that were discussed and to identify inadequacies in your own life. If you were able to do this, the book has already served one of its primary functions.

Obviously, marriage (and life itself) is an evolutionary process—one in which satisfactory completion of one stage is necessary for smooth progression to the next.

Unless the marital contract was entered into with the sincerity and understanding necessary to form the foundation of a good marriage, one could not expect a good marriage to follow without hardships and adjustments.

To be sure, most shaky foundations can be made strong by locating the weaknesses and then reinforcing them with understanding. No marriage, regardless of how well it is planned, is completely free from imperfections. But, by understanding the faults and their underlying causes, one can correct them and go on to enjoy a fruitful marriage. The early years of marriage are always trying and rarely without heartache, disappointment, and grief. But the better the understanding between mates at this phase of development, the better prepared they are to approach the responsibility of raising their family. The better the children are raised, the better the future for the couple after the children are gone. All of these accomplishments can make a foundation based on security upon which the retired senior citizen faces old age.

Now that you have thought about the structure of marriage in Part One, you can approach specific symptomatic problems in Part Two. In each case, I have correlated a problem with its probable causes, and offered some suggestions for solving it. It would be foolish to think that I could anticipate every problem that would ever arise, but it has been my experience that most difficulties fall into the categories that we shall review below.

If you feel that you are particularly interested in one specific problem and would choose to go directly to it, by all means do so. I would strongly suggest, however, that after you have done this, you do go back and read Part Two from the very beginning. By doing this, you will find much more depth and understanding of all of the problems of marriage, many of which are related to one another. Even though the principal problem may be very conspicuous, it could be compared to an iceberg, 10 percent of which is visible and 90 percent of which is beneath the surface. By the same token, you might be well aware of the major symptom, but it is possible that you would not be aware of the underlying problems that create it.

Please do not take for granted that any of the problems listed below are not your problems. Read their descriptions first, carefully analyze them, and do some soul-searching. Be honest with yourself! It's never pleasant to admit that you have a problem, but it is even more unpleasant to have to live with it.

Understanding the problems is half of the cure. After admitting and understanding the problems, a good plan, massive amounts of love, and a reasonable portion of humility will help lead to a satisfactory solution of most of them.

·1·

Boredom

Boredom is perhaps the most usual common denominator of all marital problems. It is not always recognized as such, because by the time problems have developed, their cause—boredom—has long since been forgotten.

Children who are bored usually become irritable, dull, unproductive, uninteresting, dissatisfied, argumentative, inconsiderate, gullable, prone to delinquincy, disrespectful, and generally obnoxious. When adults are bored, they are prone to all of those traits also, but on an even larger scale, and the end results from boredom can be bickering, jealousy, disorganization, laziness, depression, frigidity, irritability, alcoholism, drug abuse, infidelity, carelessness about personal habits, and loss of self-confidence.

Recognition and treatment of boredom, therefore, is of utmost importance for the prevention and treatment of other serious and more complicated conditions.

It seems to me that the more mechanized and industrialized society has become, the more prone to boredom individuals have become. It is certainly true that many jobs are repetitious and so narrowly specialized that there is little room to demonstrate initiative and originality. The person who is employed as a machine operator, for instance, and is responsible only for manipulating a few controls, might be responsible for producing massive amounts of material in his eight-hour day, which may have great economic value, but the person himself, in many cases, has been subjected to eight hours of absolute, complete boredom. Even recreation for many people has degenerated into becoming perpetual spectators in front of television sets watching unimaginative and uninformative repetitious shows as a result of the lazy habit.

In an effort to get to know my patients better, I typically ask them two questions: "What interesting things are going on in your life?" and "What are you doing for fun?" I am sad to say that approximately 65 percent of the people I ask reply that nothing interesting is going on in their lives and that they are doing nothing for fun. At first I thought these replies were thoughtless responses, rather than reflections of reality. But the more I explore these two questions, the more I realize that it is true that many, if not most people, fail to have interesting stimulation in their lives and realistically do not have fun. If this is true, it is no wonder that the divorce rate is so high and the prevalence of marital problems is so great.

As with all other problems of marriage, the approach should be directed toward recognition of the problem and establishing a good plan for its solution. Recognizing the problem is a matter of making a good, honest self-evaluation. Periodically filling out the questionnaire which appears on page xiii should be a great help to you in this, and also attempt to evaluate your mate's status with regard to boredom. Be honest and realistic about your assessment; a protective, defensive approach would only mask the condition and potentially serve as a precursor to more serious problems.

The following case is an excellent example of boredom, the problems it can cause, and the approaches to its management.

Richard had been a patient of mine for twenty years, and an acquaintenance and friend for over forty years. He was known throughout the community as a likable fellow, but one who had a tendency to drink a little more than he should at the local bar. He also enjoyed the reputation of being one of the best pool players in the community and genuinely enjoyed the social life that centered around the Golden Moon Café, which, of course, included ongoing intimacies with several women over many years. Richard was very popular among his friends and had a reputation for being the life of the party. It was assumed that "there would never be a dull moment when Richard was around!"

His wife's image of him was exactly the opposite. She considered him lazy, uninterested in family responsibilities, irresponsible with regard to his chores, and generally a very irritable, grouchy person. I could not help but be fascinated by the dual image of the same person, and I therefore took the liberty of exploring Richard's own interpretation of my dilemma. When I asked him about it he became very introspective and made the following comments: "Well, you know my friend Charlie says that there is never a dull moment when Richard is around. That's because Charlie has never visited my home. There are nothing but dull moments there, and dull hours, and dull days, and dull years. My wife's conversation never extends beyond a discussion of her sister's constipation or complaints about the neighbor's children. Her only attention to me is when she is complaining about the dull chores which are not getting done. The most excitement I can remember in my house in the past five years was the time when my daughter completed a jigsaw puzzle. There is absolutely nothing at home for me to be interested in. I suggested buying a pool table for the basement two years ago and my wife refused to hear of it because it would disturb the furniture that she already had there. Frankly, I am bored out of my mind at home and if I didn't have some place to go and something to do for some fun and excitement, I would go absolutely mad. Nothing would please me more than having my wife participate in some interesting activities with me so that I wouldn't feel so guilty about being separated from her so much, but she just refuses to budge out of her dull routine, and I therefore find no recourse but to seek some interest and excitement on my own. Without it, I would literally be bored to death."

I am not offering boredom as a form of justification for this man's behavior, but I am presenting it as a sincere, realistic explanation. I am in the process of attempting to work out a program with the couple that would make their marriage more interesting and help them to overcome family boredom which has taken such a toll. Whether I will be successful or not remains to be seen, because they have both become so set in their ways. I have, however, worked with numerous other couples who have accepted my suggestions and revitalized their lives by joining clubs, buying season tickets to the theater or sporting events, taking tennis lessons, starting home-improvement projects, taking courses, changing jobs, and a host of other activities which have helped them to overcome boredom and solve their marital problems.

In conclusion, I again warn you to be on the constant lookout for boredom in your marriage and be eager to attack it as soon as you recognize it.

·2·

Problems Associated with Housekeeping and Home Maintenance

Though the tasks associated with housekeeping and home maintenance are rarely the most serious problems of marriage, I am convinced they are among the most common. Following are a few of the comments made by some of my women patients:

"I hate housework."

"No one cares about household chores but me."

"My husband expects more of me than anyone should be expected to produce when it comes to housework."

"It has been so long since anyone thanked me for the efforts that I put into the house that I doubt that anyone ever noticed that it was done."

"If only everyone would pick up after himself, the household chores would be easy."

"My husband always objects to buying new things for the house." "The children never wipe their muddy feet as they enter the house."

"My husband constantly compares my housekeeping to the way his mother did it years ago."

"Housework is so demeaning."

And here are some comments from husbands on the same subject:

"What in the world is the matter with my wife? She is forever complaining about doing housework and yet she has nothing else expected of her."

"My wife is never satisfied. The more she gets for the house, the more she wants."

"If she would only discipline the children to help with house chores, she wouldn't have half as much to do."

"She seems so disorganized; no wonder she has trouble getting her work done."

"Instead of a wife, she acts more like a warden when it comes to housekeeping."

"She takes no interest in cooking. Why can't she get some of my mother's old recipes?"

"I know she has a full-time job too, but housework is a woman's job."

"I would be glad to help out with the housework, but she is never satisfied with any of the help I offer."

"My wife is careless. The house is always a mess."

"She demands so much in the line of perpetual home-improvement projects that we never have enough time or money left over for pleasure."

Comments such as the following have been made by sons and daughters who still live at home:

"The only time that we enjoy our parents is when we are away on vacation, and there is no tension in the home regarding housekeeping and home maintenance."

"They are forever complaining about the way I keep my room. After all, all teenagers are sloppy. It's the nature of the beast."

"My friends are offended when my mother insists that they clean up after themselves and avoid using the living room."

"I enjoy helping dad with home-maintenance projects, but he never knows when to quit. I don't mind giving up a few hours on a weekend, but I resent being asked to give up the entire weekend."

What it all comes down to is that housework irritates many people because—

1. Many families fail to set common goals regarding housekeeping and home maintenance that would be agreeable to everyone concerned.

2. Some mates are so compulsive about housekeeping as to make it unpleasant.

3. Many couples fail to adequately discipline their children early enough with regard to chores and the rules of the house. Unless these rules are established early, it becomes almost impossible to motivate the children. I firmly believe that children should be given as many chores as they are

capable of handling as early as they are capable of handling them. Sheltered children will frequently develop into functionally crippled adults when the time comes that they must use their own initiative.

4. Many people are so overcommitted to their jobs and other outside activities that they do not have enough enthusiasm and energy left over for housekeeping and home maintenance. In such cases, it would be wise to consider setting aside enough money in the budget to hire outside help to perform any jobs that you yourself cannot do. This would be preferable to putting a heavy strain on your marriage.

5. Often differences in the cultural backgrounds of a couple concerning housekeeping and home maintenance make it difficult for them to understand each other's priorities.

To resolve the problems related to housekeeping and home maintenance, I strongly suggest that you adopt a fairly rigid, businesslike plan and handle it in the same manner that industry does. If you find this plan a bit trite or difficult to follow, you might consider the alternatives: aimlessness and bickering and hard feelings or resentment when problems are not handled methodically.

My plan is to have a monthly meeting—husband, wife, and children all attending. At these meetings, chores would be assigned to all family members according to each person's abilities and available time. Money would be allotted for any necessary expenditures. Do not hesitate to write out the assignments and to make sure each family member is willing to accept his or her specific responsibility. Assignments should not include just a listing of the chores but also a definite time period in each day when they are to be performed.

I know of one family in which chore-assignment is through a contractlike agreement. Each child is asked to sign and certify that he has agreed to perform certain chores and that he does not consider them to be unreasonable. With such a plan, each person knows what he can count on and is far more inclined to develop reliability and self-respect. There should be no nagging and bickering if you establish the rule in your family that no changes in the routine are expected until the next formal meeting. The same approach is very valuable when it comes to home maintenance and budgeting, or repairs and replacement of the furnishings in the home. Husbands and wives rarely disagree on what they would really like to have in their home. Most disagreements come over the subject of when it can be done and how it can be afforded. If such decisions are made at the meetings

I propose, a budget can be calculated and a timetable set by mutual consent rather than by feuding and arm twisting. If you find yourselves unable to agree on these matters, avoid arguing, and simply set the matter aside for a week while each one tries to understand the other person's point of view. Then discuss it again; the problem may be a lot clearer this time and, if it isn't, try the same procedure for still another week.

Two key points that I made reference to above are worth repeating. The first one is, establish an agreement on the assignment of chores, and the second is, establish the time of the day at which these chores are to be done.

My long experience has revealed that one of the greatest difficulties in housework and home maintenance is lack of organization and planning. There should be a work plan, with a starting time and a finishing time, the same as there is in any other well-organized business. Anyone who works at housework from early morning until late night in the light of modern technological developments is guilty of either disorganization or poor training because such chores should just not take that long. If there are so many children or such a large house that it does take that much time, then help should be acquired in one way or another. Hiring someone to ease the burden should be considered if it is economically feasible.

In summary, the home is the entire family's concern and should be treated as such with a team effort based on mutual understanding and enthusiasm. Approached that way, it can actually be possible to have fun doing even the most tedious chores.

•3•

Interference from Family and Friends

Two's company, three's a crowd. Marriages are made between two people and two people only. Whenever more than two people attempt to share in the private matters of marriage, trouble is automatic. The exception is when a third party is a qualified person whom the couple calls upon for advice.

This brings us back to the marriage contract and the understanding of what was meant by the agreement entered into by each couple. There are times when couples marry with a verbal agreement that a widowed parent or a child from a previous marriage is to be a permanent member of the newly formed family. In such cases, there are destined to be problems, but they are mostly anticipated, and usually the couple has a prearranged agreement for their management. But unless such an agreement is part of the marriage contract, or the "outsiders" have nowhere else to go, or both, the privacy of any family unit should be preserved.

Marital interference happens for one of several reasons. The most common is that the couple is too free in discussing private problems publicly. This naturally generates commentary from parents or friends. Such comments are not necessarily malicious, nor do they constitute meddling, as a rule. But publicizing intimate matters is usually regarded as a solicitation for help.

A twenty-five-year-old woman patient, married for five years and with three children, confided that she cannot stand the way her mother attempts to run her life. She told me that her mother commented on her menu planning, the clothes she bought for her children, and even how often she and her husband had sexual relations. This apparently was a clear-cut case of a mother who needed to be told that her daughter was now married and no longer needed her guidance—which was really interference.

I said *apparently* clear-cut, because the mother was also a patient of mine, and when I questioned her, she told a different story. Furthermore, the father and the son-in-law confirmed the mother's version. The mother said that her daughter routinely discussed private matters with other people against her advice. Apparently the daughter got a feeling of importance by parading her problems to her mother and, for that matter, to anyone else who would listen. She read very little and had few interesting experiences to discuss, and therefore used her marriage as sole topic of conversation.

The mother confessed that she found her daughter's conversation boring and had no desire to force her own opinions on her. As a matter of fact, she offered opinions only when her daughter accused her of not being interested enough to help.

Against this background, I discussed the problem further with the wife. After recounting her mother's view, I advised her that the best way to avoid unwanted advice was to keep her problems to herself; if she had to discuss them with someone else, then discuss them with me, her family physician. She said she had never thought of this, but she was willing to give it a try. The result was that she developed enough maturity to keep her private affairs to herself and soon realized that she had few problems that needed discussion. In short, she realized that she had brought the interference on herself. This is so in most cases. Rarely have I known even a busybody offer unsolicited commentary on the affairs of couple unless it was solicited directly or, as in this case, indirectly.

Whenever there is a situation in which people offer unsolicited advice, the answer is simple: Tell them to mind their own business! It is not only your privilege but your duty to insist that any such person mind his own business, regardless of how closely related or how closely interdependent you are with him. Even if it be a beloved parent or an important business associate or an employer, everyone deserves his privacy and is duty bound to stand tall and demand it. And any person who permits his mate to be subjected to third-party meddling is doing an injustice to that mate (and to himself), an injustice that falls in the same category as unfaithfulness. After all, you would be permitting a third party to come between you.

At the time of marriage, many people bring outside interference right into their house by neglecting to sever close relationships with best friends. Your mate is your new best friend. And the term "best friend," when it does not refer to the mate, is a term that single people use. The "best friends" people had when they were single may have had many unwritten responsibilities to each other. But now the mate assumes those responsibilities.

The examples given above of the various forms that interference and meddling can take are merely a smattering of the most common situations that can arise. If you find examples in your own marriage, I urge you to make note of them. In summary, regardless of who is causing the interference, the answer is the same: marriages are made between two people; a mate's primary responsibility is to the mate. And so, if there is a disagreement between your mate and your children, you must support your mate. Your secondary responsibility is to your children. If there is a conflict between your parents and your children, you must support your children. Such occurrences are not so clear-cut as the rules themselves, so there will be exceptions. For the most part, however, the violation of these rules is destined to bring trouble. If you feel it necessary to violate this order of responsibilities, then seek the support of professional advice before you do so.

·4·

Bickering

By definition, husbands and wives should be partners; but in practice many could be more accurately termed opponents. It is true! The habit of bickering—"the battle of the sexes"—seems to be a way of life to so many couples that they don't even realize they are doing it. As a result, an atmosphere of tension, anxiety, aggravation, and hostility is generated, and this atmosphere permeates the personalities of the mates and of their children.

This brings to mind a young couple, Angelo and Sophie, some thirty years old, who brought their young son Albert, age four, into the office to be treated for cough and congestion. It was my first meeting with them as a family, although I had previously treated both Angelo and Sophie individually. Sophie began by recounting young Albert's symptoms, which all had started five days earlier at about two o'clock in the afternoon. At this point, Angelo interrupted and stated that the symptoms had started about five o'clock in the afternoon, and that Albert had had no symptoms until that time. I assured them that it made no difference whether it was two o'clock or five o'clock and went on to explore the problem. "Has Albert been eating well," I asked. Sophie replied, "He never eats well; he only eats an egg and a couple of pieces of toast for breakfast, along with a glass of milk or so." Angelo interrupted: "That's not so; he eats beautifully; and he really has a glass and a half of milk and three pieces of toast at breakfast." I assured them that each of the reported breakfasts was adequate and suggested that we move on. "Does he sleep well?" Angelo replied, "No, he doesn't sleep well at all. He tosses and turns and snores at night." "How would you know?" Sophie replied. "You snore so loud yourself that you couldn't possibly hear anyone else snore!" "I know more than you think I know!" Angelo exclaimed.

I had met these two on numerous occasions when they had come individually for their own illnesses, and had found them to be pleasant, intelligent people who were willing to cooperate with everything I asked them to do. Their personality as a couple was a bit of a surprise. "Does Albert take medicine well in capsule form?" "I think he probably would," Angelo said. Sophie was quick to counter, "He's never taken a capsule in his life without putting up a fight." "You don't know how to give it to him!" Angelo replied.

Just at that time, my young patient happened to be exploring my stethoscope and dropped it onto the floor. His mother was quick to tell him that he should never touch other people's property and that he was going to be in for a good spanking when he got home. "Go easy on him," countered his father. "He's just curious and, besides, he isn't feeling well." "You never discipline him at all," Sophie said. "If you did, he would be easier to manage." At this point, I assured the parents that no harm had been done to the stethoscope, and then I took the little fellow into another room and gave him some toys to play with.

I returned to the parents. "Do you people always bicker about everything?" I asked. The couple looked at each other in amazement, smiled, and Sophie said, "I guess maybe we do, but I never thought much about it. Isn't that the way married people are?" Angelo took the matter a little more seriously and said, "I always wondered about that. It does seem as though we bicker a lot, but both my parents and Sophie's parents have always acted the same way, so I never thought too much about it." "Are you happy living this way?" I asked. They agreed that they would both be a great deal happier if bickering were not their way of life. "In that case, why not stop it?" I suggested. Then I proposed that they adopt the policy of holding up three fingers if one partner found that he or she was bickering over an insignificant matter and that the other partner honor the signal and attempt to control such foolish behavior. They said this sounded like fun and agreed to give it a try.

Their next visit was three weeks later, and I hardly recognized them as the same people. They were calmly discussing family matters in the waiting room and speaking affectionately to each other. When we met in the office and I inquired about their problem, they both announced that they had never had such a pleasant three weeks in their entire relationship. Angelo confided that he had previously found himself looking for excuses to delay going home in the evening because it had been such an unpleasant place prior to the establishment of the three-finger rule. Sophie added that she had lost a great deal of enthusiasm for the romance in their life up to that point because there never seemed to be any pleasant moments together; and she, therefore, had found herself without enthusiasm for sex or for any other form of love or communication. Apparently, this had reversed itself in the past three weeks.

Five years have gone by since this incident, and I see the family at least six times a year. There is never a time that they fail to acknowledge their gratitude for having been introduced to the three-finger signal.

If, in your own case, you find that yours is a bickering marriage, I urge you to analyze it and ask yourself whether any of the subjects that you bicker about has enough merit to justify confrontation. You might also ask yourself whether anything is ever accomplished by bickering. If your answer is, as I expect it will be, that bickering has been fruitless in the past, why not discuss the situation with your mate and try the three-finger exercise? It may change your entire life.

Another interesting example of the tragedies brought on by bickering is the story of an attorney and his wife, whom I have known for the past five years. They were in their early thirties, and had two nice young children aged four and six. The couple seemed to have everything going for them. The husband was well on his way to a rewarding and lucrative career. The wife was attractive, well educated, and had a career of her own as a speech therapist. The children were bright and beautiful and seemed to be rewarding in every way. I attended them for several minor chronic illnesses, so I saw them at fairly regular intervals. I got to know them quite well and became very fond of them all.

I was therefore shocked and distressed to have Susan come in one day and tell me that Elliot had left the family approximately a month before, and that they were in the midst of all the miseries one would expect from such a separation. "How could this be?" I asked. "How can a couple who has so much together even think of separation, let alone be going through the full motions of it?" "We were having one of our usual arguments," Susan confessed, "which got more heated than most, and finally Elliot stomped out and sent for his clothes the next day." "What could possibly have been so important to argue about," I asked, "that it could lead to such a drastic move?" Susan replied (with some insight) that she would be embarrassed even to discuss with me what an insignificant subject it was that had precipitated the argument; but that it had become habit for them to bicker over the most insignificant matters and that the only important things were the arguments themselves and the hideous flaming tempers that were then revealed.

I offered to help and discussed the matter at great length with each of them individually. It was obvious that they both realized the absurdity of the situation, but each confessed that they were so headstrong they were not sure if they could modify their behavior.

When I finally felt they had enough insight into their problem, I suggested they go away for a weekend together to see if they could rekindle their romance and renegotiate their marriage. They reluctantly agreed to do this, and I felt we were on our way to a happy ending to what could have been a tragedy.

Two weeks later Susan came into the office with one of the children, and I was of course quick to inquire about the success of the weekend experiment. "It all went beautifully," she told me. "We went to the seashore and were having a delightful weekend together. We left on Friday night, stayed over Saturday and had a beautiful day on the beach, and a lovely dinner that night, and were planning to come home on Sunday. In every way we seemed to be on a second honeymoon and I was sure it was going to lead to a happier and more fruitful life for all of us. On Sunday morning, though, when Elliot went into the bathroom, he bellowed, 'You left the top off the goddamned toothpaste! When the hell are you ever going to learn how to put things back where they belong!'"

Apparently, this was ample to stimulate Susan to retaliate with the full fury of her own bad temper; and before the session was over they both agreed that they still had some maturing to do before they were ready to renegotiate their marriage and provide a happy home for their children; as well as an example for them to emulate.

It's too soon to be sure that this couple will be able to change their behavior but I am optimistic that they will, since they are both intelligent enough to realize their shortcomings and love their children enough to realize the necessity of reviving the marriage.

Not many cases are as absurd as the two presented here; however, there is hardly a couple that has not had similar sessions of bickering over insignificant matters. Realize, if you will, that no one ever wins an argument—everyone loses. Everyone loses respect, and inflicts scars on relationships that are never completely erased. Think about it. Make note of your own experiences with bickering and discuss them with your mate. Try the three-finger exercise and do all you can to avoid bickering.

·5·

Infidelity

"Thou shalt not covet thy neighbor's wife"—this must certainly be a rule that dates back to earliest antiquity. I suspect that it has been a part of every set of rules ever established for marriage. As with most rules, this one was established because of the strong tendency to do otherwise. Regarding infidelity, I think that one of the primary factors at the time of marriage is the agreement to maintain exclusive fidelity to each other. Therefore I shall attack the problem of infidelity not as a moral issue, but rather as a violation of the basic marital agreement. There are three classifications of infidelity. They are the following:

1. Premeditated infidelity—in which one or both partners neither promises to be, nor expects the mate to be, exclusively faithful.

2. Infidelity generated by lack of satisfaction with the marriage and therefore yielding to the temptation to look elsewhere for satisfaction.

3. Circumstantial infidelity—which results from unexpected circumstances and that happens as a pure surrender to temptation at a time of low ego strength.

In the case of premeditated infidelity, I feel that couples are getting what they bargained for. Those who choose to marry in spite of a courtship fraught with unfaithfulness and lack of depth with regard to a monogamous commitment are simply asking for trouble. If such a couple is willing to attempt to find happiness in marriage on these premises, that is their affair; however, I have rarely seen it work.

An example of such circumstances is Arthur and Nancy, who met at a singles' club six months prior to their marriage. Arthur proudly told me that he considered himself a "male whore." Nancy was a little more subtle but confessed numerous times prior to the marriage that she had great confidence in the "new morality" and felt it important to have multiple sexual experiences before finally accepting one man to be her husband. "How else would I know who the right one is?" she quipped with cocky arrogance. During their six-month courtship they made no pretense of being faithful to each other, in spite of the fact that they did profess being in love and seemed sincere about plans to establish a solid marriage. After the wedding it was no surprise to anyone when Arthur continued to carry on an extramarital affair with an old girl friend. Nancy attempted to be broadminded, but her tolerance wore thin after a few months.

As she continued, Nancy lamented that Arthur had never really promised to forsake all others on her behalf, but she had thought that time would solve the problem. So she had retaliated by accepting an extramarital lover of her own, whom her husband soon began to resent. When Nancy finally came to tell me of this dilemma, I asked her what she intended to do, and she honestly had no idea. Frankly, I wasn't sure at the time as to how they could continue their current pattern of behavior, based on their present philosophy, and simultaneously build a good marriage, and I told her so. "We can't go on as we are," she acknowledged, "it's driving us all crazy." Finally, I suggested the following alternatives:

1. Dissolve the marriage completely since it had been founded on such unrealistic grounds and was indeed an unworkable arrangement.

2. Renegotiate the marriage with a new set of rules, by which they both might live and abide; rules that would include fidelity and understanding as to whether the marriage was to be permanent or to just last until it became too unpleasant to bother with.

3. Make an agreement to resolve all the interpersonal conflicts they had been bickering over since the inception of their marriage.

In spite of the fact that their problems had stimulated observations about the realities of life and marriage, these were still very selfish and immature people who were not ready to agree to anything that would require humility and sacrifice. I urged them to think seriously about the three proposals that I had made and to return in two weeks with a plan of attack.

Much to my surprise, they did return in two weeks with a long list of points on which they had agreed and told me that they had decided to renegotiate the marriage contract, and this time they were going to write their own. Although they considered themselves original in the points they chose to agree upon, the contract turned out to be almost a carbon copy of a traditional marriage contract that people have been agreeing to for years.

I have never seen a happy marriage based on any agreement in which premeditated infidelity is accepted. To be sure, I have seen many people tolerate infidelity, but not happily. If this is your situation, I would urge you to think about the two choices that I offered the couple in the above story. Either separate and stop hurting each other, or be honest and renegotiate the marriage by rules that you feel you could live by happily.

Infidelity due to lack of satisfaction in marriage is a completely different type of problem. There are hundreds of reasons why people would lack satisfaction in marriage and, therefore, an equal number of reasons why people would be willing to justify breaking their pledge of fidelity and attempt to find happiness and satisfaction with someone else. When the lack of satisfaction is purely sexual, a reasonable solution would be to turn to pages 167 through 186 of this text to review sexual adjustment and try to find the answer to your own problem. If you are not successful in doing so, consult your family physician for individual counseling.

As unpleasant as it is to be forsaken by one's mate, it is even more unpleasant to destroy the chances of happiness in marriage by holding a grudge and lacking the humility to admit the cause is lack of sexual satisfaction and not doing something about it.

If dissatisfaction in marriage falls into other categories, such as feeling unloved, feeling unimportant to your mate, feeling a lack of respect, or being bored, or constantly aggravated, or any of the other problems that appear in Part Two of this text, please review them one by one and attempt to put more satisfaction into your life. Adopting the solutions in the Golden Rules of Part Three into your daily living could also be valuable in your attempt to rebuild a debilitated marriage.

The third type of infidelity is circumstantial infidelity. There are those who would say that no such thing exists, because any sexual surrender outside of marriage would of its very nature constitute a form of premeditation and a violation of the marriage contract. It could further be argued that even the most circumstantial conditions might also be an effort to compensate for lack of satisfaction in marriage. I will not refute either of these hypotheses; however, I have known some cases in which infidelity was purely circumstantial.

One such case involved a twenty-five-year-old man came to me in great anxiety and with the following story. He said that he had been away with his National Guard unit for their annual two-week summer camp. On the weekend, it was traditional for the fellows to go into town and "raise hell at the local gin mill." This had always been a highlight of the summer camp experience in years gone by, so he certainly did not hesitate when it came time to join in the fun this year. The only difference was that instead of waking up in his bunk with his usual annual hangover, he awakened in a motel room in bed with a strange woman.

He was embarrassed and horrified at the possibility that he may have contracted venereal disease from the woman and was terribly worried about the possibility of transmitting it to his wife. He was equally upset for having fallen into this predicament and dreadfully worried about the possibility of his wife's finding out about it and responding with justified anger. For all I know, he may have been telling me a phony story in an attempt to justify his circumstances; however, I believed him. Fortunately, he did not have venereal disease, and I saw no reason to do anything other than reassure him and advise him to be more careful in the future. He had the good judgment to accept my advice; and, as far as I know, there have been no repetitions of infidelity.

In conclusion, I would like to emphasize that infidelity, though possibly not the worst indiscretion of marriage, usually carries with it the greatest consequences; namely, the possibility of pregnancy, transmission of disease, and the generation of anger on the part of the faithful mate. It is grounds for divorce in every court of law, and all told, a very unpleasant affair. If you have the misfortune to be a victim of infidelity in your marriage, I urge you to face up to it and to be honest. Try to classify it with the criteria outlined above, and then utilize the rest of the text to aid you in solving your problem. Infidelity in itself is not the end of the world unless you let it be, and unless you cannot develop a positive approach to its solution. It is not uncommon for the so-called faithful partner to be as guilty in causing the circumstances that precipitated the unfaithfulness as it was for the weaker partner who succumbed. The total marriage must be evaluated honestly and approached realistically if there is to be a happy resolution.

Do not give up hope. Some of the strongest marriages I know of have had episodes of infidelity. Even though the recollection of infidelity remains as a scar, it is possible to live with it and to build happiness in spite of it. Do not be eager to destroy your marriage and your family. Be thorough. Think it out. Talk it out. Get some help if you need it. If you pray, pray about it. If you follow these suggestions, there will usually be a satisfactory solution in store.

·6·
Unequal Development

Most couples in a marriage of choice begin their marital career on the premise that they complement each other's needs, but the years that follow frequently bring about inequalities in the development of their personalities and make communication, companionship, and even mutual respect a challenging problem.

With rare exception, inequality is not planned nor anticipated, but rather is an unavoidable circumstance. Inequalities fall into several categories.

Inequality due to age difference is common and predictable. When a marriage takes place between two people of significant age difference, it is to be expected that the years to come will precipitate inequalities in personality development. If, for instance, a thirty-five-year-old man marries a woman of twenty, people will not think this too unusual, especially if the girl is mature for her age. But stop! Look at this couple again when the husband is sixty and the wife forty-five! Or later, when the husband is seventy and the wife fifty-five! Obviously, their ages then would place them in different phases of life. Their interests, desires, and ideas all would be different.

Many years ago I met two nice people with such an age disparity. At the time they met, George was a fifty-year-old executive—very popular with all his colleagues. Mary was twenty-five, bright, cheerful, and mature beyond her years. Perhaps this was why her contemporaries had passed her over as a marriage partner. George had been widowed for five years, since the death of his forty-two-year-old wife, whom he had adored through their twenty-two years of happy marriage. Now he wanted and needed a second wife because he was obviously unhappy living alone. Mary was very receptive, for George seemed to possess all the qualities she had dreamed of in a husband. After courting for eighteen months, they both felt certain that they could handle any potential hardships that their age difference might create. And so they embarked on a life together.

The first fifteen years of the marriage were very happy ones. There were mutual friends whom they knew from work, and their age difference had little impact on their lives. George was able to sexually satisfy his young wife; he loved her tenderly, and told me he frequently thanked God for being able to have a second life of happiness. Up to that point, Mary also acknowledged her delight with life and was thankful to have found such an attentive man to give her the security she had always craved.

When George retired at sixty-five, Mary was forty. Although George's retirement income was adequate to support them both, Mary admitted that she enjoyed her work and the independence that came with having an income of her own. Since they had no children, she chose to continue working. Immediately, the age gap became far greater than ever before. When George surrendered his job, he also surrendered a great deal of his youth and status and became an older citizen. Mary's career, on the other hand, was now in its prime; she had been promoted to a position of significant responsibility. Having reached early middle age, she no longer wanted, or needed, to be considered older than her chronological age.

All the problems that one might anticipate in a situation of this type now seemed to arise. George aged rapidly, became embarrassed by his advancing years, and lost the self-confidence that once had been the backbone of his personality. Mary, because of her comparative youth and her capability, was forced to assume many of the so-called masculine responsibilities, and this she resented. What had been strong love degenerated into resentment, frustration, and overall unhappiness.

Not much could be done to remedy the situation, for it had deteriorated to the point where both George and Mary were actually happier when they were apart. It was senseless to recommend that Mary surrender her job and her security to become her husband's attendant. And George, a fine and honorable man, was far too proud to consider asking her to do so. Their only recourse was to pursue their separate paths and to live together nominally as husband and wife. Fortunately, they were able to do this because they were both mature people of principle. Let there be no mistake, however, in the later years of their marriage it was not a marriage at all but a peaceful coexistence.

It was obvious that George and Mary reaped the fruits of a good marriage for a number of years, but the time came when they were forced to pay the price because they had defied the laws of nature. They were fortunate in that they could pursue separate interests. They were also fortunate in having guidance to the understanding of their problems. George realized that his wife still enjoyed outside activities in which he no longer was able to participate; he himself was content to stay at home and watch television while she went off to the seashore. Although they neutralized their frustrations with such courtesies and kindnesses, each confessed to me separately that understanding and accepting the needs of the other was the only salvation for their marriage during those difficult years. Without this approach, the situation would have been absolutely impossible.

But not all couples are so lucky. I have, in fact, seen cases fraught with so much unhappiness as to make one of the partners commit suicide.

Who is to say what is the proper age difference between mates? Certainly not I. I can state, however, that if a couple has this problem, the answer is to understand it and substitute healthy and honorable outside interests for the necessarily missing mutual portion of their lives. Such gaps are not always in chronological age. They can also exist with people of the same age.

Premature aging can be either physical or mental.

We have all had the experience of knowing a couple in their late sixties, where one mate is feeble and even showing signs of early senility, while the other has been fortunate enough to remain substantially youthful. The interests and desires of these two people, even though they may have spent a lifetime together in happy marriage, will at this time be quite divergent. The secret, if there is one, is to recognize this divergence at a time when some separate interest can be cultivated rather than taking the path of bickering and blaming each other for the frustrations. Try to satisfy your obligations without compromising your own life entirely.

Unequal development can also exist in intellectual, social, cultural, and environmental capacities. It is not uncommon for people to embark on a marriage of choice with a well-suited mate and to find after several years that their development in the above-mentioned areas are completely unequal—much to the frustrations of both.

I knew a couple who had such a problem. I have watched them develop over many years. Katherine and Albert were high school sweethearts. After graduation, Albert went on to college to study to be a chemical engineer, and Katherine went to work as a secretary. After Albert completed his second year of college, Katherine had progressed in her job to a point where her salary was adequate to supplement Albert's part-time income so that they could be married during his last two years of college. They were deeply in love, knew each other thoroughly, and had a strong, sincere motivation in their marriage.

The first two years were happy ones, and they enjoyed working together and making the sacrifices required to make ends meet. Upon graduation, Albert found a job with great opportunity as a chemical engineer, and within a few months Katherine was pregnant. They were absolutely delighted. Katherine, of course, quit her job, and they planned to have a large family. In the succeeding years, they did indeed have five children.

Albert became quite successful. He received regular promotions, and was frequently required to attend many out-of-town meetings. Meanwhile, Katherine, who had previously been proud of her ability to deal with people and had enjoyed her own interests and accomplishments, found that she had to devote her entire time to being a mother and housekeeper. She had no time for personal indulgence or self-improvement; she never even got a chance to read the newspaper. Albert, on the other hand, was daily put into a position of personal self-improvement that was required for his job. Katherine had always been trim and style-conscious, but Albert had considered himself something of a slob. Now, however, job circumstances had caused Albert to become quite style-conscious, while Katherine was overburdened to the point of personal neglect. She had grown corpulent, and her wardrobe had become shabby.

Their daily routine was one in which Albert would get up with enthusiasm to go to his job, and Katherine would approach each day haggard and overburdened. Even so, she loved her husband and children, and did not approach her household duties resentfully. At the end of the day, Albert would arrive home eager to recount his interesting achievements, only to find that Katherine had stories of her own to tell about the children being sick or misbehaving, or about how the washing machine broke, leaving her with the chore of washing two-dozen diapers by hand.

When weekends came and social opportunities arose, Katherine routinely would balk at accepting invitations. She imagined herself conspicuous among Albert's friends and associates because she felt she had become a dull, unattractive, and uninteresting person. She became depressed and sincerely believed that she had let her husband down by not keeping up with him intellectually. She was resentful too because Albert seemed to be reaping all the benefits of her sacrifice while she herself seemed to be sacrificing only and not realizing any direct reward from her tasks. Albert was genuinely confused by Katherine's feelings when she related them to him. His view was that he had been doing his very best to provide for the family and advance himself for the benefit of the family. He could not understand why his success should not make the entire family happier. The question he asked was, "What more could a man possibly do that I am not already doing?"

The truth of the matter is that both of them were indeed doing their best, and no one could possibly question their love and devotion to each other. They had kept their bargain and followed the plan they had initially agreed to. Their problems seemed to be those of circumstance, which were made considerably worse because it was a long period of time before they sought help. Please note at this time that their present complaints were frigidity on the wife's part, the underlying cause of which was her feeling of intellectual inadequacy; bickering brought about by mutual frustration, and Katherine's fear that Albert was taking an interest in other women. Fear of another pregnancy was also a contributing factor.

Once they were cognizant of the basic underlying problem of unequal and divergent development, and were able to work on this problem as I outlined it above, and frigidity, the bickering, and the fears of infidelity soon cured themselves.

After we exposed the dynamics of the problem, the couple themselves provided the suggestions for the cure. Here they are:

1. They hired a housekeeper to help with the housework two days a week.

2. They established Saturday night as a date night. They would go to a preplanned activity, without the children.

3. Katherine would enroll in an art appreciation course at the local community college on Wednesday evening while Albert took care of the children.

4. Katherine would have a definite clothes budget to use solely for herself.

5. They were to go to the PTA together and share in responsibilities for the children.

6. They would plan a weekend away from the children every two months.

7. They would agree on a safe birth-control program.

8. Katherine would enroll in an exercise class and take tennis lessons to restore her figure.

Fortunately, these were very methodic, determined people who kept to the above plan religiously. The positive results were soon obvious, and tragedy was avoided.

In summary, the solution to the problem of unequal development is to be found in a humble, realistic assessment of the needs and frustrations of each other, and the subsequent resolve to cure what can be cured and to learn to work around the problems that have no solution. From the two cases above, it is obvious that improvement is usually possible, but that restoration to an ideal state is rarely 100 percent possible. But, for that matter, how many completely ideal marriages are there?

Please reevaluate your own marriage periodically. The earlier the problems of inequality can be recognized, the greater the possibility of rectifying the situation.

·7·

Marriages with Built-in Inadequacies

It is said that some marriages are made in heaven while others are made at the bargaining table. We would all like to believe that every marriage was a great romantic event between two people predestined for each other, and who go on to live happily ever after. In truth, however, a high percentage of marriages are ones of negotiated convenience. And people accept the mate as only the best, realistic substitute for the man or woman of their dreams.

Many circumstances, of course, make people willing to settle for marriages of this type; for instance, people who approach their late twenties or early thirties and who have never had a truly satisfying romantic relationship and who realize that they are well beyond the time when most people do marry. They want to be married and, therefore, are willing to accept any mate who is available rather than go on waiting. After all, if he or she has not arrived by that time, he or she may never come.

Another set of circumstances that brings about the bargaining-table marriage is when someone has been rejected by a lover and flies to any potential partner for the reassurance of being wanted at all. A third instance is when a person feels completely inadequate and is willing to accept any offer of marriage. This person truly doubts that he or she will ever have another offer. A fourth example is the couple who marry because they have conceived a child and feel obliged to make a home for the child. And a fifth instance is the couple who marry because their parents have arranged their marriage. (This is uncommon today in the United States but still prevalent in other parts of the world.) There are numerous other examples of marriages that are made at the bargaining table rather than in heaven. If your own marriage to some extent or other fits into this category, make notes and refer to them as you read through the remainder of this chapter.

It has always been my belief that marriage is indeed a sacrament, a sacred act blessed by God and reinforced by both the hardships and satisfactions of everyday life. By virtue of this, most marriages, even though they be entered into on less than a perfect foundation, work out to be quite satisfactory. People who are honest about their marriage vows usually find a great deal of pleasure in the sacrifices of marriage, and the union naturally grows stronger as children are born. Mutual sacrifice in time of need actually makes good marriages better.

When problems do arise because one person has accepted a less-than-ideal mate, they invariably take the form of resentment. This resentment is frequently responsible for the severe abuse or neglect of one mate by another, and in some cases it seems that only an act of God can make their life together tolerable.

Several years ago I had as patients a couple, about thirty-five, who were both schoolteachers. Their problem was the husband's uncontrollable depression and complete loss of self-confidence. He stated that his wife was a wonderful and capable person, and a leader in the community; and that he was completely undeserving of her. He said that everything he attempted "seemed to turn out wrong." He was so discouraged that he had given serious consideration to suicide as the only way out of his misery. When I later spoke to his wife, I observed that she was indeed a vivacious, sophisticated woman. She displayed self-confidence and a charming personality—in short, she was all that her husband had said she was. He himself, in her eyes too, was the "world champion clod." She laughed about his inadequacies and delighted in telling how the children would frequently make fun of him in the classroom. He was also so clumsy as to be accident prone. She was eager to add that he was not at all handy around the house and that it really fell into her domain to do most of that work too.

As she related her story, I became more and more aware of the fact the she seemed to be enjoying the tale of her husband's misfortune and was speaking of him without feeling, as she would speak of a fictitious character. She was not speaking the way a woman would speak about a husband with whom she was in love. When she finished her story, I asked her, "How did you ever get involved in such a mismatch in the first place?" She was somewhat taken aback by the question, but after a moment of thought she had an explanation. It was this: when she and her husband were in college, she was deeply in love with another young man who was bright, aggressive, witty, and quite her equal in charm and personality. He was, in short, everything she wanted in a husband, and they had a romance that for her seemed to be absolutely perfect. She was understandably heartbroken, therefore, when at the end of three years, he started dating another girl whom he married shortly thereafter.

She went on to say that she was bitter and depressed until she decided to prove her femininity by choosing another man and enticing him into marriage. Poor Benjamin was the victim. Prior to their marriage, Benjamin was a passive person, average in most ways. His grades were satisfactory; he had a few friends; but he was certainly no scintillating personality. He wanted to be a schoolteacher, nothing more, nothing less. He was delighted when Selma showered her attentions on him, and indicated she would be agreeable to marrying him. In his own words, "She was so much more than I had ever hoped for in a girl." From the time of their marriage, Selma attempted to make her husband into the image of the boyfriend who had jilted her. Benjamin obviously never made it, and she never ceased to remind him of his inadequacies. It was no wonder, therefore, that he gradually lost all self-confidence and sank deeper and deeper into depression. It was interesting that he never blamed Selma for his illness and never uttered any resentment of her constant criticism. His only explanation of his problem was, "I'm just not good enough."

Both mates received psychotherapy, but the outcome was a rather sad one. Benjamin, it was realized, would always feel inadequate and inferior as long as he was subjected to Selma's criticism. Selma concluded that she could not spend the rest of her life with such an inadequate person. She would always feel compelled to drive him into being the man she had always wanted. As Benjamin had the opportunity to review his years of marriage and his attempts to fulfill his wife's desires, he came to realize that Selma had never really loved him but had only wanted him to imitate the former boyfriend. (The marriage contract was, therefore, one into which she had entered fraudulently.) Even though he loved her desperately, Benjamin could no longer stand the constant failure complex.

By mutual consent they separated. Benjamin subsequently found a woman who was willing to accept him as he was and love him for it, and to the best of my knowledge they have found a fair degree of happiness together. Selma, on the other hand, married a successful salesman whom she had had her eye on for five years prior to her divorce.

The case above is not characteristic of all such bargaining-table problems. It was unfortunate, of course, that the problems of this particular marriage were unsolvable, but what the wife wanted and what the husband had to offer were so completely far apart that there had been really no basis for the marriage in the first place.

The purpose of this story was to give an example of just how bitterly cruel resentment in a mismatched marriage can be. This case, of course, was an extreme one because the wife was absolutely drunk with resentment and acknowledged no desire at all to be a wife to her husband. It was, therefore, a completely hopeless, as well as loveless, marriage. There have been few marriages that I have considered as hopeless as this one, but one could argue that it never really was a marriage. By the wife's own admission, it was never her intention to have and to hold her husband, nor was it her intention to stay by him, for richer, for poorer; in sickness and in health. She admitted that when she married, she had told a girl friend that she was going to make him do as a husband until someone better came along. If this were the limited extent to which she was willing to give of herself, how in the world could anyone attempt to transform such a petty bargain into a marriage?

In most marriages of this type, however, there is some common ground on which to work. There is usually some common interest. Most people are successful in building on the good features of the marriage and are willing to work around the shortcomings. The secret to doing so is to understand your mate's needs, as well as your own, and to accept them. Then look elsewhere in your life for healthful and socially acceptable activities to compensate for what is missing in your marriage. Give this some thought, if you will: Was your marriage founded on a flimsy basis, or was it founded on solid ground? Determine whether your problems are centered on unrealistic expectations of your mate. Remember that he or she was probably never aware of your expectations and that it may be impossible, given his or her personality, to fulfill them. If there are some aspects of your marriage that fit into this category, make note of them and reconsider them from time to time. Chances are that years of nagging could have done little to change your mate, so why not accept him or her "as is," all the while emphasizing the compatible points and overlooking and forgiving the incompatible ones?

If you are unwilling or unable to do this, and if you find that life is intolerable with your mate, and if you also find that your marriage agreement was such that neither you nor your mate really ever agreed to be what the other intended, I suggest you seriously evaluate whether you have or ever had a real marriage. (Homosexuality, for instance, might be another irreversible and intolerable inadequacy.)

As I have said already, I have strong faith in the sacramental state of marriage and do not personally condone divorce; however, I also firmly question the validity of many marriages founded on a shaky agreement at the time of the wedding ceremony. For marriages of this type, I strongly recommend that the whole agreement be reconsidered and renegotiated. It might well be that when people are presented once more with the decision of spending the rest of their lives together, with a free choice this time, they might find that they can accept a good mature agreement of choice with more enthusiasm. If, on the other hand, it was a marriage that never was meant to be, there is nothing to be gained by the daily insult and frustration of attempting to be what one cannot be.

Marriages that have produced children are not easily dissolved, regardless of the basis for the original marriage.

It is nearly impossible to turn one's back on parenthood. Therefore, the solution, if there is one, is to renegotiate the marriage in order to live with each other's inadequacies and attempt wherever possible to avoid aggravating and magnifying them.

The Golden Rules that constitute Part Three of this text will be helpful in aiding couples with these problems. It is never too late for courtship. Read Part Three before you give up on any marriage and give it a try!

·8·
Marriage in Which One Mate Is Transplanted from His Native Environment

In this day of world travel, it is not at all uncommon for couples from completely different cultures to meet, fall in love, and marry. Following the marriage, one or both of the members are faced with adjusting to life in a completely new environment and must learn different folkways and mores. This was very, very obvious during World War II and the Korean War and afterward when soldiers returned home with wives whom they had met overseas. Their romances were very close during their time abroad, but when the couples were faced with the problems of coming back to the United States and fitting into conventional society, with all of its traditions and prejudices, the task often became difficult.

The problem for the transplanted mate was twofold: in addition to becoming an American, the foreign wife had to meet the husband's family and friends and attempt to make herself acceptable. This meant adjusting to the American attitudes toward hygiene, housekeeping, and child rearing. It also meant that she had to surrender all the family ties of her former life. Her family and friends were too far away to help; people and places she had known her entire life were taken away from her, and, in short, she was forced to surrender everything for the privilege of being married to the husband of her choice. The problems which ensued were obvious. Loneliness, resentment, depression, disappointment, and even despair were the cardinal symptoms. The husband frequently found himself embarrassed at his wife's different cultural background. It was strange and conspicuous in his own country, and he was frequently guilty of attempting to force her to conform to the ways of his friends and family. The wife, on her part, would frequently rebel with the explanation that he promised to love her as she was at the agreement of marriage and that it was unfair for him now to expect her to be otherwise.

These examples represent the extreme of environmental transplants, but practically everyone is forced to embrace to some degree a new society and a new culture after marriage. This involves a necessity for adaption and a necessity for tolerance, which usually go far beyond what was anticipated at the time of the marital agreement.

The answers to these problems are several: (1) Never expect of your mate something that he or she never promised to give. In the case of one couple, of whom the wife was a naturalized citizen, this was evident in a somewhat amusing but expressive way. The couple met in Italy while the husband was in service, and they enjoyed a delightful early courtship and happy early marriage. When they moved to the United States, his family immediately embraced the new wife and did all they could to make her feel welcome. It seemed that the marriage would be a happy one—that is, until one of the husband's sisters criticized the new bride for not shaving under her arms; she explained that girls in the United States shaved their armpits, and it is considered a sign of femininity. Maria explained that in the part of Italy from where she came, women do not shave under their arms, and she saw no reason why she should. She said that when they were married in Italy, the subject never came up and she felt it would be unfair of him to expect her to do this. When the husband became aware of his sister's criticism, he became embarrassed by his wife and prevailed upon her to conform. She rebelled, stating the criticism was unjustified. This was the beginning of a long series of such problems. Fortunately, they were both clear-thinking people, very much in love, and willing to compromise on many issues. Their strong love for each other and their willingness to understand each other's needs and desires spared the marriage from deep and irreparable troubles. (2) The second rule, therefore, is bring the problems into the open, discuss them freely, come to a mutual decision, and adhere to it. (3) The couple should remain primarily faithful to each other. If there is conflict between the mate and family or friends, the rights and privileges of the mate must take priority. With this as a foundation, time and understanding cure most other problems. Difficulties of this type are usually temporary and easily solved by people who are humble and realistic enough to work on them.

If there are problems of cultural difference in your own marriage, list them. Discuss them openly with your mate and try to agree upon a mutually satisfying plan for their resolution.

·9·

Jealousy

Jealousy, as it will be used in this chapter, means resentful insecurity with regard to the faithfulness of one's mate. The symptoms of this type of jealousy are suspiciousness, hostility, depression, frigidity, paranoia, and sometimes even spiteful infidelity.

Jealousy falls into two basic categories. First, jealousy resulting from one mate teasing the other with acts or threats of infidelity and unfaithfulness, and second, jealousy resulting from one member feeling inadequate and unworthy of the mate.

Once a person has been jilted by any partner (before or after marriage), he or she is supersensitized to the possibility of being disappointed again. A woman who had been jilted by a former boyfriend might always be suspicious and jealous of her husband even though he never gives her any valid reason to suspect unfaithfulness.

People who are products of homes in which the parents have been unfaithful to each other are also suspicious. The mechanism of thought and behavior can be summarized by the statement, "I know by my experience that members of the opposite sex are not to be trusted. After having been hurt once, I will be on guard never to be hurt again."

If your problem is jealousy of this nature, you must first analyze it and determine whether the object of your resentment is really your mate, or the phantom of a premarital experience, or the recollection of parents who were unfaithful to each other. If you are judging your mate by someone else's conduct, be reasonable and make your judgment on his or her own merits. All men are not alike; neither are all women. And each person must be given the benefit of being considered honest and honorable unless actions prove otherwise.

If your mate has ignited jealousy in you, it is ordinarily the result of flirtatious teasing, which might simply be the product of ill-timed humor and bad taste. For some people, it is a habit from premarital years. Also, some people have a psychic necessity to constantly prove their sexual identity; they have to feel desirable to the opposite sex.

In some instances, this flirtatiousness represents a genuine frustration from an inadequate marriage; if this be the case, I urge you to review the general status of your marriage. Flirting might be only a symptom and not the underlying cause. If this be the case, analyze it and conduct yourself accordingly. Correct the inadequacies if you can.

If the jealousy results from actual infidelity, I refer you to the chapter that deals with this subject exclusively and urge you to understand infidelity and work toward its solution. If the jealousy is over a resolved infidelity from the past, you must realistically evaluate whether such an infidelity might recur. If there is reason to suspect infidelity or its probability, you must, of course, work toward its resolution. If there is no reason, then you have little choice but to discipline yourself to not punish your mate for past sins—"The world is weary of the past." There is an old adage in psychiatry that if you give a person a good name to live up to, he will do his best to live up to it; and if you give a person a bad name to live up to, the chances of his accepting this image in his own mind are almost as great. So even though your marriage may have scars from the past, but if there is no reason for suspicion now, for goodness' sake forget it. Enjoy the present. You might inadvertently create a recurrence if you are continually suspicious without cause.

The last category of jealousy is that which a person feels as a result of doubts about his or her adequacy as a husband or wife. Conceivably, there are reasons for feelings of inadequacy. They may be due to a basic difference in cultural background, or there might be a significant illness, or there might be a difference in developmental maturity. Unfortunately, when one feels undeserving of one's mate, symptoms of hostility, suspiciousness, and depression frequently develop, and create further alienation.

The more profitable course would be to analyze the situation at face value. If there is a disparity in personality development, or if either partner has permitted himself or herself to deteriorate cosmetically or intellectually, an effort should be made to go on a self-evaluation and a self-improvement program. This is never impossible: after all, if two people once loved and respected each other enough to consummate a marriage, there must be enough residual attraction remaining to once again bring about equality. Unfortunately, these matters are usually left as skeletons in the closet —unspoken, undiscussed, and often not even admitted.

If there is to be a solution, the problem must be brought out into the open and acknowledged. You might find that you are overemphasizing something of no consequence, or, at least, of no importance whatsoever to your mate; your feelings of inadequacy may be groundless. If you're too fat—lose some weight. If you feel dull—read, or take an interesting course and learn something. If you think you are unattractive for other reasons, get advice from someone who can show you how to make yourself more attractive. A positive attitude will give you a feeling of self-satisfaction; and the more satisfied you are with yourself, the less likely you are to be jealous of your mate.

One of the most common and difficult forms of jealousy to cope with is jealousy of a mate's work, hobby, or other outside interest. Even a mate's interest in the children can be a source of jealousy. In short, anything that competes for one's time and attention could be a problem.

If jealousy exists in your marriage, diagnose its cause and treat it promptly before you become consumed by it. If you cannot handle it on your own, get help soon. It will never resolve itself without understanding and a good plan.

Please write down your own experiences with jealousy. If you understand the mechanisms of past problems, any future ones will be easier to handle.

·10·

Financial Problems of Marriage

When he heard that I was writing a book on marital problems, a friend commented that marriage was 10 percent romance and 90 percent finance—and that the best premarital counseling would be a course in accounting for both men and women. I think his percentages were somewhat exaggerated, but his point was certainly well made.

In laying the foundation for your marriage, good advance planning—as well as understanding of and mutual agreement on all plans—is essential. To begin, you and your future mate should agree about the economic level on which you will be living. (Differences in economic background will often create difficulties unless both partners can reconcile the differences to each other's satisfaction.) Then you must both be willing to accept this level and adjust your spending and income goals accordingly; in other words, decide on your priorities as far in advance as possible and stick to them. Finally, you should agree to the apportionment of your budget and avoid impulse spending—unless it is for something you both really want for your mutual benefit.

The twentieth century has given us the educational opportunities and the rights to equal employment for women; and birth control procedures have provided a great deal of latitude for couples in selecting the economic plane on which they would like to live. It is to a great degree a matter of choosing what you would like to have and how much you are willing to sacrifice to have it.

To some people material wealth is so important that they are willing to exert a high percentage of their total effort toward making money, and they are willing to defer the joys of parenthood and housekeeping. To others, being able to have children is of vital importance, and many men prefer their wives to stay at home and take care of the children; to such men this is far more important than anything money could buy.

These contrasting philosophies are well demonstrated by two couples of my acquaintance, of similar age and background. Both husbands are teachers in one of our local high schools. The men were college classmates, good friends, and consider themselves equal in most ways. The girls they married, while still in college, also received degrees in teaching.

After they married, couple number one decided to have four children early on—while they were still young and could "grow up" with them. The wife would work as a full-time homemaker, and the family would contrive to live on the husband's salary. Couple number two, more interested in the material things of life, was in no hurry to start a family; the wife retained her job. Their combined incomes are double that of couple number one and, in addition, the husband, working part-time as an automobile salesman, earns some $6,000 a year beyond his teaching salary. (He says that since they have no children and live in a fairly small apartment, there isn't that much for him to do in his extra time, and he enjoys meeting the people he sees in his part-time job.) With a total combined income of better than 225 percent above couple number one, they are able to live in almost unlimited luxury. They always take an expensive summer vacation, and they have a substantial savings account and investment program.

Fortunately, both of these couples are content with their decisions and would want it no other way. The purpose of the story is to point out the wide variation that two otherwise parallel couples have to choose from. The important thing with these two couples is that they made their choice willingly and embraced the results without reservation. They knew what they were choosing, and this is why they are happy with the results.

Another major factor in marital financial matters is the problem of contenting oneself with the practical economic plane that is chosen. Couple number one could potentially have a serious problem if either mate's background was on an unduly high economic plane. If their choice was to live as a six-member family on a schoolteacher's income, then, this is what they must be mature enough to realize and work their economic planning accordingly. So often we see couples do great harm to themselves by failing to face up to their own decision to live within their economic bounds. Husbands are frequently too proud to admit that there just isn't enough money in the family income to keep up with the Joneses, and wives are frequently too unrealistic to appreciate the economic limitations of their husbands.

The agreement at the time of marriage should, and usually does, include the acceptance by both partners of the economic level on which they are to start out living. "For richer, for poorer" is self-explanatory; there is practically no correlation between overall economic achievement and the success of a marriage, but there is a big correlation between marital success and the *attitude* toward the economic status.

A friend of mine works as a machinist in a nearby industrial plant; his income is double the current minimum wage for a forty-hour week. He and his wife and two children live in a modest but pleasant home that is kept in beautiful repair. Although the furnishings are not elaborate, they are in good taste, comfortable, and functional. The lawn is always well tended, and the flowers show the care and interest that the couple has in gardening. The wife has long accepted her husband's economic limitations and has adjusted her desires accordingly. She says she would not want a fur coat because she knows how many work hours the price of such a luxury would represent and therefore would not feel justified in demanding it. The couple enjoy an active social life, consisting of church socials, having friends in for cards, and visiting the homes of their friends. They also take a family camping trip each summer for their vacation.

The husband told me that he has never regarded lack of monetary wealth as detrimental to the family social life. As he put it, "It just requires a bit more advance planning to get the most out of our recreation dollars." He further pointed out that when he and his family go camping for a weekend, their total expenses run approximately one day's pay, which is just about what dinner for two in a fine restaurant would cost.

Wealth is not necessarily having a large income. Wealth is learning to be happy with what you have. If you find yourself brooding about what you do not have, take a lesson from the family above; and count your blessings, make the most of what you have, and enjoy it.

The last item to discuss concerning finance is budgeting the family income. As with most other facets of marriage, the secret of good budgeting is good planning and mutual agreement. Figure out what you have to work with, what your needs are, what you want to put into savings, and what extras you can afford. It all sounds so simple, but it is absolutely the reverse of what most people do. Common practice these days in our credit-card society is to buy what we want with little regard for payment. The retailers have succeeded in convincing the potential buyer to think in terms of "Do we want it?" rather than "Can we afford it?" Credit is a convenience, but it is a very abused convenience and creates a multitude of problems. Therefore, couples with substantial incomes can have budget problems too.

Another important factor to consider in family budgeting is having a plan by which each family member is allotted an allowance for his or her private use. Such an allowance will permit every member of the family to have the dignity of being able to take care of his or her personal needs (clothing, personal grooming, savings, recreation, gifts, and so forth). Even children, as soon as they are old enough, should be given an allowance and receive guidance on its use. Although personal allowances may be limited by necessity, each person should be entitled to a regular amount of money without having to ask for it.

Probably the most common source of argument in any marriage is money; and the plan outlined above should help to avoid such disputes.

In summary, the most likely solution to any financial problem is talking it out. Sit down with pencil and paper and make some mutual decisions. If there are points on which you disagree, write them down and then discuss them. If you still cannot agree, wait a week and each try again to grasp the other person's point of view. Be honest and keep trying! Sooner or later, the wisest solution will surely surface.

·11·
Alcoholism

"In Sickness and in Health, till Death Do Us Part." There are many types of illnesses that people are exposed to during their lifetime. Some illnesses are curable; some are not. *The illness of alcoholism is often manageable, but the predilection for the addiction is rarely, if ever, curable.*

An *alcoholic* has been defined as being any person who drinks alcohol for the purpose of experiencing relief of tension and thereby craves it for that purpose. This, of course, includes people who have never been drunk in their entire lives. It is, however, the difference between an alcoholic and a party drinker. With this definition, it is easy to understand why the statement is true that not all alcoholics are drunks and not all drunks are alcoholics. A person who looks forward to the relaxation obtained from a cocktail or two before dinner after a good day's work might well be an alcoholic if he is dependent on this cocktail for relaxation. The party-goer who gets drunk on New Year's Eve and drinks to be the life of the party is not likely to be an alcoholic since, presumably, he or she is drinking *because* of the party and not for relief from any underlying tensions. With this background, it is easy to appreciate the fact that alcoholics fall into two categories. The first category, which fortunately includes the greatest percentage of alcoholics, may be classified as *ambulatory, or functional and socially acceptable, alcoholics.* It is OK for a couple to look forward to, say, two cocktails before dinner to relax. But they must stop short of impairing their senses. Even though many can contain themselves within these bounds, they are usually dependent on and habituated to the alcohol.

Many folks acknowledge a need for this evening relaxation and are quite convincing in describing its therapeutic value. Though I would offer a strong word of caution about its potential abuse, I would not insist that people who fall into this category be forced to abandon their drinking habits so long as they are kept within tolerable limits.

The *uncontrolled, nonproductive, socially incompatible alcoholic* is the one who drinks for relief of tension and permits himself to become drunk and have his senses altered on a regular basis.

We have all known of marriages, businesses, and assorted people who have been ruined by the abusive use of alcohol. Society in general looks with disfavor and disgust upon anyone who drinks abusively and soon ostricizes that person socially. Because of this irresponsibility, he has great difficulty keeping or progressing in any sort of work, and so he very quickly finds himself with economic problems as well. Any outsider would say that this is indeed a fool who would be so self-destructive.

Herein is the greatest misconception. Even though society deems any person a fool for ruining his or her life with alcohol, alcoholism is an addiction that the person cannot control. The alcoholic has neither will nor choice. He cannot decide to take or not to take the next drink. The addiction decides. The alcoholic understands better than anyone else why he should not drink and what alcohol will do to him in the future because he knows what it has done to him in the past; yet he is powerless to prevent it. This is why an alcoholic is usually the world's most accomplished con artist. He fully understands and endorses all the reasons why he should not drink, but his common sense is overruled by his compulsive addiction.

Now that we have a working definition of *alcoholic*, we can examine how such a person functions in marriage. Ten years ago, James came to my office in a stuporous drunken state, attended by his mother. At that time, he was twenty-five and a handsome young man in spite of his condition. His mother stated that he had been drunk for three weeks and that she had just retrieved him from jail in a nearby city where he had been confined for boisterous behavior. Since he was medically debilatated as a result of his prolonged drunken state, I hospitalized him for seven days in order to dry him out. This gave me time to get to know him. After the third day in the hospital, James had his senses about him and was able to tell me his story. He had started drinking at the age of fourteen in imitation of his father. (A high percentage of alcoholics are the sons and daughters of alcoholics. Even though alcohol may have caused endless grief and suffering that the future alcoholics both observed and may well have suffered from when they were children, the urge to imitate the wayward parent is frequently uncontrollable.) James stated that he had first begun to drink as a form of mischief and as a way of having fun, but he soon realized that alcohol gave him the facility of overlooking worry and seemed to supply him with a degree of self-confidence that he otherwise lacked. (Relief from worry and tension and artificial self-confidence are two of the cardinal addicting properties of alcohol.)

He stated that all through his life his performance was below what he thought his level of attainment should be and that he had great difficulty accepting his imperfections. When he was eighteen, he went on a weekend drunken spree with a blind date, and the result was that the girl became pregnant. Even though they hardly knew each other, the couple went on to marry and to have a total of four children in a relatively short period of time. He said that he had been drinking heavily all through the entire marriage to date. He wasn't sure whether or not he really loved his wife, but he was sure that he could not stand her incessant nagging him about his drinking and irresponsibility. His wife was constantly reminding him of his inadequacies, making his life intolerable, and forcing him to drink for relief. (It is not uncommon for alcoholics to blame others for their urge to drink, even though they readily admit that the criticism is justified. Sometimes they provoke such criticism as an excuse to drink.) He claimed to be a reasonably successful salesman who, although he had difficulty keeping a job, performed well when he was working. Actually, he had a reputation for being an excellent salesman, thanks to his winning personality and "nice guy" image. (Alcoholics typically present a "nice guy" image because they need the approval of others since they disapprove of themselves.) During his hospital stay, James began to appreciate the sufferings of his family during his drunken escapades. He admitted his guilt over neglecting his children; however, he stated that he never really had any feeling of satisfaction nor compassion from his wife. He said that he realized he had been a mess to live with and probably didn't deserve much from her, but that he had a strong feeling that there was more from life than he was getting and he desperately needed to pursue happiness. He had to have a better plan, he said.

I discussed the overall status of the situation with his wife, who said that she was fed up with the marriage and generally fed up with her husband. She said that after the hell she had been through over the past seven years of marriage, she had been hurt and disappointed so many times that she had no desire to try any more. This was understandable because she had indeed been through more than should be required of anyone. I asked her, however, what she thought of a program whereby her husband would live with his parents until he had been sober and rehabilitated for a three-month period. Would she then be willing to renegotiate the marriage? She was agreeable, but felt it would be impossible for him to stay dry for three months. When I proposed the three-month drying-out period to the patient, he was delighted, because he didn't feel prepared at the time to accept the responsibilities and aggravations of his marriage.

James went to live with his parents in an atmosphere that was virtually devoid of problems. His mother and father were very eager for his rehabilitation and agreed to spare him aggravation of any type whatsoever. He took to this marvelously; and with the aid of psychotherapy and tranquilizing medication, he was on his way to a rather remarkable recovery. He got a job with a fine company, and within two months he was their top salesman. Success and the flattery that goes with it were exactly what he needed, and he thrived on it. He gained back the weight he had lost over the years and became the picture of health. He was bright, alert, and witty; and it wasn't long before women started to make advances. Everything was going exactly as I had planned, and it seemed almost too good to be true. It was. When I thought the time was right, I asked James' wife to see me again so we could discuss the possibilities of renegotiating the marriage. Her attitude, much to my surprise, was wary. She recalled seeing James sober before, and even though he was now "putting on a good act" for everyone, she was not enthusiastic about attempting to renew the marriage. She was convinced that James' present good behavior was due to his being permitted to think only about himself without having to give any of himself to his family. She called my attention to the fact that he was enjoying a good salary from his new job and was indulging in many luxuries, such as eating in high-priced restaurants. Moreover, he had contributed nothing over the past few months to the support of herself or their children. (This is characteristic behavior of the alcoholic. Invariably, alcoholics think only of themselves and do not—or cannot—accept responsibility.) I told her I was aware of James' egocentricity, but that I felt a sustained period of sobriety would motivate him to reassume some of the family responsibilities.

She was still skeptical, and it made me wonder whether she really wanted a husband at all—regardless of his qualifications. The tale of these two people was beginning to take a different turn. I challenged her with the question, "If you'll just tell me what you want in a husband, I'll see what we can do about remaking your husband to fit those specifications." Her answer was well put. "If I have to have a husband at all," she said, "I would like one who would provide me and my children with an adequate, stable income and one who would not cause any trouble." "What about love?" I asked. "Wouldn't you want someone who would be affectionate and need your love and be willing to give love in return?" Her answer was, "Not if I could help it." As we discussed the problem further, I became aware that she never complained about her husband's alcoholism, only about their incompatibility. She never did complain that she was disappointed in not having an adequate husband but only that she had to put up with the one she had. (This is not at all uncommon among the mates of alcoholics. Surprisingly, many are unable to give of themselves sexually and emotionally, and find a fair bit of consolation in the fact that their spouses are drunkards. This way, they need not feel guilty about not being a dedicated mate. Who could argue that the alcoholic deserved one?)

(This is, in fact, an archetypal story in the study of alcoholics. The wives of a fairly high percentage of rehabilitated alcoholics are so inadequate as women that they [the wives] literally drive the husbands back to drink and thus absolve themselves of the responsibility of having to be a wife. The same is true for husbands of female alcoholics.)

At my suggestion, after three more months of sobriety had passed and James was still steadily employed, the couple dated on five occasions without their children. The purpose of this was to attempt to establish a new relationship, upon which they might be able to negotiate a worthwhile marriage. It turned out, however, to be a failure. The wife stated that her husband's immaturity and selfishness irritated her to the point where she could hardly stand his presence, let alone want to reestablish a marriage with him—all this despite her feeling that her children should have a father. The husband stated that although he had practically conquered the urge to drink for relief of tension, his need for a drink to help him get away from it all became practically intolerable after five minutes in his wife's presence. He was convinced that sobriety and the company of his wife were mutually exclusive. The marriage was impossible for him. She agreed, and they divorced within a year.

Following the divorce, I have seen the wife on numerous occasions, and she is quite convincing as she tells of what a relief it is to be free of the burdens and aggravations of marriage. But she meant *all* marriages. When I asked her if she would be interested in a new mate if one were to come along, her answer was a definite "No." She said that she enjoys parties, and even an occasional date, but has no desire to be anyone's wife again. As she lamented her story of marriage, which more and more became a denunciation of the whole concept, she said that she really never wanted to marry in the first place. The reason was that her introduction to marriage as a child, that is, the observation of her parents, was a tragic one. And she always feared she might involuntarily imitate it. Her father was a drunkard, and abused her mother cruelly. She resented her father bitterly and came to resent all men and all masculinity. Her view of men was that they were all self-centered, animalistic, sex-driven creatures whose main purpose in life was to abuse and take advantage of women. She confessed that her marriage was an accident and a mistake, and even though she agreed to go through the motions that she never had any intentions of surrendering herself as a wife to her husband and had little intention of doing so in the future. Might she have been a good wife to a sober individual? (This is a single case; however, the personality pattern and the attitude toward marriage that this unfortunate woman expressed has been repeated to me so many times by wives of alcoholics that I wonder sometimes if such women don't intentionally choose to marry alcoholics so that they might convince themselves through a self-fulfilling prophecy that their impression of men is a real one.)

James continued to do well for quite some time. However, he began to neglect his job little by little and find ways to spend more and more time at the racetrack—a new addiction. He rationalized that by being the best salesman in the company he could accomplish more in half a day than his colleagues could in a full day. He saw no harm in treating himself to frequent afternoons at the racetrack. It was not his intention to bet heavily, he said, but he thoroughly enjoyed the game of chance as well as the thrilling excitement of horse racing. (It seems to be a basic urge of alcoholics to resist conformity and the disciplines of regular employment. For that matter, they even seem to rebel against prosperity, security, and responsibility.) After some months of sobriety, James' health was excellent, and he was indeed, as I said before, a handsome young man. It was not long before he had an attractive girl friend, and they were considering marriage.

When he consulted me about getting married again, I suggested that he was not yet ready because he had not yet disciplined himself adequately to become a responsible husband. He still had debts, and his job had become insecure because of his poor attendance. Most seriously, his attitude toward his responsibilities was not good. I suggested that if he could get rid of all his debts, and have $5,000 in the bank, I would recommend the marriage. At that time, he was $3,000 in debt, but his income was $45,000 a year; and he had no expenses other than the $200 a week that he had been ordered to pay his wife for the expenses of his children. My recommendation, therefore, was not unreasonable. His parents were not charging him for maintenance, and they even did his laundry.

He agreed that if he could meet these requirements, it would constitute a sign of his maturity and that he himself would feel more comfortable in approaching the responsibilities of a new marriage. One month later, he admitted that even though he had $500 a week left over after meeting his obligations, he was not able to save so much as $5 a week, only 1 percent of his income. He added that he had analyzed himself and concluded that he would not be content with the self-discipline I had recommended. He was therefore going to take his chance at the second marriage—just as at the racetrack—and trust to luck that it would work out. I wished him well but told him that he was foolish not to be able to guarantee his actions to himself before possibly jeopardizing the security of a new wife.

His fiancée said that she realized they had a difficult road ahead but that she loved him so much she was willing to accept whatever she got. (Personal disciplines are nearly impossible for the alcoholic personality to accept, even if the alcoholic has enjoyed a prolonged stretch of sobriety. The cure for alcoholism must extend far beyond the cessation of alcoholic abuse. It must also include a remolding of the basic personality and the cultivation of discipline and responsibility.) The new wife was a sincere and warm individual who was steadfast in her commitment to stand by her husband in sickness and in health, for richer, for poorer, till death do they part. She had not, however, had a firsthand experience with one of his drinking sprees.

That occasion came the tenth week after the honeymoon. James was drunk for a solid week, and when he returned, with the aid of the police, his wife was heartbroken but determined to do her part in his rehabilitation. She was panicked, however, because she was already pregnant, and she interpreted her husband's carousing as an insult to her and to the pregnancy as well. In addition to this, she did not feel well during her pregnancy and was, therefore, a reluctant sexual partner. She was frequently irritable.

At this time James decided that if he could limit himself to one drink a day, on his way home from work, it would relax him enough to be able to tolerate his problems at home. (Even though it is true that alcohol is an excellent tranquilizer, it is equally true that James had ample tranquilizer capsules at his disposal, which would have done the job just as well. Alcoholics who choose to drink have an endless number of devious methods of tricking themselves into thinking that they can get by with just one or two drinks. In reality, when an alcoholic takes the first drink, his alcoholism takes over, and he usually drinks until his behavior is socially unacceptable. He often ends up doing damage to himself and will not quit until that end comes. AA refers to this as "stinking thinking.")

As expected, it was a matter of some two weeks before James' two drinks at the end of the day progressed into full-time daily drunkenness. Each night, as he came home from work strongly under the influence of alcohol, he would approach his wife sexually. At first, in her desperation to avoid alienating him, she would attempt to accommodate him; but she quickly found out that he was unable to perform sexually while under the influence of alcohol. (This is very common. The alcoholic, male or female, frequently turns to thoughts of sex and the sex act, but males are frequently unable to perform.) Shakespeare described it thus: "Drink spurs the desire but dulls the performance."

In the midst of his embarrassment about his inability to perform sexually, the alcoholic often becomes hostile to his mate and sometimes is violent to the point of physical abuse. After a few episodes of this type, the mate will usually find it intolerable to even attempt sexual involvement and therefore rejects it. The result is often that the drunken mate will become paranoid and accuse his mate of not wanting him because she is carrying on sexually with someone else.

The couple I am illustrating unfortunately followed the classical set of events described above; and it wasn't long before James became physically abusive, and his new wife became heartbroken and depressed. This was aggravated by James' losing his job, as a result of his drinking, and it seemed as though he were right back where he started with the former mate.

There were, of course, differences. This time James had a woman who truly wanted a husband and was willing to convey this feeling to him. Furthermore, this second wife had the knack of making her husband feel more important than their new baby. Instead of presenting the child to him as a competitor for her attention, she presented the baby as someone who admired him even from the time of birth. This was motivation enough to induce James to join Alcoholics Anonymous and attend the meetings regularly.

Fortunately, James had had enough psychotherapy to appreciate that he had much reason to stay sober. At the time of this writing, he has been sober for over five years. He has been reinstated in his job, and they are living as a happy family with their three sons.

Above all, he achieved the one essential prerequisite for alcoholic rehabilitation—humility. He admitted he was an alcoholic and that the first drink he would take would cause complete decompensation. Let there be no mistake—his personality was not completely changed! He is still irresponsible with money and not above taking a few days off from work for the weakest excuse imaginable. But his wife has learned to assume the responsibilities he cannot handle; she does not punish him for not being what he cannot be. Her actions spare him the agonizing frustration that frequently decompensated him in the past.

And so, their marriage has been saved by her understanding as a wife. When I asked him if he was done with alcohol forever, he looked at me, smiled, and said, "I know the situation well enough to know that I could never say yes and be sure of it. Like any alcoholic, I am only one drink away from being right back to where I was years ago—a drunkard."

And when I asked him what advice he would give other alcoholics and their mates, he replied, "Join an Alcoholics Anonymous group. Take each day as it comes, promising yourself twenty-four hours of sobriety at a time. Be honest and be humble, and stay away from that very first drink."

I have attempted to give a review of alcoholism by citing the above case because it includes most facets of alcoholism. It is, however, far from a complete discussion of all the problems of alcoholism and should not be accepted as such. For this, I would refer you to the Alcoholics Anonymous chapter nearest your home for further guidance. Alcoholics Anonymous is listed in almost every phone book in the country. I have never known a call to any AA group to go unheeded, and I have never known AA to give up on anyone, regardless of how bad he had once been.

It is an excellent program, and it works. In all of my experiences, I have never seen a better spirit of camaraderie that equals that of a good AA meeting.

In summary, if you are an alcoholic, admit it. Join an AA group to get insight into your problem and work toward its resolution. If you are married to an alcoholic, never argue with a drunk. But when he or she is sober, insist that the person undertake a therapeutic program, and don't take "no" for an answer. Tolerance only keeps the alcoholic away from a program of help. Join an Al-Anon group. It will help you to understand the problem and establish your own plan for managing it. If you do not resolve the problem early in your marriage, it may well destroy the marriage. At best, you and your children will be subject to a lifetime of misery.

If your alcoholic mate refuses help, make up your mind early on whether you choose to live with a drunk or not. Don't hesitate to deliver the ultimatum of "Take it or leave it" and, if necessary, proceed into separation until his state of prolonged sobriety has been established. If you choose to live with the alcoholic in spite of drunkenness, then you have chosen your lot in life and should not complain about it.

If your once alcoholic mate establishes a state of sobriety, try to make his life pleasant and satisfying enough, so that he will have reason to stay sober. Never resurrect old sins or magnify inadequacies. Such actions will only reopen wounds and drive the alcoholic back to the bottle. The alcoholic must be judged for what he is today. In short, you must follow the AA plan and take one day at a time.

Finally, I must acknowledge that people who have a religious commitment are more successful than others in handling alcoholism and drug addiction. The strength of prayer and faith can be far more effective than psychotherapy in many cases of this type.

·12·

Marriage with a Depressed Mate

Depression is a state of uncontrollable, distorted mental activity in which the person assumes an attitude of pessimism, lack of self-confidence, lethargy, uncontrollable craving for sleep, insomnia, irritability, and mental confusion. It is difficult for the person to think clearly or organize activities, and he manifests a general state of nervousness. My purpose here is not to present a complete psychiatric summary of depression, but rather to give a bit of insight into the mechanisms that bring it about, to offer an understanding of it as an illness rather than a willful act of antisocial behavior, and to offer some suggestions regarding its management and cure. We shall consider depression as falling into three major categories.

1. The depression that one would experience following a violent personal tragedy, such as the loss of a loved one, the serious illness of a mate or parent or child, a serious accident or a personal debilitating illness, or the loss of a job. These are surely tragedies, and depression can be regarded as a normal reaction to them.

2. A pathologic depression that is really a serious psychiatric entity or a form of mental disease. This form of depression is unrelated to any serious environmental situation, even though it is not uncommon for a person to single out a scapegoat as the cause. This type of depression must be recognized for the illness it is, and proper medical and psychiatric care must be sought. Recent medical research is clearly pointing to a biochemical imbalance being present in such cases. Therefore discussion, reasoning, environmental modification, and even good fortune rarely help. It is very definitely treatable with medication, and the prognosis is fairly good. An early visit to your family physician, therefore, is an absolute necessity.

3. There are many times in life when depression must be considered

almost a natural state. Women have far more occasion to experience this than men do because their physiologic functions predispose them to depression. In the ten-day period prior to the onset of the menstrual flow, the female hormones function in such a way as to create the retention of excess fluids. Many women say the sensation is that of having full and heavy breasts and puffing or bloating of the lower abdomen. During this period, they are also subject to fluid retention in most other organs of the body, and a physiologic state known as *premenstraul tension* exists.

Premenstraul tension frequently includes uncontrollable depression. One woman told me, "Approximately ten days prior to my period, I am downright bitchy, and I know it. I don't know how my family tolerates me at that time because I find it nearly impossible to accomplish anything, and I become hostile to everybody and everything." Hers is an extreme case, of course, but I think it would be fair to say about 75 percent of all menstruating females experience some degree of premenstrual tension and therefore some degree of personality change prior to the menstruation. For some women, it is a ten-day period; others perceive it to be only a one- or two-day period prior to the actual onset of menstrual flow. Statistics compiled a few years back proved that the percentage of female suicides during the premenstrual period was considerably higher than otherwise. Likewise, the precipitation of marital separation was much higher during that period. If, in your marriage, there is a marked difference in your relationship and that difference is cyclical, be mindful that the premenstrual period might be the cause. If it is, simple medical help is readily available. This is certainly a mood that the woman had no desire to be in, so she should not be judged on her behavior, but helped instead.

The first three months of pregnancy can also present a physiological cause for depression. A major part of this depression is explained on the same basis as premenstraul tension; however, there is also the real factor of the personal discomforts of pregnancy. There is the challenge of increased responsibility, and sometimes the possibility that one or both of the expectant parents might not desire the pregnancy. The physiologic aspect of this can be helped by a physician's medication; however, the real personal problems of early pregnancy are best treated by the husband's reassurance of his wife's attractiveness and security. He must also assert his desire for the unborn child and detail a reasonable plan for how the increased responsibilities can be handled.

Postpartum and postoperative depression are well known to and well understood by the layman. Almost everyone has known a woman who had had postpartum blues, that depression which often follows childbirth. Several factors play a part in postpartum depression:

(1) During pregnancy the body experiences hormonal stimulation that makes it possible for the mother to nourish and provide for her own body as well as that of the unborn child. After delivery, the body reverts to its nonpregnant state, and a rebound phenomenon of depression can, and frequently does, exist.

(2) Anesthesia renders a person temporarily helpless. To many people, this is a shock from which they don't easily recover. We all derive self-confidence from our ability to maintain control over our minds and bodies. Under anesthesia, one loses control, and this somewhat challenges his self-confidence, and the result is depression.

(3) The realization of the responsibilities of caring for a newborn child can be frightening and depressing. Very quickly, it becomes apparent that childcare is a twenty-four-hour-a-day, seven-day-a-week job from which one cannot resign. If there are already children in the family, this burden is augmented by a feeling of guilt that they will have to share in the problems of the new baby, whether they want to or not.

(4) Sometimes a woman becomes subconsciously jealous of her husband's attention to the new child and feels that she is being forced into a position of secondary importance.

(5) The nine months of pregnancy is a long time to feel less than perfect, and the physical exhaustion from labor and delivery can leave a woman feeling physically and mentally exhausted—reason enough for depression.

The treatment for postpartum depression is both medical and environmental. It is the physician's job, of course, to reassure the woman of her basic good health and provide her with the medical assistance to make it as good as it can possibly be. It is the husband's job to understand the condition himself; then to reassure his wife and do everything he can to make her burden easier. It is the job of the couple together to make life interesting enough to abort the depression before it gets too deep. Following delivery, my usual prescription for a patient is to urge her—as soon as possible—to get hold of a reliable baby-sitter, get herself dressed up in her prettiest outfit, and go out to dinner with her husband. This can solve a multitude of problems. First, it proves to the woman that the baby will eat and sleep and cry and breathe without her constant attendance. This reassurance alone will often prevent the feeling of claustrophobia that comes from having a young baby. Second, it gives her time alone with her husband. They can be as boyfriend and girlfriend for a while, and return home to the baby with renewed energy. There is no time like the beginning of parenthood to recognize the necessity for this communication. Third, it gives the new mother reassurance that she is still attractive when she can get into a pretty dress. After having a distorted body for nine months, she might not fit into it so well, but the very fact that she can wear it at all is quite therapeutic.

Menopause brings with it a form of physiologic depression too. Hormonal change plays a part much the same as it does during pregnancy and the premenstrual period, but the environmental factors also play an equal part. It would seem to many that freedom from the threat of pregnancy in later life would be a relief rather than an impetus for depression. But the truth is that it is often depressing for a woman to realize that her childbearing years are over and that she is now passing into the category of older age. For some time, she has perceived her body losing its youthful tone. To many women, this is even more of a threat because their husbands, having become important in their careers, are quite "attractive" to younger women. They often admire him, not for his masculinity, of course, but for his power and maturity.

During the menopausal years women are also subject to symptoms of physical discomfort, including hot flashes, body aches, weight gain, arthritis, and menstrual disorders. If a woman is grouchy and depressed during this time, she certainly has good cause to be so. The treatment is not in scolding discipline, nor in threats to leave her—all this would only compound her miseries and insecurities. The treatment is:

(1) Proper medical management under the guidance of an interested physician.

(2) Sympathetic understanding by husband and children.

(3) Reassurance of the husband's love and devotion.

(4) An understanding on the part of the woman that the menopausal symptoms are actually short-lived. (The symptoms will vary in duration from four months to three years.)

(5) Encouragement to regard this phase of life as an opportunity to enjoy new rights and dignities, and maturity. Do not let her pursue the fruitless quest for youthful femininity. This is not to say that people should jettison all attempts at looking young but rather to understand that youth is a state

of mind. People stay young by being interested in life, and they keep their minds alert by continual stimulation.

In summary, depression is an illness. It can have a definite cause, a definite treatment, and a fairly good prognosis when properly treated. Like most other illnesses, it can be properly treated only if it is properly diagnosed. So, if you—or your mate—are out of sorts, short-tempered, hostile, irritable, constantly fatigued, and hard to get along with, try not to respond to one another with hostility. Seek help from your family physician to ascertain if depression might be the cause. If so, and if properly treated, you are almost certain to save yourself a lifetime of suffering.

The suffering that menopause brings is a special subject in itself, and will be discussed in the next chapter.

·13·
Adjusting to Menopause

Menopause is the phase of life during which a woman makes the transition from the childbearing years to older age. It is during this phase that menstrual function ceases, which announces the cessation of ovulation and fertility. The ovaries reduce function. They stop producing eggs and reduce the production of estrogen, the female hormone responsible for breast development, maintenance of vitality to the genital organs, maintenance of the feminine body structure—all of which is characteristic of the sensuousness of females in the childbearing age group.

The withdrawal of estrogen from the body's metabolism causes a change in the female's general body habitus as well as some physical and emotional changes which occur in a less specific way. The blood vessels, for instance, become unstable and tend to dilate and profuse the skin with extra circulation. The result is hot flashes, which is an overwhelming feeling of uncontrolable warmth that occurs regardless of ambient temperature. Women are also notoriously depressed during this period, and the depression is exhibited by symptoms of functional irritability, headaches, a lack of interest in life, a lack of interest in sexual relations, a general mood of pessimism, an insatiable craving for sleep in spite of insomnia, diffuse and intermittent joint pain, and a general mood of hostility.

A great deal of study has been made of menopausal women in an effort to determine which of these symptoms is the result of hormonal change and which represents a purely emotional response to advancing age. Although such studies are not conclusive, my opinion is that 80 percent of the symptoms are physiologic and, therefore, uncontrollable, unpreventable, and without the aid of medication, all could be related to the chemical changes which are occurring in the menopausal female. Psychotherapy, therefore, has generally been very inefficacious in helping during the menopause. Drugs that counteract depression chemically are of great help. Replacement therapy with the estrogens which are no longer being made naturally but can be given artifically is helpful; however, there is considerable risk in using these drugs. There are dangers of malignancy from the drugs, and the transition of menopause is prolonged by them.

Symptoms of menopause vary significantly from woman to woman. It would be reasonable to say that 50 percent of all women are fortunate enough to go through the changes with a minimum of discomfort and inconvenience, and are aware of menopause only by the cessation of menstrual periods. Another 25 percent are made uncomfortable enough to seek medical help for a short period and are able to cease medication after four to six months. The last unlucky 25 percent become incapacitated by the condition and require prolonged medical help in order to function satisfactorily. Fortunately, modern psychiatric drugs permit us to manage this condition reasonably well and prevent most of the tragedies that were seen a generation ago.

The menopausal age is usually forty-two to fifty-two years of age for most women, with the average age being between forty-five and forty-eight. Is it any wonder that this is considered to be one of the most difficult periods of life to manage? Many women during this time are absolutely unable to control their own thoughts and behavior. Husbands are unable to cope unless they have a good understanding of the condition and boundless love and devotion for their wives. It is the time when the husband and wife need their family doctor most of all. It is a time when the husband should accompany his wife to the family doctor with a great deal of humility and ask for help and understanding. If your family doctor does not respond to your requests for his time and compassion, you should find another who is willing to provide the necessary interest in your problem.

A good example of the menopausal problems is the case of Allen and Patricia who came to me for help about two years ago. This was a forty-eight-year-old couple whom I had known for some fifteen years. During that time, they enjoyed a satisfactory marriage and raised a fine young son, who was sixteen at that time, and a beautiful young daughter who was fifteen. Allen had his ups and downs economically over the years. He was a salesman who enjoyed some years of success followed by some years of business disappointments, which included several periods of unemployment. Patricia responded with understanding on all occasions, and went to work without resentment to supplement the family income. In the years just prior to Patricia's menopause, however, Allen attained a degree of success and economic stability far beyond their most ambitious dreams. They, therefore, enjoyed not only the luxury of their unquestioned love for eath other, but saw the results of their sacrifices bear the fruits of economic success as well. They were also especially proud of their two children.

I first learned about their current problem through a call from Patricia, asking me to prescribe a tranquilizer for her. She explained that she was getting ready to see her attorney about obtaining a divorce from Allen. I of course told her that I could not prescribe any medication over the telephone without first seeing her. (Please, please, *please* never ask any physician to do this!) I then suggested that she come to the office so we could discuss the problem further, and she agreed to do so. When she arrived, I hardly recognized her. I had always known her to be a meticulous and proud person whose appearance reflected her personality. On this occasion, however, she was disheveled; her hair poorly done; her clothing spotted and wrinkled. Her face reflected fatigue and distress. She appeared to have aged five years in the five months since I had last seen her.

She told me that she had decided to leave Allen because she could no longer tolerate life with him. He was spending more and more time at his office or playing golf, and seemed to have lost sexual interest in her. His vacation was approaching, and he had asked her if she would mind if he went on a golfing vacation with a group of men from the country club instead of spending it with her. Most of all, she resented the fact that he never seemed to be interested in listening to her problems.

This was a surprise to me because I had always known Allen to be a very attentive family man who loved his wife dearly, demonstrated a great deal of interest in their children, and cherished his time together with them. I then proceeded to take a more detailed medical history on Patricia.

She revealed that she was experiencing hot flashes, that she had joint pains, was sleeping poorly, cried easily, was more irritable than she had ever been in her life, and that she could not remember the last time she felt well. She said that she had an intolerable headache that did not respond to aspirin and other home remedies.

Menopause was the obvious diagnosis. When I asked her how she was getting along with her children, she said she found them ungrateful and distant toward her, and that they seemed to prefer the company of their father. She had decided, in fact, that after the divorce she would move out of the home and leave the children with their father. She was sure they no longer had any interest in her.

Sensing the acuteness of her problem, I spent a great deal of time explaining menopause to her; and I assured her that medical help for her physical problem was indeed available. I persuaded her to cancel her appointment with the attorney until I could look into her problem further and discuss it with the rest of her family. I prescribed a mood-elevating drug along with a mild tranquilizer, some mild pain relievers for joint pain, and insisted that she get to bed by eleven each night and force herself to respond to an alarm clock that would be set for 7:00 A.M. She agreed to all this and would have her husband call me the same day for an appointment to discuss the problems.

Allen was delighted that his wife had come to me for help and was grateful for my interest. He said he loved Patricia dearly, and that there was no limit to the sacrifices he would be willing to make to restore their marriage to its once happy state. In discussing her behavior, he said that she had become very hostile in the past year, that she never felt well because of headaches and insomnia, that she was irritable with the children, and that she seemed to be constantly looking for someone to blame for her unhappiness. She was rejecting not only him but also their children, relatives, and friends.

Patricia had indeed undergone an almost complete personality change that was destroying her marriage. Allen admitted that he was spending more time at the golf club and that the children too were finding reasons to stay away from home only because conditions at home had reached an intolerable state. I explained menopause to him, emphasizing that his wife did not have voluntary control over the things that were happening to her, but that with his cooperation and understanding I should be able to help her to overcome the depression as well as the physical discomforts that she was experiencing. He was very grateful and assured me of his cooperation. In three weeks' time, Patricia was sleeping better, her mood was brighter, she had long since forgotten her plans for divorce, and the family was functioning as a unit again.

Allen insisted on accompanying Patricia to the office for all subsequent visits, so that he could better understand her problems and participate in their management. Their mutual understanding and tolerance was every bit as therapeutic as my medicine, and the end result was that they were able to reestablish not only the closeness they once had but also an extra dimension of happiness based on the realization that they had survived a challenging experience.

I urge you to be aware of the menopausal years and to be constantly on guard for any symptoms that require medical management. Also, be ready to provide an extra measure of tolerance and understanding. If handled gracefully and early, the conditions can be solved with a minimum of stress. If handled improperly, a lifetime of love and sacrifice can be destroyed in a very short time.

·14·
Male Involutional Syndrome or Male Menopause

Between the mid-forties and the mid-fifties, men too experience a syndrome of mild physical decline and come to realize that their limitations in life have already been established. At this age, sexual performance declines somewhat. It is not uncommon for men who have never before had difficulty performing sexually to now have occasions where the spirit is willing but the body fails to react, much to their embarrassment and frustration. Even though this may happen as infrequently as one out of every twenty attempts at sexual intercourse, its emotional effect can be devastating. It is also a time when a man becomes aware that many of his contemporaries are dying and coming down with serious diseases, thereby reminding him of his own mortality. At work, men who are not already in a favorable career position by the age of fifty or fifty-five are unlikely to expect much advancement from now on. For most men, it is also a time in life when it is too late to change careers, and they are therefore forced to accept the realities of their limitations.

On top of all these troubles, it is a time when most men usually find themselves married to a woman going through the menopause, which has all of the hardships discussed in the previous chapter. Is it any wonder, therefore, that under such circumstances men respond with anxiety, depression, loss of self-confidence, embarrassment, and panic. At times, they are tempted to go off on many foolish tangents in an effort to prove their continued masculinity and to ward off old age.

The most common responses that we see in troubled males at this time are the following:

1. Attempting to regain youth by flirtations and extramarital affairs in an attempt to prove their masculinity.

2. Imitating the youth of the day by adopting their clothes, hair styles, and even their jargon.

3. Embarking on hobbies, fads, and slang of the day, which might be inappropriate to their age group.

4. Compulsively immersing themselves in their work in an effort to prove superiority and gain the recognition they have so desperately craved.

5. Becoming members of clubs and seeking prestige by running for office in those clubs.

6. Frequenting bars and nightclubs in order to be a part of the "scene."

7. Compulsive gambling for the feeling of power and importance that comes with winning.

Not all of these activities are socially unacceptable, nor are they without merit, for indeed anxieties must be allayed and needs must be satisfied. Please understand that the problems of the menopausal male have been elaborated upon and exaggerated intentionally for the sake of demonstrating the magnitude of the problems that exist. Obviously, most men are mature enough to realize that their needs change with each phase of life, and are able to find ways of satisfying those needs without resorting to absurd behavior. This is a time, however, when a wife's understanding and encouragement are most important. It is a time when a wife must be very sensitized to the needs of her husband and shower him with affection and acknowledge his virtues.

Similarly, the younger members of the family must help, for this is when a man can feel very inadequate if he does not get acknowledgment and respect from those in whom he has invested his entire life. The keynotes of management are acknowledgment and affection. If he is given enough, most of the problems of male menopause should be prevented. If the problems do manifest themselves in a socially unacceptable way, the treatment is still affection and acknowledgment and, whenever possible, a massive amount of understanding on the part of everyone involved. It is very important that this become a team project because mismanagement has destroyed many a family at the time when they should realistically be enjoying the fruits of all of the sacrifices that have come throughout the many years of married life.

Two examples come to my mind of cases of the male involutional syndrome which are very descriptive of the problem. One was unfortunately mismanaged and the other is an excellent example of how things can turn out when a team approach is used.

Elmer Johnson's wife, Joan, came to my office one day to tell me her problems. It seems that Elmer, who was fifty-three years old, had become extremely irritable with her. He was also making it a habit to go out alone in the evenings, and showed obvious signs of drinking. She suspected that he might also possibly be on the verge of having an affair with a woman from his office. I had known this family for many years and it was my previous experience with them that they had always been a close-knit family that had not previously experienced any problems of this sort.

"Had Elmer been having any personal problems," I asked, "which may have been giving him other frustrations in his life?" Joan said she did not think there was anything serious going on, but she felt that perhaps he might have been offended by the fact that he was passed over for a promotion at work and that a younger man had become his supervisor. She observed that ever since that happened, Elmer seemed to be compulsively trying to impress everyone with how important he was, and that he repeated the same old stories about his past achievements. "Frankly, he bores us to death," she concluded. At my request, Elmer came to see me a few days later and told me a slightly different version of the same story.

"Life has been a bit difficult for me lately," he said. "I have reached my peak at work and it is humiliating to realize that I still have thirteen years ahead of me until retirement with no chance for further advancement. I have attempted to discuss it with my wife, but she always finds a reason to change the subject. In fact, rather than trying to understand, she scolds and belittles me for not being more aggressive. She just doesn't understand. The children now have lives of their own and don't seem to be very interested in me; therefore, I stop at the bar on the way home for some companionship and understanding."

When I asked about the relationship with the woman at work, he was somewhat embarrassed, but then made the following statement. "Things have been going very badly with my wife and me. Joan criticizes me and makes me feel like such a fool that I have difficulty performing with her sexually. When I am with Susan, however, she seems very interested in everything I have to say. She finds me attractive and tells me so, and I therefore have developed a craving to be with her. I know it seems foolish, but sometimes it seems as though I need that flattery and attention to maintain my sanity."

It is still too early to know just what the outcome of this case will be; however, it seems obvious that the only solution will come from a team approach, one in which the wife will attempt to understand her husband's needs and fulfill them to the best of her ability. It may be too late, because Joan now must compete with another woman who is already fulfilling these needs quite satisfactorily. The children, too, instead of criticizing and judging their father, must attempt to include him in their lives and show respect for his age and experience. This is not an easy project, but at least the topic is being discussed and everyone seems interested in trying to salvage the marriage.

Fred had a somewhat similar problem but his family was astute and handled it differently and prevented the situation from getting out of hand. His initial complaints were feelings of restlessness, discontent, inability to perform sexually with his wife, occasional dizziness, and worry about the fact that his brother, who was two years his junior, had recently died after a heart attack. Fred also had problems in work. He too had progressed as far as he could as a machinist and was bothered by the fact that his present supervisor was ten years younger than he was.

After examining him thoroughly, I assured Fred that his physical health was excellent, and explained the male involutional syndrome to him. I also asked for the privilege of seeing the rest of his family. When they came in, separately, I told them of Fred's problems and his need for love, understanding, reassurance, and a feeling of importance. "We could certainly take care of that," they assured me, and they certainly did.

The two sons frankly admitted that they had never thought of their dad as having needs before, but now that they realized the situation, they made it a point to invite him to go bowling and to play tennis on a regular basis. They also set up some weekend fishing trips. His married daughter asked him to participate in the planning of a new addition that she and her husband were making on their home. Fred's wife was the most helpful of all. She fussed over him in every way imaginable and impressed upon him the fact that they were enjoying a wonderful time of life, without the responsibilities of young children and with free time and money to do all the things they had always hoped to be able to do. She also made it a point to plan interesting and rewarding projects, which included some weekend vacations, refinishing the basement, and taking dancing lessons.

Within five weeks, Fred was free of symptoms and life improved for him in every way. It also improved for all the other family members. They had done everything right to solve the problem. Their program reassured Fred of his masculinity, it provided him with recognition for his positive attributes, and it gave him a plan for the future. He had no need to look elsewhere for a feeling of importance or sexual satisfaction. He had no need to attempt to impress anyone with his importance because his family acknowledged it freely. He had no need to look elsewhere for attention and affection because he was getting as much as he could handle from his family. This was not done artificially, but from the heart. It was not that his family previously did not feel all of these things, but they took it for granted and that was not adequate.

So if you—or one of your loved ones—are experiencing the signs and symptoms of male involutional syndrome, work on it as a family group with a plan based on understanding the problem and compensating for the needs of the individual. The results will be very rewarding to everyone concerned and it will spare endless turmoil and heartache.

·15·

Peer Pressure and Media Pressure Against the Stable Marriage

Never before in the history of the world has there been such an onslaught of media pressure to destroy marriage and morality. It is virtually impossible to be exposed to radio, television, movies, or the press without hearing stories that glorify extramarital sex, alcohol abuse, and drug abuse. This is having such an effect on the young, as well as on married people of all ages, that some genuine confusion is developing about what is right and what is not. It is not my purpose to attempt to preach morality, but if the text is to be of any value at all, it should certainly serve as a tool to help people to determine what makes sense and what does not. Equally important is the determination of what is a workable way of life and what is not. It is not difficult to lose proper perspective when one considers the magnitude of that brainwashing apparatus that the media possess. Even commercial advertisements are replete with sexual and immoral innuendos. It never ceases to bewilder me that people are so gullible and mindless as to accept this media and peer pressure.

Approximately a year ago, I was attending a thirty-four-year-old woman whom I shall call Helen. She told me that she was nervous and unhappy because her husband had become inconsiderate of her. She was a wholesome-looking schoolteacher with three children whose ages ranged between five and ten. She was modestly dressed and very well-spoken. When I asked her to elaborate, she told me that she and her husband had been happily married for ten years, but two years ago they began to experience boredom and frustration. They discussed their boredom with some friends who promptly diagnosed the cause as old-fashioned thinking;

they were not modern enough. The cure was simple: their friends guided them into reading pornographic books and associating with a swinging crowd; next, they were both sexually involved with other members of the group.

Helen went on to say that another, "more-advanced couple," had suggested that they switch sexual partners as an experiment. In their effort to be "modern," they tried this on several occasions. Helen said that she had found these experiences unsatisfactory. Even though she was fond of the other couple as friends, she was at a loss to reconcile the mate swapping. She said, "There must be something wrong with me because from everything I read, it is obvious that it is the thing to do if you are going to be modern."

An example of her husband's lack of consideration was that the two of them, together with their children, visited the other couple for a weekend. The husband of the other couple was a repairman of some sort and went out on a service call immediately after dinner. When the remaining three adults ran out of conversation, the friend's wife suggested that she and Helen's husband go up to the bedroom for some private recreation. Although, as I said, they both had been sexually involved with others, this time Helen rebelled. She said that she was appalled by her husband's willingness to accept the hostess's request and leave her alone with the children.

This led to a violent argument when the couple returned home, which precipitated Helen's visit to me. It was not, however, until I challenged her with the question of whether she thought her activities were proper that she expressed any doubt over them. She replied that she had been of the opinion that if this sort of activity was acceptable enough to be in the movies, on television, and in books, then it must certainly be the acceptable thing to do. She was only trying her best to be one of the crowd and avoid being thought of as stuffy. Her husband too was trying just as hard; he had often said he would much rather stay home than force himself to be part of the swinging set. After a few sessions of ventilation, and several large doses of common sense, they decided to take tennis lessons and remodel the house for their social activities and seemed significantly better off for it. At this time, they have completely withdrawn from their "swinging friends" and have started thinking for themselves and are reconstructing their lives with some success.

This story may seem incredible, and somewhat foolish, but it is true. I deliberately tell it to point out just how gullible and susceptible people are to peer pressure and media pressure.

Other examples of these influences are all around us. Probably the most grotesque is the growing public acceptance of extramarital sexual involvement, with the explanation that since it is so openly portrayed on television and in the movies, it must certainly be all right. Many therefore completely ignore the traditional morals and common sense, which indicate that the personal and emotional trauma involved in extramarital sexual affairs is much too high a price to pay for the momentary sensual thrill.

Another obvious example of peer pressure and media pressure on society manifests itself in the widespread use of marijuana and other illegal drugs, sometimes to the point of self-destruction. Whenever I question the users of these drugs, they justify it by saying, "This is the way people do things these days. It is the 'in' thing. Everyone else is doing it. Why shouldn't I? It can't be wrong if so many people are doing it." The results of this type of thinking are obvious—catastrophic!

He who stands for nothing will fall for anything. I think that that probably states the problem with regard to acceptance of peer pressure and media brainwashing. Unless you have a code of personal ethics that you are willing to live by, regardless of what the rest of the world is doing, you are vulnerable to self-destruction by the whims of those who control the brainwashing apparatus. How does one decide what code to follow? Obviously, it will vary from person to person and from culture to culture. Probably the simplest and most practical way to decide for yourself what a realistic code for life should be, would be to ask yourself, "What advice would I give to my children, if and when I had some, under these same circumstances? Would I tell my daughter that extramarital sex was certainly harmless and that she should simply follow her urges? Would I tell my son or daughter that they should experiment with drugs and make their own decisions about whether or not it was right for them? Would I tell my married son or daughter to keep their marital commitments only as long as it was convenient and to abandon their mates and children if they became bored with married life? If my married daughter were to come home and tell me that she and her husband were invited to a partner-switching party and asked me what I thought of it, what would my reply be?"

There is, no doubt, a strong element in our media today that thrives economically because it is literally able to sell the idea that religions, philosophies, morals, and time-honored rules are all things of the past; and that the world at large is swinging in a different direction and marching to a different tune. Perhaps they are right, because the statistics regarding marriage failures have certainly followed the trend which they seem to be advocating.

If, however, your marriage means something to you; and you are working toward happiness in a stable marriage, I would urge you to review the questions that I have proposed and answer them in the same fashion that you would answer them for your children. After all, do you deserve any less common sense than you would like them to have? Then plan your life accordingly.

Most of us have lived long enough to see what has happened when people have lived in a brainwashed society. Adolph Hitler, Joseph Stalin, and Mao Ze-dong were all powerful enough to suppress religion, family ties, and traditional values, and thereby completely change the worlds in which they lived. People were so thoroughly brainwashed that they no longer had the ability to think for themselves. Hitler even had his people brainwashed to the point where they were willing to commit themselves to annihilating the entire Jewish race with no feeling of guilt.

Since the institutions of marriage and parenthood are being challenged to the point where they must struggle for their very existence, I feel that our only hope for the survival of a sane society lies in a resolute resistance to the brainwashing and a resolute dedication to live our own lives with dignity, morality, integrity, and common sense. Think about it. Talk about it. And then set up your own standards in the same manner that you would hope your loved ones will follow.

·16·

Homosexuality

Ten years ago, when I first began to write this text, I did not consider homosexuality an appropriate subject to include in a marriage book. It was true that I knew marriage partners who seemed to lack strong sexual identification, such as the effeminate male or the masculine female. But usually they were only slightly different from the norm and had seemed to work out a healthy heterosexual relationship that appeared to be quite functional. It seemed that people who lacked strong sexual identities would deliberately choose mates with whom they fit very nicely and who compensated them for their own weaknesses. This slightly different but socially acceptable relationship has no doubt always existed.

Until recently, practicing homosexuality was considered a social disgrace; and there was considerable peer pressure against experimentation with it, as well as legal enforcement against it. In recent years, however, homosexuality has come to be a socially acceptable way of life for many; and, therefore, more and more people have experimented with it. It is not my purpose to comment on the pros and cons of this. My major interest here, however, is to comment on the problems which ensue when a homosexual individual attempts to participate in a heterosexual marriage.

Homosexuality, by definition, is a person's predisposition to act and react in a manner resembling that of the opposite sex, and to prefer a member of the same sex as a sexual partner. So far as its cause is concerned, there are many theories. Some say that it is a personality deficiency, precipitated by an overbearing parent of the same sex whom the child would have an impossible task emulating; instead, he or she withdraws from such competition and chooses to emulate the parent of the opposite sex. There are others who claim that it is an inborn freak of nature, which is neither preventable nor treatable. Another theory suggests a biochemical imbalance. And still another theory suggests that all of us carry within our basic personality makeup the ability to align with either sex and, if given the chance to experiment, one might find himself or herself imitating the opposite sex.

All of these theories, and countless others that I have not alluded to, are helpful in explaining the possible cause of homosexuality. The important thing, however, insofar as marriage is concerned, is that if a person with homosexual tendencies chooses to embark on a heterosexual marriage, he or she must do so with the full intention of being honest about the past and sincere about the future. Many people with homosexual tendencies have been able to overcome them and opt for a heterosexual life that they find more rewarding. Many become excellent mates, fathers, and mothers. The problems, when they do exist, usually fall into two categories:

1. The category in which the homosexual mate who has doubts about himself or herself does not admit the concern over the ability to perform in a heterosexual marriage. (This problem should be discussed in great detail with the fiancée and the person offering premarital guidance. Failure to do so is tantamount to fraud.)

2. The homosexual who marries with the intent to carry on a heterosexual marital relationship but finds it is not possible to do so.

In either case, the marriage by very definition is not a marriage at all since it is not between a functioning man and woman; and therefore it is null and void. I know of no civil law nor religious law which would not embrace this as grounds for divorce or annulment.

I am put in mind of the very sad case of a young couple who met while in college. They were both art students and had many other common interests. Charles was a gentle person who had many effeminate mannerisms and who had participated in some homosexual activities prior to his romance with Janet. They didn't talk much about that, however, and enjoyed being best friends for the last two years of college. Janet had been a patient of mine for quite some time and told me of her plans for marriage, describing Charles as a delicate and gentle fellow, with a beautiful mind and a love for art and culture which they shared. In fact, she said that she had felt comfortable with him because he was the only fellow that she had dated since she was in college who had not made a vigorous effort to lure her into his bed.

Both Charles and Janet were eager to maintain their relationship after college, and they married one month after graduation. Six months later, Janet came into the office with the sad story that they had had very infrequent sexual intercourse, and that Charles had confessed that, although he loved her very much as a friend and felt dependent upon her, he preferred homosexual relationships that he had had with males and that he could not envision himself ever being able to overcome that preference. He subsequently had four visits with a psychiatrist who seemed to understand his problems but had no answers for their resolution. "What can I do?" Janet asked in desparation. "I respect Charles as a friend, and I would not want to hurt him; but there is a great difference between having a friend and having a husband." She had always hoped to have children and the securities that would come with a good solid marriage. She had also hoped to enjoy the pleasures of an active sex life with her husband.

I took a very dim view of their future after discussing the problem with Charles. He said that he suffered as much as Janet did by his inadequacies and realized that the marriage was a mistake because, in essence, he had promised to be something that he could not be. The two of them also consulted with their pastor, who was quick to agree that they would only continue to hurt each other if they attempted to pursue their marriage. It is sad, but they parted and had the marriage annulled. I am pleased to add, however, that Janet is now the happy mother of two daughters and a son, and the wife of a man who loves her very much. She enjoys a rich, healthy heterosexual marriage. Charles has apparently found happiness and success in his art work and has a circle of friends in Greenwich Village. To the best of my knowledge, neither he nor Janet is sorry about their decision to dissolve the marriage.

Solving such a problem is never easy. But if the marriage cannot work because of homosexuality, I can see nothing but tragedy and disappointment in store. It is nearly impossible to reverse this unfortunate freak of nature. Since such a marriage has no validity anyway, its dissolution might possibly be the only practical answer.

·17·

Coping with the Problems of Having a Permanent House Guest

In Part One of this text, I emphatically stated that a family should avoid living with another family or taking in a permanent house guest. I feel very strongly about this, for the privacy that a couple needs to carry on a successful marriage is extremely important and should not be compromised unless there is absolutely no recourse.

There are times when there is no choice, specifically when caring for a dependent parent or offering refuge to one of your adult sons or daughters who is temporarily down on his or her luck. Even under those circumstances, however, every effort should be made to maintain privacy by giving the guest a private section of the house that he is responsible for and may treat as his own home during his stay. It would also be wise to schedule several days a week when mealtimes would be separate, so that the family might function as an independent unit. From the very beginning, the family's independence from a guest should be established in such a way that major decisions are still made without interference. Though it may seem inhospitable to greet a house guest and then proclaim these rules, I am sure you will find that doing so in the beginning will pay dividends throughout his stay. These are problems that cannot be avoided and must be reckoned with sooner or later; so why not be honest about the terms of the unwritten contract from the very beginning? In fact, it should be discussed before the house guest arrives; that way a better result will follow. Do not be afraid of being offensive by discussing it before he comes. The guest is usually as concerned as the hosts. Obviously, if he does not accept the rules of the house before his arrival, he would accept them even less as time goes on. And if he is not compatible with these rules, it might be wise to look toward the possibility of another arrangement before the inevitable problems arise.

The story of Ed and Lucille Wagner demonstrates the hardships that I have been referring to. They were a good-hearted couple in their early fifties who sympathized with the plight of Ed's mother after the death of her husband. Mother seemed so desperate and demoralized with her loss that Ed and Lucille expressed their compassion by inviting her to come live with them. Mother was reluctant to give up her house, but quite desperate for companionship, so she agreed to move in with the Wagners. Two of their four children were already married and the remaining daughter and son were in the ninth and eleventh grades respectively; therefore, the Wagner's home had ample room to accommodate Mother.

The total family group was compatible for approximately a month, with all family members being very polite about the situation. And then the inevitable problems started. Since I was serving as family physician, I had occasion to hear everyone's complaints, and their comments tell the story very well.

Fifteen-year-old Jane made the following statements: "Mother and I never seem to have any private time to just sit and talk anymore; and, besides, mother always seems irritable. She never used to be. Grandmother is nice, but she has the knack of offering unwanted advice at the worst times. I am embarrassed to admit it, but she annoys me."

Lucille had the following comments: "It's not my mother-in-law's fault, but I just don't seem comfortable in my own home anymore. The children seem to make up excuses not to be home as they used to be. My husband, the children, and I always had such a good time at the dinner table; we always seemed to pour our hearts out to each other. The mealtimes now seem to be more stiff because for some reason we are not as at ease in grandmother's presence. My husband and I seem to be bickering about very minor things now, and this was never our problem in the past."

Seventeen-year-old Jimmy said, "I always felt free to bring my friends home before, but now I am always concerned that our music will disturb my grandmother; and besides she doesn't seem to like my friends very much anyhow. So I spend most of my time over at Charlie's house. I feel more comfortable over there now even though I would rather be at home if things were like they were before."

Grandmother was my patient too. She was a lovely woman, one who had always had a reputation for being kind and gentle, bright and loving. She said: "It was a big mistake for me to give up my home. I miss my old friends and neighbors and all of my familiar surroundings that meant so much to me. My son and his family are wonderful, but I just don't feel completely comfortable there even though they do their best to make me feel welcome. I would not feel free to invite friends in and entertain as I always did at home. The children are wonderful kids, but frankly I cannot stand the noise. My daughter-in-law is polite and generous, but I can understand what she is going through. I wish that I knew the answer to making everyone comfortable and happy again. I miss my husband very much and find that I have periods of depression that upset the entire family. If only I had some privacy, I would be so much happier."

Her son was the last member of the family to discuss the matter. He was as nice as could be, and very dutiful to his mother, wife, and children. To me, he looked as though he had aged six years in the past six months because of the problems that were going on in his home. "I love them all," he said, "and I understand everyone's point of view. It seems as though I am forever trying to appease one person or another by begging everyone to be more understanding of everyone else's problems and point of view. It has become an endless task. I don't seem to have any fun anymore because of the tension involved; and, in fact, I find that I stop on my way home from work each day now for a couple of drinks to help me get through the evening. I never did that before, and I know it is not right, but I certainly need something to make the whole situation tolerable." This family and I are still working to resolve the problems, and I think that we are reaching happy solutions.

It is interesting to note that their neighbors the Cavanaughs, who live a block away in the same split level community, had exactly the same problem of having to offer a home to a widowed mother. They too had four children, and the older two had already left home for college. They handled the matter very differently, however. They talked over every foreseeable detail before extending the invitation to the mother to come and live with them. Instead of inviting her to become an addition to their family, they offered her a makeshift, two-room apartment in the lower level of their split-level home. It required a few modifications, which cost a month's salary, but it permitted her to bring her favorite pieces of furniture with her, to have her own private bathroom, a small kitchen, and a private entrance. The result was that she had the twofold advantage of privacy as well as the closeness of her family. The Cavanaughs too were able to retain their own privacy, and yet fulfill their obligation to the widowed mother. The children would go down and visit with her and spend more time with her than if she lived upstairs. She has made friends in the neighborhood and always seems to have a guest of her own whom she is entertaining in the privacy of her own small apartment. Both the Cavanaughs and their guest have maintained their privacy and dignity; and therein lies the secret of their success.

In summary, if it is ever necessary for you to have a long-term house guest, talk over all the foreseeable details and explore the potential hardships before you extend the invitation. Discuss it with everyone concerned. Do not be blinded by a feeling of guilt and obligation. If it is obvious that the arrangement would not work, explore every other available option. After all, your children's needs are all-important; do not compromise their welfare. You only get one chance at raising them, and if you alienate them by not providing the happy and comfortable home they deserve, you will have done them and yourselves a great disservice. At all costs, never compromise your marital privacy and remember your responsibility is to your mate and your children before any guest.

·18·

Problems Associated with Geographic Change

Our American society has become a mobile one out of necessity and by choice. With the availability of cheap and convenient air travel, people are exposed to all parts of the world and very often will relocate for convenience and opportunity. People tend to relocate for convenience during the retirement years because couples choose to move to more favorable climates and to live in communities more oriented towards a retirement life. Young people, now too, are seeking favorable climates as well as convenience-oriented living.

Moves of necessity are ordinarily undertaken by younger couples. Such moves result from a job transfer, or from the need for employment opportunities when there are none available in the present area. For the family who is relocating by choice, the problems are usually few inasmuch as they have usually researched the new region very carefully and have assessed their plans to adjust to it accordingly. However, even with the best-made plans, my observations have been that adjustments to a new environment almost always carry with them a great deal of challenge, and, not infrequently, have very distressing side effects. It is never easy, after all, to leave family, friends, and familiar environment, regardless of what the benefits might be.

For the family who must move against its will, the problems are ever so much greater, for it is very difficult to embrace a new environment and give up the old if it is not of your own choosing. The children usually rebel and do everything within their power to avoid moving, and reject the new home.

The tensions between husband and wife are usually great, not only because of the unwillingness to give up their old home, but also because of the physical inconvenience, expense, and major annoyance that is associated with moving. If they are forced to leave the proximity of some family member who may be dependent upon them, the complexities are multiplied further.

How does a family go about coping with this problem? Is there any easy way? Is it ever solved without a great deal of hardship? I don't think so. I have rarely seen it solved without a great deal of hardship, even if the move means that the family will be more economically secure or be able to live in a finer home, or in a better climate, or whatever. It is still rarely easy. But, neither is it impossible. Suffice to say, if there is any way to avoid an unwanted move, I would strongly recommend that you do everything within your power to avoid it at all costs. If it is not avoidable, I urge you to embrace it and make it a team effort as did the Johnson family.

Bob Johnson was a forty-four-year-old junior executive with a paper processing company in New Jersey when his employer informed him that they were closing down their New Jersey operation, and that he was going to be transferred to Oregon to become general manager of the paper mill there. This, of course, meant that Bob, his wife, and their four teenaged children would have to leave their home in New Jersey, which they dearly loved, as well as their family and friends, and move to a small community in the woodlands of Oregon that had a climate that none of them even liked. To say the least, they were individually and collectively upset and resentful of the fact that fate could have been so unkind to them. It was this upset that brought them to my office.

Bob came in with all of the signs and symptoms of early peptic ulcer—a result of the upset. He brought with him his sixteen-year-old daughter Judy who had broken out in hives—also a result of the nervousness and emotional upset precipitated by the situation. It was obvious that medicine alone was not the answer to their problems, so I suggested that the whole family come in and we talk about it as a group. During our group meeting, we all agreed that unfair as it was, the necessity for the move was beyond question and that the only way to make it tolerable was to investigate every possible positive aspect of the new community and embrace it as much as possible. This was not easy because there wasn't much to like about "Dullsville," Oregon, at least from a distance.

We established a format for our meeting in such a way that we would all take turns offering a positive suggestion about how to make the best of a bad situation; the following worthwhile suggestions were presented:

1. To write to the pastor of the church in Dullsville, telling him of their situation and asking if he might be of some assistance in helping them to get socially oriented.

2. To write to the Chamber of Commerce and request a list of community services and organizations.

3. Bob proposed that he would also write a letter to some of his co-workers-to-be and solicit suggestions from them about adjusting to the new community.

4. Each of the children would be allowed to have a guest from New Jersey visit for a week in the coming summer.

5. Bob commented that there was a lake in the new community where sailing was a popular sport, and they all agreed to join the local sailing club and buy a sailboat.

Around and around went the suggestions on how to make the best of the move and by the time the family left my office, I think it would be fair to say that they had some enthusiasm for their new project. And one thing for sure, they were functioning as a cooperative family that understood each other's problems because they were all sympathetic to the overall situation rather than just individually feeling sorry for themselves.

Recently I heard from the Johnsons by mail and also spoke with one of their summer guests. She had had the time of her life in Oregon with the Johnsons. She went intending to stay a week and ended up staying a month because there was so much to do. Dullsville, it turns out, is a great place. The correspondences that we had planned were extremely fruitful, and the family was welcomed into the community from the very first day because the groundwork had been done so well. The Johnsons summed up the problems and their answers very well on the back of their Christmas card this year, in which they told me that they would still much rather be in New Jersey but that a family in which everyone loves one another, and has a good plan, can not only survive but prevail anywhere.

And that is my advice to you if you are forced to make a move. Make it a team effort. Embrace your new community in every way possible. Be close to each other and try to understand each other's problems. Get to know your new community and all that it has to offer. Be aggressive about joining clubs and taking part in the community activities. Force yourself to have a positive attitude toward the community, and the community will eventually have a positive attitude toward you.

·19·

Coping with the Problems and Failures of Children

Regardless of how much a husband and wife love each other, and how close their relationship is, probably one of the most trying situations is the one in which their children are having problems or experiencing failures. Obviously, this is a time when the parents must muster all their resources and do all they can to help the child in trouble. A team effort is obviously the best, and usually the only, approach that can bring about a satisfactory result. Unfortunately, human nature is not always so reasonable as to be able to figure that out; and in times of such stress, parents will often resort to blaming each other for the child's problems and argue interminably over their resolution. Once this pattern becomes established, it could go on for years and destroy the marriage as well as the lives of the children.

This brings to mind the story of Jack and Shirley, whom I have known for the past twenty years. I first met them when they were young lovers, and saw them develop throughout their marriage. The marriage had been a typically happy one until the eldest of their four children began to have troubles in school, in the seventh grade. At that time, the couple had a major disagreement on how the daughter's performance problem might be handled. Jack thought that she needed stronger discipline and attempted to impose it upon her. Shirley was far more sympathetic and forgiving, and thought that Jack was unjust in using harsh disciplinary measures. She blamed the child's academic problems on the inadequacy of the school and teachers. They bickered back and forth about the problem incessantly, yet never agreed on a definite plan of action. The result was they were constantly contradicting each other over the child's management and confusing her immeasurably. In desperation she would play one parent against the other and contribute to the dilemma.

The parents and the child finally became so defiant to one another that a complete family turmoil resulted. The sad outcome was that Shirley eventually decided that she could no longer stand the whole situation and left Jack and the children to pursue a life of her own without them. When she discussed her decision with me, she said it was not that she did not love her husband or the children but that she felt she could not stand the entire predicament and had chosen to leave them.

The rest of the story is a tragedy crashing upon tragedy, and beyond the scope of this text at this point. The main issue, however, is that a marriage between two people who still loved each other was annihilated by the mismanagement of a child's school problems. I doubt that any family in which there are children has ever been completely devoid of these problems, and so I am offering some straightforward rules for their management.

1. Discuss the matter privately before approaching the child with a plan of attack. Discuss it until you reach a steadfast agreement on what the plan of attack should be. If it is impossible to reach agreement, seek the help of a third party, preferably the child's teacher, or your family physician, or your clergyman, or anyone else you respect who might be familiar enough with the problem. Then formulate for yourselves a mutually agreed upon plan of attack *before* approaching the child with a solution.

2. Never blame each other for the child's problems, even though the child's rearing can contribute somewhat to his eventual problems. The problems are primarily his and his alone, and it is wrong to blame yourselves directly for these problems.

3. Be sure you understand the child and his problems before attempting to offer a solution to them. Try to see his point of view. Investigate what he says before coming to your own conclusions.

·20·

The Problems of Children from a Previous Marriage

If there are children from a previous marriage, a myriad of challenges and difficulties can be anticipated. This is so whether that marriage ended in divorce or at the death of one of the partners. The subsequent emotional involvement of all family members is complex and sometimes without a satisfactory solution. With this in mind, I shall attempt to attack the problem by discussing the dynamics of the parent in charge, the surrogate parent, the absent parent, and the child or children involved in an effort to offer some measure of understanding. Then I shall present a list of rules that can be used by each involved party. With understanding and guidance, I hope to make this difficult situation more tolerable and manageable.

The parent with whom the child lives usually feels obliged to compensate the child for being deprived of the benefits of being raised by both natural parents. This parent usually attempts to maintain a sense of balance between the child and the new mate and tries to foster love and compatibility between them. In many cases, there is also the problem of competing with the child's other natural parent. This is particularly a challenge if the other parent presents a threat to the child's rapport with his newly formed family.

The parent is often troubled with the subject of priorities too. Does the responsibility of parenthood in this situation take precedence over the responsibility to the marriage? Indeed, this is a question that should be considered prior to marriage; and the marriage contract must be negotiated with this problem in mind.

For the surrogate parent (the new mate of the parent with whom the child lives), the problems are also manifold. The primary problem is usually to attempt to cultivate a form of love that would be necessary to fulfill the role of a surrogate parent successfully. This is rarely easy, for it involves an attempt to develop affection for a person who is not always likely to return it. The surrogate parent must also cope with the smoldering resentment that the child naturally feels toward this person who has deprived him of the privilege of sharing life with both of his natural parents. Another serious challenge to the surrogate parent is the establishment of the child's respect and willingness to submit to his or her authority. Finally, perhaps the greatest problem for the surrogate parent is the fact that his or her mate must share love, interest, and attention with the children. It is natural, therefore, for competition to exist.

For the estranged parent (the parent with whom the child is not living), the problems are usually as follows:

1. A feeling of personal guilt and discontent based on the realization of the less than perfect conditions under which the child lives.

2. Difficulties relating to the child and coping with the child's problems.

3. A feeling of competition or resentment with the child's other natural parent and his or her mate.

4. Justifying to the new mate that he or she has obligations to the child. And there is the greater matter of maintaining an adequate relationship between the mate and the children.

5. Coping with the problems that may exist between the child and the children from the next marriage, if there be any.

The hardships experienced by the child himself are probably the most complex and most difficult of all. The child typically feels confused by the complexities of his life, particularly with regard to who deserves his allegiance, respect, love, and obedience. He also resents his natural parents for not being able to provide him with a stable, uncomplicated life. In many cases, the child has a specific resentment and rebellion predicated on a realistic state of neglect, one in which the parents become so preoccupied with their own needs and desires that they have inadequate time, interest, and resources to devote to the essentials of parenthood.

Please note that all of the upsetting, interpersonal drama referred to in the above discussion is superimposed on all the normal, natural, everyday drama of coping with marriage and raising children. These challenges alone are more than many people can handle, so it is certainly not a surprise that the additional burden of the problems of children from previous marriages stretch one's ability to cope to the absolute limit and sometimes beyond.

A very difficult case that demonstrates the plight of a marriage with a child from a previous marriage is the story of the Smiths. I first came to know the Smiths five years ago when their family consisted only of Lewis and Marilyn Smith, who were thirty-five and thirty-four years old respectively, and Marilyn's son, Clarence Jones, age seven. (Marilyn had been divorced from Clarence's father Henry Jones for the past four years and had been married to Lewis Smith for the past two years.) Their first visit to me was precipitated by a request from the child-study team of Clarence's school. Clarence's teacher had referred him to the study team because his academic performance was below par and because he was quite disruptive in class. Physically, the boy was in excellent health; however, his overall demeanor was really quite bizarre. He grimaced inappropriately, made grunting and whistling noises while his mother and I were talking, and proceeded to tear apart the current edition of *Fortune* magazine, which lay on my desk. During our initial meeting, it is no exaggeration to say that Mrs. Smith said, "Clarence, don't!" or "Clarence, stop it!" no fewer than 875 times. The purpose of this visit was to reassure the family of Clarence's physical well-being, but it was obvious that the emotional well-being of the entire family required diagnosis and therapy. I therefore invited Marilyn to return with her husband at a later date, and she agreed to do so.

When Marilyn and Lewis returned several days later, they gave the following account of their home life. During their courtship, most of their activities were private ones from which Clarence was excluded and was consequently resentful. After the wedding, the boy seemed to be on a constant, attention-getting campaign in an effort to reassure himself of his mother's love and affection. The more he demanded attention with his misbehavior, however, the more resentful Marilyn and Lewis became of him and therefore proceeded to punish him precisely for that absurd behavior. The punishment, it seems, gave the child a feeling of rejection and made him even more desperate for his parents' attention. He responded by continuing to demand this attention with bizarre behavior such as insomnia, climbing into bed with Marilyn and Lewis in the middle of the night, and refusing to eat at the dinner table. (This attracted his mother's attention to the point that every mealtime was one in which the only topic of conversation was Clarence's reluctance to eat, thereby making the entire experience an unpleasant one.)

After Clarence started school, he continued his attention-getting routine in the classroom by annoying and disturbing the entire class. His academic performance was also below his capabilities. In desperation over her son's poor school performance, Mrs. Smith solicited help from the teachers and put herself on a daily routine of attempting to help Clarence with his assignments. During that period, the boy was able to have his mother's undivided attention and seemed to deliberately avoid learning his lessons so that he might have more of his mother's undivided attention as a secondary gain. The story up to this point is very typical of many children who react both consciously and unconsciously to the desperation of not feeling wanted, needed, or loved.

Lewis Smith was a gentle, mild-mannered fellow who claimed to be happy with his marriage generally but was overwhelmed and frustrated with the problems of being a surrogate parent.

I explained to the Smiths the mechanisms that were at work here, and advised them that I felt that the situation would doubtlessly get significantly worse unless we were able to get a plan together to reverse Clarence's basic feelings of insecurity and obviate his desperate quest for attention. They understood my explanations well and expressed not only a desire but an eagerness to adopt a plan to make things better. My suggestions were the following:

1. Insist on a regular schedule for the family that would be rigid and reliable. It should include:

A. Regular mealtimes with everyone sitting at the same place at the same table for each meal. No in-between eating should be allowed. (A growing child who is not permitted to eat between meals will eventually become hungry enough to do justice by each meal that is offered.)

B. A regular bedtime with no deviations.

C. A regular time for planned recreation, and a regular time for homework. (Children function much better and feel a sense of order and security when they operate within the parameters of a definite schedule.) No matter how much the child rebels or how difficult it might be, the schedule is an absolute essential.

2. Employ a tutor to help with the homework. (The parent makes a poor

tutor, particularly if problems exist, because both the parent and the child have too much emotional involvement with each other to be able to concentrate adequately on the tasks of teaching and learning. Likewise, the child's ability to learn should not be contingent upon whether or not he is loved by his parent and *vice versa*.)

3. A conference should be held with Clarence's natural father, Henry Jones, in an effort to establish some form of uniformity with regard to Clarence's management during his visits with the Joneses. (The confusion that children experience when the rules are different with one parent than with another parent is dreadfully upsetting. A child must know what he can count on, and what is right, and what is wrong.)

4. I suggested a parent-teacher conference so that Marilyn could advise the teacher as to the approach they were taking with Clarence and strongly suggest to her that she invite him in privately at least twice a week to talk to him on a one-to-one basis for the purpose of reassuring him that she did not dislike him. If she could convey to him the understanding that she was simply doing her job and that he could make it a lot easier for her by attempting to contain himself and not disrupt the class, it would be a great help to her. It was also suggested that the teacher might help the child's self-image by giving him some chores to do in the classroom, such as wiping off the blackboard, carrying out trash, running errands, and so forth.

5. I suggested that Clarence be enrolled in a fun-type learning experience, such as swimming lessons, or cub scouting, so that he might develop some self-confidence and also master the technique of learning without self-consciousness.

6. Marilyn was asked to completely avoid ever saying "Clarence, don't!" for it was obvious that it was a little game the mother and child were playing to attract each other's attention. She was also advised to establish a rule that there would be no mention of Clarence's eating habits. The only rule that was to be followed with regard to eating was that he was not to be permitted any in-between-meal snacks. (It is human nature that anyone told that he must eat will have an aversion to food. It is likewise a very obvious fact that if a person were to fill his stomach with in-between-meal eating or a glass of milk at the beginning of a meal, he would be unable to approach his regular meal with enthusiasm.)

7. Since Clarence was fascinated with my Dalmation and my Siamese cat, I suggested that they consider getting a family pet and permit him to be responsible for its training. It was my hope that he could probably get from a pet all the attention that he was demanding from others, and at the same time realize that a creature truly loved him without reservation and with boundless enthusiasm. (Of all my suggestions, I think this one was the most successful, for there is hardly a time when I saw Clarence from then on that he didn't have a story to tell me about his beagle and all of the antics that they enjoyed together.)

Fortunately, they accepted all my suggestions and were successful in their efforts to make them work—all except the suggestion of establishing an agreement with Henry Jones over maintaining Clarence's schedule during his visits with the Joneses.

The results were remarkable. The boy's school performance gradually improved. His self-image changed from that of an unwanted, irritating nuisance to one of a self-confident, contributing young citizen at school and at home. Within nine months after our first meeting, Marilyn told me that Clarence was now quite acceptable in every way, with the exception of the week following visits with his father. The inconsistency that he experienced during these visits made the ensuing week a difficult one.

At this point, I requested that Henry Jones come in to see me to discuss Clarence's problems, and he did. This is how he described the situation: "I feel bad about the boy because I know that I don't do everything for him that a father should. After all, I only get to be with him every two or three weeks, so I try to make up for it in the short time that we are together. That is why I let him stay up as late as he likes and let him have anything he wants while he is with me. I know that Marilyn says that he is allergic to chocolate and gets stomach aches from it, but I figure a little bit once in a while can't be all that bad for him, so I let him have it. My wife, Sara, can't stand him because of his irritating ways, so that too makes the whole situation very difficult. I can't stand to think of him calling Marilyn's husband 'Daddy,' so I do everything I can to try to make him like me more than he likes Lewis Smith. Sara's two daughters don't like him either because they say that I allow him more privileges than they have, and he seems to do everything he can to irritate them. I guess they are just jealous."

"Are you satisfied with the boy's behavior and performance when he is with you?" I asked.

"Of course not," he replied. "It's a constant disaster."

"Okay then, why not try my suggestions and see if we can't make things better."

He agreed to try and here were my suggestions:

1. Maintain the very same rules that the boy is required to follow at home for meals, bedtime, general behavior, and personal responsibilities.

2. Spend at least one hour per day privately with him during the time he is with you, so that you might listen to him and participate in the things that he is doing. Understand his interests and his problems and understand them in a realistic way, not as a fairy godfather who can solve all of the problems with the wave of a twenty-dollar bill.

3. Meet with Marilyn and Lewis Smith from time to time and discuss Clarence's progress. Whether you like it or not, it is a joint project; and it stands a much greater chance of success if you develop mutual respect and stop competing.

4. Develop a father-son hobby. Putting models together would be okay. Going to sporting events. Playing a game. Anything that you are both interested in; but find a mutual interest that you can both enjoy rather than attempt to push him into a relationship with your wife and stepdaughters, which thus far has been unsuccessful.

5. Come back to see me in six months and tell me how things are going.

I am pleased to say that he did return in six months and with a very favorable report. He said, "Things are certainly not perfect, but they are 200 percent better than they were. I now feel as though I have a realistic father-and-son relationship with the boy. Before, it seemed as though it was just a pretense at a relationship. Even my wife and her daughters are now willing to accept him and include him in family events."

With the benefit of this type of guidance, Clarence has developed into a better than average student with a reasonable amount of self-confidence and an adequate social life. The Smiths and the Joneses are also enjoying happier marital relationships because the disappointments and exasperations of Clarence's problems now no longer plague them.

In conclusion, I would like to offer the following list of recommendations for all people who have problems of adjusting their lives around children of previous marriages:

1. Be honest and forthright with the child. Do not attempt to cover inadequacies of the situation with pretense and appeasement.

2. Never compete with the other parent for the child's attention. Try to

maintain mutual understanding about the child and be consistent in your efforts to establish some form of mutual respect.

3. Never neglect the child. Allot him a reasonable amount of your undivided attention on a regular basis so that he knows he is loved and has no need for absurd behavior.

4. Be consistent and attempt to establish one set of rules that both parents and stepparents agree to.

5. Insist that the child realize the parents' need for privacy and respect.

6. The surrogate parent must assume the responsibilities of a natural parent and the authority and respect that go along with it, so long as the child is living under the same roof.

The approach that I have offered is a utopian one. It is out of reach for many people; however, my experience has shown me that it is the only way that the thorny situation can be handled successfully.

·21·

Role Sharing and Role Reversal in Marriage

Since marriage is indeed a partnership, it is often necessary for mates to compensate temporarily or permanently for each other's inadequacies. I am sure that this has been so ever since the idea of marriage originated, for it is one of the implied components of the marital contract. After all, to be faithful to each other for richer or for poorer, and in sickness and in health, requires that mates substitute for each other in certain activities. In my experience, when mates have the opportunity to complement each other generally and care for each other during times of trouble specifically, the depth of love usually increases; and the bonds of marriage are tightened.

In modern American society, equal opportunity for both sexes is the law of the land, and it is understandable that the traditionally polarized roles of husbands and wives overlap more than ever before. In addition, equal educational opportunities have allowed both sexes to be equally able to provide economically for the family. And modern technology, rather than the woman or the man, does many household chores. It is important, therefore, to recognize the world as it is today and, within reason, adjust to it. All of this is so obvious that I am sure most couples figure it out on their own, and have no need for the aid of a text to remind them of the necessity to exercise mutual respect and fair play in marriage. In my experience, I have come across several cases that represent the many couples who are not able to figure it out for themselves and who subsequently jeopardize their relationship.

An example is the case of the Schultzes, a nice family made of Alvin, age thirty-nine, Elizabeth, age thirty-seven, and their two children, ages fifteen and seventeen. The Schultzes thought that since the children were old enough to be self-sufficient, the time had come when Elizabeth could go to work as a saleswoman to supplement the family income. This would allow them to afford college for the children, as well as give Elizabeth some stimulation and satisfaction, which she felt she needed. Both husband and wife agreed on the plan; however, problems arose when Elizabeth found that she could no longer perform all of her household duties and still be out working at a full-time job. Her husband was not inclined to do any "woman's work," and the children, who had never been required to do any of the housework either, seemed unwilling to inconvenience themselves with what actually were necessities of life. Alvin stated that his father never did any woman's work nor did any other man in his family, and he wasn't about to be the first. He felt that if his wife's working meant that she could not do these traditional chores, then she would have to resign her job, and the family would simply have to do with less. This was better, he insisted, than to crack what he considered to be the very foundation of their life-style.

We talked about this problem at great length, but Alvin was not willing to budge; neither mate was interested in motivating the children to help. It was obviously a lost cause, so Elizabeth resigned her job reluctantly and resentfully.

A few months later, she came to me with a new plan. She said that she and her family had reconsidered the situation; it had become apparent to all of them that economic needs made it necessary to increase the family income, and that the most practical way to do so was for her to work again. The children realized that there were things they could not have without extra money, and so they agreed to do some of the household chores. Alvin also decided that there were many things he could do without compromising his masculinity. Elizabeth returned to the same job, but this time it was with the blessing and assistance of her family.

I am pleased to report that, after a year, their arrangement seems to be working out; and everyone seems to be the better for it. Elizabeth has a new air of self-confidence. The children have matured sooner because of their added responsibilities; and Alvin has taken pride in the fact that he has refurbished the basement and started some home-improvement projects. This is a good example of role sharing.

Role reversal is quite a different matter. This is a situation in which the wife becomes the primary breadwinner, and the husband becomes the primary housekeeper. To be sure, this life-style receives a lot of exposure in the media, but in reality it rarely occurs in the complete state. In the few instances that complete role reversal does occur, however, it is usually for one of the following reasons:

1. A situation in which the husband is unable to work outside the home because of illness, loss of employment, or inability to cope with the outside world.

2. The situation in which the wife has a trade or profession that yields an income much higher than what the husband could possibly match.

3. The case of the husband who has basic feminine interests and personality traits and whose wife is more contented to assume the burdens of the traditionally masculine role.

These are all very specialized situations that must be handled individually and very delicately. I do not think that there is any clearly defined, right or wrong, dogmatic principle to follow so long as the end result is one which is mutually satisfactory. If both partners are happy with the situation as it is, and if they mutually decide that it is the most ideal set of circumstances that can be worked out, then they should leave well enough alone. If one or both members, however, is unhappy with the arrangement, it would be wise to take a good long hard look at it and weigh the viable alternatives.

·22·

Carelessness, Laziness, and Procrastination

It has always been my impression that carelessness, laziness, and procrastination are basically different forms of the same thing, and would be better classified under the heading of *disorganization.*

The entire animal kingdom, especially human beings, are essentially creatures of habit. Once ingrained in the personality, all habits—bad as well as good—are difficult to break. This is unfortunate in the case of bad habits, of course, but most fortunate in the case of good ones. Good habits such as, for example, being reliable and punctual, should become automatic. Bad habits, such as procrastination—"the thief of time," someone once said—have to be strongly attacked and overcome.

Obviously, it is easier to live with someone whose personal habits are organized; who adheres to a strict schedule—a time to arise in the morning, a time for meals, a time to go to the bathroom, a time to go to work, a set time for extra-curricular activities, recreation, and bedtime. Many people will resist such a strict regimen; however, I remember a wise old teacher telling me one time that, "Like it or not, we all live on a schedule. The only difference is, some of us live on good schedules and some of us live on jumbled schedules." When you tabulate the activities of people over a long period of time, it is indeed true that their personal habits do repeat approximately the same schedule from day to day and week to week, and it is true that the major difference is in their organization.

If all the bad habits of disorganization are a problem in your family, I would urge you to discuss it and set up a written timetable by which all of you could live more productively and happily. Write it down. Agree to it. Recheck yourselves from time to time to see whether or not the plan is working. If it is, great! If it is not, or if you are unhappy with it, revise it, and establish a new timetable, but at least have something that you can reliably count on and adhere to. This is even more important for self-employed and unemployed people than it is for those who are rigidly forced into a schedule by a demanding form of employment. Think about it, and jot down in your notebook your own suggestions for family scheduling. Ask your mate to do the same if you feel that he or she would benefit from it. If your experiences are like those of many people with whom I have worked over the years, my guess is that you will find your lives happier, more productive, and more satisfying.

·23·

The Role of Drugs in Marriage

Our present society has been justly described as drug-oriented. If we define a *drug* as any chemical that, when taken into the body, modifies the functions of the mind and body, it becomes apparent that practically every adult American is exposed daily to drugs in one form or another. And all of these drugs have potential side effects as well as the therapeutic effect for which they are used.

The drugs I am referring to fall into three basic categories:

1. Foods with druglike properties, such as those that contain caffeine (coffee, tea, and cola drinks), alcohol, hot pepper, red dyes, chocolate, and others.

2. Medications prescribed by a qualified physician.

3. Drugs used for social purposes, both legal, as in alcohol and tobacco, and illegal, such as marijuana, narcotics, stimulants, sedatives, and other so-called street drugs.

It is not within the scope of this text to individually analyze the above-mentioned drugs, but I would like to comment about each category briefly. All of the drugs mentioned have the capacity to modify a person's behavior and basic health, and, therefore, generate problems that might affect a person's mood, intellectual capacity, sexual performance, work performance, reliability, and acceptability as a mate. I recommend therefore that you always be mindful of which drugs you and your mate and your children are exposed to at all times. Know their effects and side effects and evaluate your family's performance accordingly. Be objective. The fact that everyone does it or everyone has always done it, does not necessarily make it right or acceptable for you and your family.

Of the food drugs most commonly abused, I feel that the caffeine-containing foods, that is, coffee, tea, and cola drinks, are the most dangerous. Caffeine is definitely addicting. It causes irritability, nervousness, tremor, sleeplessness, peptic ulcers, and even possible impotence. I am not suggesting that it should be outlawed or completely forbidden in all homes; however, if you or any member of your family drink more than three cups of coffee a day or feels a dependence on any of the caffeine-containing foods, I urge you to omit it. This can be easily done by simply switching to a decaffeinated brand of coffee, tea, or cola, or simply changing to another beverage entirely.

Alcohol, too, has many obvious side effects, such as drowsiness, predisposition to many illnesses, particularly, liver disease, gastrointestinal disease, emotional disorders, and impotence. People vary in their susceptibility to these side effects; however, everyone is vulnerable to them in one form or another. Unfortunately, in the case of alcohol, the person experiencing the side effects is often not the best judge of whether or not the side effects are indeed occurring, and will very often deny that any of these symptoms that I mentioned is directly attributable to the alcohol for fear of having to give it up. It therefore becomes the responsibility of the other family members to forcefully observe for these symptoms and handle them accordingly.

Medications, whether prescribed by a qualified physician or self-administered in the form of over-the-counter preparations, also have a multitude of side effects. An old pharmacologic rule of thumb says that almost every drug has the capability of having an opposite reaction to the one for which it was prescribed. If you are going to take over-the-counter medicines, I urge you to take them only according to the instructions given, and only when a true indication exists, and never, never take any over-the-counter item for more than four days without the approval of your family doctor.

In the case of medications prescribed by a qualified physician, I would urge every patient to always ask his doctor what the medicine is, what is its purpose, and what side effects can be expected. Every medication is required to have a specification sheet, approved by the Federal Drug Administration, that lists all effects and potential side effects of the drug; but it is neither necessary nor possible for any doctor to review the entire pharmacology and all of the potential side effects with every patient. The important thing is to have at least some general understanding of the nature of the drug and what to expect from it, so that if you do experience any adverse reactions, you would be able to determine if the medication might be the cause.

If problems exist in your family, and if either you or your mate takes any medication (even if prescribed by a qualified physician) you should contact the physician and discuss your problems with him and ask whether there is a possibility that the medication might be contributing to your problem. Never assume that there is no correlation between your problem and the medication, because it would be impossible to know this without adequate training. For example, here is a list of potential side effects from the more common medications used to control high blood pressure: drowsiness, irritability, loss of appetite, nausea, vomiting, diarrhea, skin rash, depression, nasal congestion, headache, abdominal cramps, numbness and tingling, blurred vision, tremor, loss of consciousness, frequent urination, convulsions, and serious blood disorders.

Obviously, some of these side effects are quite rare, and the benefit of the medications far outweigh their potential risks. This, of course, is why the Federal Drug Administration has approved their use under careful guidance of the physician. The important thing, however, is that if you have any discomfort, or any unexpected reaction to a prescribed medication, you should immediately consult with your physician so he can decide what should be done about it.

A typical case is that of a forty-five-year-old woman who complained that her husband was irritable, lazy, never wanted to do anything, and had lost interest in sex. The marriage had become generally unsatisfactory, and there was constant nagging, bickering, and hostility. The woman stated that they had been very happy until eighteen months ago, when all of these problems suddenly developed. Her husband was not a patient of mine, so I had no idea what was going on with him. However, he came to see me and we reviewed the situation thoroughly. He was embarrassed, but defensive, and said, "I don't know what's wrong with me. I guess maybe I'm just getting old and crotchety." I always do a complete physical and history on all patients who come into the office whether they are in for a medical or a personal problem, and, of course, I did so with this patient. Thus I became aware that he was taking three blood pressure medications prescribed by his previous physician, who, in addition, had authorized unlimited refills of the prescriptions. I recognized the possibility of his problems being those of medication side effects and, therefore, recommended that he discontinue all of them. Within three weeks, he told me that he felt like a completely new man. In retrospect he told me, "It's as though I have been in a fog for the past eighteen months. I did not recognize the difference as being due to the medication because the drowsiness and irritability came on gradually." This is not uncommon because medications of this type do have a cumulative effect. Fortunately, his blood pressure was able to be controlled by omitting salt and caffeine, a weight reduction diet, and regular sleep habits.

That case had a happy ending, but I have been exposed to many similar cases in which the marriage was completely destroyed by a condition that could have been easily corrected by understanding the effects of the medications and taking the appropriate measures of either changing them or eliminating them entirely.

Every danger and potential ill effect of the drugs mentioned above also exists with the illegally used and abused street drugs, such as marijuana, stimulants, sedatives, narcotics, mood modifiers, and other assorted compounds. The major difference, however, is that unlike the ethically distributed drugs used for therapy in disease, the so-called street drugs are usually unlabeled, untested, unprescribed, and have no indications for use or instructions with regards to dosage or frequency of use. To make things worse, people using them usually deny their use so that the diagnosis of side effects from these preparations is established purely by the observations of friends or loved ones or a particularly astute physician. Even though the use of alcohol and tobacco are currently legal in our society, their abuse is so rampant that I would be inclined to include them in this discussion. If, therefore, either you or your mate or your children are involved with the use of "street drugs," I would urge you to carefully evaluate what you are doing. Evaluate behavior, health, performance, achievement level, job performance, general hygiene, mental attitude, sexual performance, and overall happiness. If there is a deficiency in any of these categories, and there is indeed drug exposure, I would recommend that you do your best to eliminate drugs from your lives. If you are unable to eliminate them on your own, seek the help of your family physician and be honest about your problem and work on it. If you do not, the chances of it destroying your family are tremendous. Do not be shy about soliciting help, as embarrassing as it may seem to be. Your physician has had experience enough to realize that all people are vulnerable to problems of all sorts and that it is his job to help with them.

In conclusion, never abuse legal social drugs (alcohol, caffeine, tobacco, etc.). Understand the medications prescribed by your doctor and use them only as directed. And *never* permit yourself or any member of your family to become involved with illegal drugs in any way.

·24·

The Subject of In-Laws

The relationship that one has with in-laws can range from being completely satisfactory, rewarding, comfortable, and affectionate, to being thoroughly catastrophic. The complexities involved are too varied to be included in the context of this chapter, but motivation, cultural background, and basic personalities are the most common and most important variables. With all of this in mind, I offer the following suggestions which could be of great help in getting along with your in-laws:

1. *Always be polite and respectful.* Even though you may be attempting to have a reasonably close relationship with your mate's family, you must never be led into the false sense of security that your indiscretions will be automatically forgiven. Therefore, it is of utmost importance to be as polite as possible and very respectful to all of your mate's family. There may be times when you do not feel that they are deserving of your courtesy and respect, but take it from me, these are the times when they are the most important. You will also find that courtesy and respect are contagious, and if you express these traits to your in-laws, your chances of having them returned are excellent.

2. *Never criticize your mate to his or her family.* Regardless of how justified any criticism is, or how sympathetic to your plight your mate's family may seem, complaining about your mate to his or her parents, brothers, or sisters will almost always turn out to be catastrophic. It is natural for family members to protect each other and, therefore, your criticism of your mate will very often backfire and cause you considerable grief. Always be discreet.

3. *Never offer unsolicited advice to your in-laws.* Regardless of how well meaning it may be, if your advice is not solicited it can well be interpreted as an intrusion upon the privacy of the person to whom you are giving it. This is invariably offensive and should be avoided if at all possible.

4. *Preserve your privacy.* One of the most common complaints that I hear from people with regard to their in-laws is that they are forever intruding on their privacy. This is obviously annoying; however, it has been my experience that many people bring it upon themselves by discussing their own intimate affairs with their in-laws and therefore soliciting the intrusion upon their privacy.

5. *Never criticize your in-laws.* Whether you like it or not, your mate's family becomes your family once you are married, and you therefore must be understanding and tolerant of their shortcomings and indiscretions. Some of these things may require a great deal of patience, but it is of utmost importance that you be faithful to each other and do not criticize each other to a third party. It really serves no purpose and could ultimately lead to lack of respect and confrontation. Likewise, the person to whom you complained about your in-laws could very well lose respect for you as well because of your own indiscretion.

6. *Always be willing to forgive and forget.* The relationships between in-laws are so delicate that it would be inconceivable that they could be 100 percent free of incompatibility and misunderstanding. The only possible way an unpleasant relationship can be made tolerable is to be willing to forgive and forget and to start anew with understanding and respect at every opportunity.

7. *Unless it is absolutely necessary, never share living quarters with your in-laws.* This subject is covered elsewhere in the text and therefore will not be elaborated upon here. But let me emphasize: unless there is absolutely no alternative, never share a home with your in-laws.

8. *Never give nor take too much from your in-laws.* Generosity and caring for each other in time of need are wonderful, beautiful expressions of love, and I certainly encourage them. However, I have seen so many cases where people will give to or accept from their in-laws more than is healthy or reasonable. For anyone to feel beholden is extremely unhealthy and it is equally unhealthy to condemn one's in-laws as ungrateful for all they might have been given. With this in mind, I urge you to maintain a sense of balance about what you give and what you get with your in-laws, be it parents-in-law or children-in-law. Be careful to neither give nor accept more than is reasonable.

9. *Attempt to love one another.* All of us would like to accept our own

mate's family, as well as our children's mates' families, as being true loved ones. It would certainly be ideal if such love were as automatic as the love which exists between parents and offspring. Unfortunately, it is rarely the case, and these relationships deserve a great deal of unselfish initiative on the part of all persons concerned. Realistically, it is not always possible, but out of respect to your mate and your children, you should always keep on trying to develop a love that could enrich your life many times over.

I am sure that all of you have your own pet rules for getting along with your in-laws and I can't think of a more important thing for you to do than to enter those rules in your notebook. There will probably come a day when you will be advising your own children on how best to get along with in-laws, and your own comments at this time may be invaluable to you in the future.

·25·

Sexual Maladjustment and Frigidity

Sexual maladjustment and frigidity have been deliberately left as the last problems of marriage to be discussed. The reason is that proper understanding of all the problems discussed up to this point is necessary to fully comprehend the problems of sexual maladjustment.

Sexual problems fall into two basic categories: (1) those that affect people who have never enjoyed sexual satisfaction on a regular basis, and (2) those that concern couples who at some time past have enjoyed regular sexual satisfaction but for one reason or another have lost the ability to do so.

Couples differ markedly in what they consider to be their goals in sexual relationships, and this is a matter that must be taken into consideration when deciding whether a real problem exists. There is little question, however, that the problem is a widespread one because a recent survey indicated that out of a large group of women who were interviewed, only one-third stated that they had experienced complete satisfaction from sexual intercourse, including orgasm, more than 50 percent of the time. The second one-third said that they had achieved orgasm less than 50 percent of the time, and the last one-third stated that they had never achieved orgasm throughout their entire married lives. Mind you, some of these women had been married for a number of years, and most of them had borne multiple children. The remainder of the chapter will be devoted to classifying the many reasons for sexual maladjustment and offering suggestions for a positive therapeutic approach to each one.

Primary Frigidity and Sexual Maladjustment
The most common causes of primary frigidity and sexual maladjustment

are (1) medical and physical, (2) hostility toward the opposite sex, (3) unpleasant premarital experience, (4) poor sex education, (5) sexually incompatible partnership, and (6) fear of pregnancy.

Medical and Physical

Hormonal imbalance, exposure to numerous drugs, circulatory disorders, and many other disease states can make it impossible for people ever to have satisfactory sexual experience unless they are corrected.

There are many other reasons which are related to structural physical problems that cause people to have unsatisfactory sexual relations. The not infrequent occurrence of an inadequate opening of the female vagina, and its cure by simply stretching it by incision in the doctor's office, has already been discussed. Many women have a prepuce (a fold of foreskin overlying the clitoris) that prevents adequate exposure of the nerve centers. This too is easily repaired. Many women have a retroverted uterus. This is a condition in which the uterus is bent backward instead of the usual forward-flexed position. The result is that deep penetration of the penis bruises the uterus and causes it to be bumped against the vertebral column and therefore causes back pain with intercourse. The cure for this is simply advice about different coital positions—for example, the female on top of the male is most satisfactory—and maneuvers; sometimes a collarlike bumper can be mounted on the penis to prevent deep penetration.

Many women suffer from tender breasts. When the husband touches his wife's nipples in love play, she experiences painful rather than pleasurable sensations, and her natural reflex, therefore, is to push her husband away. Consequently, the husband feels rejected and concludes that his wife is frigid. The truth is, since she experiences pain when her husband touches her, it is impossible for the woman to experience sexual stimulation regardless of how deeply she is in love or how deeply she craves sexual stimulation. Most breast tenderness is treatable with medication. All tender breasts should be examined by a physician routinely because there is the possibility of more serious diseases of the breast, of which tenderness is an initial symptom.

The internal pelvic organs of the female can also be tender for other pathologic reasons. Such problems are easily diagnosed and not at all difficult to treat. Causes of such tenderness include ovarian or uterine infection, uterine fibroids, adhesions, constipation, bladder disorders, and vaginal infections.

Some women lack the ability to manufacture adequate lubricating secretions in the vagina, and, therefore, experience an abrasive, burning irritation during intercourse. This is easily corrected by the use of a water-soluble jelly, spread about the vulva before intercourse. (KY Jelly and Lubritene are two of the many jellies available.) Women can also be sexually inhibited by back disorders, orthopedic problems, and claustrophobia.

Men, too, can be deprived of sexual satisfaction by problems that can be medically and surgically corrected. One of the most common problems is *phimosis* (a condition in which the foreskin of the uncircumcised penis has too tight a ring, and therefore prevents painless stripping back for the exposure of the head of the penis where the nerve centers are located). Other physical diseases, such as disfigurement of the male genital tract, could be responsible for the male's dissatisfaction and inability to perform sexually.

The final, and probably the most common physical disorder on the part of both males and females that makes sexual satisfaction difficult is excessive obesity. Aside from rendering the mate unattractive, obesity also makes the physical contact awkward and often unpleasant. Obesity to this degree is always treatable, and its neglect is unforgivable.

No one could possibly know how much sexual maladjustment is caused by the physical problems discussed above, but I assure you that it is a lot. The sad part of it is that most of these problems could have been recognized and cured if only the couple had gone to their family doctor for a good *premarital* physical examination. Even if they had gone to their doctor at the *first* sign of trouble, most of these problems could have been quickly cured. Unfortunately, most people with this kind of problem suffer from frustration and embarrassment. They procrastinate for a long time before they seek medical help. Sometimes they live a whole lifetime suffering from an easily curable problem and never experience the joy of a satisfactory sexual experience.

Hostility toward the Opposite Sex

People who are the *offspring of a bad marriage* very often have so much hostility to heterosexual relationships that they find it nearly impossible to surrender themselves to their mates. A girl, for instance, whose image of masculinity is a vivid remembrance of her father abusing her mother, could understandably find it difficult to completely surrender herself sexually.

She may have agreed to marry because of the other advantages that marriage offers, and not have thought about her future sexual behavior. Even though her husband may be respectful, patient, and have none of the characteristics of her father, her subconscious barriers frequently cannot be overcome unless they are brought out into the open and debunked.

Males, too, can miss the true satisfaction of sex if they are inhibited by hostility toward females. Even though they can perform the sex act and reach orgasm, the experience as a whole can completely lack satisfaction. It might be wise to discuss these matters openly with your mate and try to come to some mutual understanding. Most people, unfortunately, will not have the objectivity to completely analyze such a delicate situation on their own, and therefore the aid of an interested family physician, a therapist, or a psychiatrist, would be very helpful. Evaluate your mate on his or her merits alone. Do not punish your mate for the wrongdoings of your parents or of any other person in your experience.

Unpleasant Premarital Experience

People who have had *unpleasant premarital sexual experience* sometimes find it difficult to relax and accept a healthy sexual relationship in their married life. This is apparent if you think in terms of a girl whose first sexual experience was being raped. Such a horrible, vivid experience will probably never be erased from her mind; and for her to relax and surrender to a husband and discover that sexual intercourse is a wonderful, beautiful thing is extremely difficult, if not impossible. Fortunately, few women suffer such a traumatic experience in their first exposure to sex. However, many people do have a premarital sexual relationship that they very often come to feel guilty about. They frequently judge themselves as having done a dirty, illicit thing; and consequently they reject their legitimate marriage partner. Thereafter, they continue to have a feeling of panic and restraint associated with sexual intercourse.

Poor Sex Education

Preparation for marriage must include *adequate sexual knowledge* if the adjustment to an active marital sex life is to be a graceful one. It is true that in many cases, men and women who have never been told a single word about sex education will reach a satisfactory adjustment by simply letting nature take its course. But in this day, I doubt that anyone, especially in the United States, could reach the state of lying in a honeymoon bed without knowing something about sexual intercourse. The unfortunate part, however, is that most of the learning comes from pornography, and the net result in many cases is that many people are misinformed about sexuality—love is *not* lust. In obscene writings, there is little practical discussion of male and female anatomy and physiology. Therefore, people who learn about sex this way are ignorant of their own body functions.

Unfortunately, many parents who intend to enlighten their children about sex find that they never get beyond discussing the dangers and disgrace of premarital sex. They rarely get around to telling the children of the beauty of proper love-directed sex in marriage. I would venture a guess that fewer than one out of every thirty people, at the time of marriage, has been given a word of parental advice about the importance and methods of the sex act and about the emotional involvement of sexual surrender. Isn't it a gross inequity that so much emphasis is put on avoiding sex at the improper time, but so little emphasis is put on the importance of enjoying sex at the proper time?

Proper and adequate sexual knowledge is not found in pornography. Neither is it found in dirty jokes, gossip, or burlesque shows. By the same token, it is not necessary to become a fully trained gynecologist to be prepared for satisfactory sexual adjustment in marriage. In my opinion, good sex education is composed of, first, an adequate understanding of all facets of sex in marriage and its goals, which I hope this text will have been successful in providing; and, second, a basic understanding of the anatomic and physiologic aspects of both male and female sexual organs and their functions. I have made reference to many aspects of sexual adjustment throughout this text, but if the discussion has left you still feeling unprepared with regard to sex, you should consult your family physician.

Sexually Incompatible Partnerships

Some marriages are just plain *poor marriages* insofar as sexual compatibility is concerned. Much is spoken about this overemphasized fact in an attempt to justify premarital sex. Those who endorse this view maintain that to "try before you buy" is sensible. Maybe it would be if people were products, but they are not. It is rare to find a completely sexually incompatible couple. When there is such a case, the cause can be an extreme difference in cultural background; an attitude toward sex as an unclean, even animalistic, act; or lack of imagination by one or both partners in love play.

A common example of this is the sexually shy woman whose husband is too impatient for love play. He wants to "get to it" and satisfy himself without attempting to sexually stimulate his wife. She finds it almost impossible to achieve orgasm because of his complete lack of consideration for her. It might be that this same woman, if she were married to a more considerate and imaginative man, could be easily and regularly satisfied. Actually, the same could be said of the man. It might well be that even though he achieves ejaculation (orgasm) on a purely physical plane, his own psychological craving for affection and mutual surrender could be completely lacking. His experience could be the exact opposite if his wife guided him to a more exciting love play. It is well known that an impassioned partner has a reciprocal effect on the mate.

Another cause of fundamental sexual incompatibility is the forced marriage in which there is no basic love or respect. If you are experiencing this type of problem, it would be wise to analyze it to the best of your ability. Then make an honest effort to understand your mate and help him or her to understand you. If there was enough feeling between you to precipitate marriage, there might be enough left to rekindle the effort to have a satisfactory sexual relationship, thus creating a more secure marriage.

Fear of Pregnancy

Finally, *fear of pregnancy* is one of the most common reasons for failure to enjoy the sex act. If it is understood that the basic natural purpose of sexual intercourse is the procreation of children (as well as a way of expressing love for each other), it is understandable that people who have no desire for children and a real fear of having them would also have hesitations about the sex act. Improved birth-control measures have made contraception more aesthetically acceptable and more natural, so there is far less sexual frustration than there used to be, and many people practice contraception so they can enjoy sex to it fullest. I would urge you to read pages 29–36, and review the various methods of contraception. If you and your mate can select the method best suited to your needs, your fear of pregnancy should be greatly lessened and your enjoyment of healthy sex vastly increased.

All cases of primary frigidity and sexual maladjustment should be treated with the help of sympathetic but objective professionals. Any healthy cohabiting couple who had gone through even a month of marriage without experiencing complete sexual satisfaction can assume that he or she has a problem that is not likely to rectify itself easily. Attendance in a group therapy program might be the answer; but a simple visit to an interested family physician would most assuredly be of great help.

Secondary Frigidity and Maladjustment

Secondary frigidity or maladjustment is the situation in which a couple that has once experienced sexual satisfaction on a regular basis has lost the ability to do so. The reasons for this are many. The most common are as follows: fear of pregnancy, loss of mutual respect, loss of self-respect and self-confidence, lack of privacy, fatigue, lack of imagination in love play, impotence and loss of libido, lack of mutual physical attraction, physical and mental illness, old age, and infidelity.

When people have a secondary sexual maladjustment, it is safe to assume that since they once had satisfactory sexual adjustment, they certainly know how to perform the sex act. So-called sex educators often seem to believe that if a couple knows the mechanics of the sex act everything will turn out well. This belief is very comforting to the instructor, but it has been my experience that it doesn't offer much help to people because "where to put it and what to do with it"—something people learn very, very quickly—is rarely the cause for lack of satisfaction.

The cause for lack of satisfaction lies in the conditions listed above, and the cure of a secondary sexual maladjustment lies in the understanding and correction of these conditions. In the pages that follow, I shall attempt to review them in some detail and offer some suggestions for their cure.

Fear of Pregnancy

Fear of pregnancy is a more serious matter after the birth of one or more children. Both husband and wife are now often fearful over the responsibility and inconvenience that come with having more children than they can handle, and this plays a big part in their attitude toward sexual intercourse. If an overburdened and insecure woman regards her husband as being an ever-present source of an unwanted pregnancy, it is easy to see why she may cringe at the very sight of him, and panic at the thought of exposing herself to the possibility of pregnancy. Men, too, suffer fears and anxieties over the burden of having more children than they can handle. Quite often, they will discipline themselves to suppress their sexual desire by distracting themselves with activities outside the home rather than succumb to the temptation of sex and the threat of pregnancy to follow. It is indeed a sad thing to watch couples who started out with a strong foundation of love and all the other solid building blocks of marriage, drift apart when they become preoccupied with the fear of pregnancy. I know of couples who have deliberately thought of excuses to not sleep together for this reason. Husband or wife will sleep on the floor, or on the living-room sofa, or crawl into bed with one of the children, simply to avoid the temptation (and threat) of sexual contact.

Much to my surprise, however, only a very small percentage of these couples actually admit their fear of pregnancy. It seems as though they deliberately create other reasons for their separation, become quite inconsiderate of each other, and resentful over the entire situation. But for some reason, they are reluctant to admit their fear of pregnancy and find excuses to avoid it.

In a previous section of this text, I alluded to the reasons why people refuse to confess their fear of further pregnancy. To many couples, it is a genuine fear that God will consider them ungrateful for the children they have and, therefore, permit something bad to happen to them. It is by this reasoning that parents feel guilty about fearing pregnancy. It is the same feeling of guilt that is most often responsible for a couple's purposeful neglect to adopt a program of practical birth control. (Various methods have been discussed on pages 29 to 36).

If this matter has not been carefully discussed and understood by both mates, their mutual frigidity can continue even after they institute a birth-control program. There are two reasons for this. First, is that experience has shown us that no method is completely foolproof; therefore, even though the possibility of conception might be slim indeed, it is risky enough to the couple involved to assume tragic proportions. And second, if the couple chooses a form of birth control that strikes one participant as unsatisfactory, the whole mood of the sex act might well be lost. A third consideration deserves attention too. Many people enjoy sex primarily for the exciting possibility that they could be conceiving a pregnancy. Without this feeling, their sex act becomes a reasonless indignity, and the thrill is completely lacking.

The adoption of a satisfactory birth-control program would certainly be very easy to accomplish. I have already mentioned in some detail the various methods of doing so.

The question of the morality of birth control is one that varies considerably with the backgrounds of the mates involved. Since our religions too differ so much on this matter, the churches seem to be in a dynamic state of flux over the birth-control issue, because of the socioeconomic needs of the times and the methods of birth control available. I would urge all people who have moral hesitations about birth control to seek guidance from a spiritual leader in whom they have confidence, as well as from the family physician. Please do not make the mistake of going to a dogmatist who does not understand your culture nor your own basic training. More harm than good can be accomplished by getting bad advice or advice that does not suit your particular culture. There is a great range of interpretation of the rules in every faith, and if you are going to follow someone's advice on such a delicate matter you must carefully choose the person who is to give you the advice.

I am put in mind of a young couple, both age twenty-four, who already had four children, and who were taking a sensible and methodic approach to family planning. They went to their pastor, however, who had never been married himself and who was notorious for his unbending rigidity and indiscretion. This man was a very forceful speaker on a pulpit, but he had little or no understanding of the problems of marriage. They told him of their problem and requested advice on how they might morally approach their family planning. The pastor rose to his feet, shook his forefinger at them, and proceeded to tell them that the children that they had already been blessed with were the ultimate blessings that could be given to any couple through the grace of God. And that since they had received and appreciated and enjoyed their children, it was their duty to accept and endure any and all who might come hereafter—and they should not interfere with the will of God. He went on to tell them that he knew of many couples who attempted to interfere with the will of God and who were punished by losing the children that had already through horrible accidents and illnesses. After this browbeating, the young couple found themselves embarrassed for even having brought up the topic, and so they thanked their pastor and left with a feeling of guilt and dejection.

Another couple with a similar problem went to their pastor for advice. This clergyman was a younger, more compassionate man. Mind you, the two pastors were from different churches but of the same religious denomination. Upon hearing their problem, the second pastor's response was, "Yes, of course, you already have more children than you can rear comfortably; so to put yourselves under the burden of still more children would be a gross injustice to yourselves and to your existing children. It would be morally wrong to be inadequate parents to six or more children. It is your moral obligation to limit your family to a sensible number." He then referred the couple to their family physician for more specific guidance on the exact method of birth control they should employ, which would still be acceptable by church doctrine.

If you are going to seek moral guidance, for goodness' sake, seek it from someone who will be understanding and compassionate enough to really help—not that you are seeking someone who will prejudge the matter in your favor, but someone who will be open-minded enough to not prejudge the matter at all.

Whether or not you have a problem of sexual maladjustment, if you have a fear of pregnancy, or feel unsettled in your family planning, this is a matter of utmost concern and importance; it should be discussed at great length until mutual agreement is reached.

Loss of Mutual Respect

Since sexual intercourse is an act of love-making, there can be no surprise about the fact that sexual relations are far less likely to be successful and satisfying if other expressions of love between the two mates are not all they should be. One could easily consider sexual adjustment as being the end product of mutual love and respect, and overall marital adjustment. So if things aren't going well for you in general, and you also have a problem of sexual maladjustment, it is easy to blame the lack of sexual satisfaction for your basic problems. But is far more likely that other marital problems are causing the sexual ones.

Lack of Self-respect and Self-confidence

Lack of self-respect and self-confidence is another common cause for lack of sexual satisfaction. This is particularly so in males who suffer frustrations and indignities in their work. Those who are unemployed are even more afflicted. When someone is personally demoralized, it is difficult to maintain the self-confidence necessary to be a good husband and lover. Protection and virility are usually associated with the male image in sexual love play.

Women experience the female counterpart of such mechanisms and react in very much the same way. Obesity and a feeling of unattractiveness, however, are contributory causes of the female lack of self-confidence. Women are also prone to this symptom if they have suffered the embarrassment that comes with infidelity on the part of the husband, or problems with their children, or less definable inadequacies and failures of their own. The solution to this problem, of course, is not to drive yourself crazy through feelings of compounded guilt and inadequacy; do not fixate your frustrations on your sexual disappointments. Instead, analyze the causes of your lack of self-confidence and work out a good plan to regain it. It is not always easy to do so, but do not let yourself get into a tailspin from which you cannot recover. Your family physician can help you. The chances are that in solving that problem you might solve your sexual problem as well.

Lack of Privacy

In spite of the mammoth business that pornographers have created out of demonstrating the sex act in magazines, films, and other means of communication, the fact remains that for people to truly express love for each other in a satisfactory way, they must have privacy. In a family with small children, this privacy is often hard to come by. For a couple that lives with parents, it is almost impossible. Consider this in evaluating your own problems. If you find it difficult to achieve the proper mood for sex, ask yourself whether or not the setting is an attractive one. If it is not, for goodness' sake, take measures to make it so, even if you have to send the children away for a specific time. You might simply tell the other adults in the house that you and your mate need time alone together. People often are embarrassed to admit the need for privacy, and they shouldn't be. Insist on your privacy; it is an absolute essential. Don't neglect it.

Of all the subjects that I have discussed in this text, this must be one of the most obvious. However, it is surprising how many people fail to recognize it as a cause of many problems. It sounds incredible, but one man actually told me that he and his wife had so little privacy that, out of sexual frustration, he got himself involved with another woman with whom he eventually had regular sexual intercourse. He said that he had very little feeling for the woman and only had an appetite for her sexually. He also enjoyed the privacy of their illicit romance. He said, rather innocently, that he would have preferred to have sex with his own wife, but that in the past *seven* years he had never been able to get her alone long enough to be able to make love to her. I believed him. I have visited their home, and have seen that there is no privacy. Their bedroom has no door because his wife feels obliged to listen out for the children, in case they have problems during the night. They have several teenaged children who apparently never get to bed before one A.M. The youngsters awaken at six, and have complete freedom of their parents' bedroom. When I approached the wife with the problem, she admitted that she craved her husband's sexual attentions, but was frustrated by lack of privacy. However, she had no idea of how to solve the problem. My suggestion was that they get a door with a lock on it for their bedroom and hang up a "Keep Out" sign when they did not want to be disturbed. I also suggested that they inform their children that there are times when privacy is a must, and they would have to respect it. The husband lost no time in following my instructions and, so far at least, they have solved their problem.

I have another friend who is somewhat more affluent. He has six children, and he was more imaginative in solving his problem. He actually hired a baby-sitter every other Saturday night to stay with the children while he took his wife to a plush motel which is only six miles from their home. They would come home Sunday morning, after reading the newspaper and having breakfast in bed. Of course, they were subjected to a lot of teasing about this, but they were emphatic in saying that it has completely changed their marriage, and that they look forward to their weekend honeymoons with such enthusiasm that they feel like newlyweds.

No matter how you go about it, *insist on privacy.*

Fatigue

Probably because it is the only time that most married couples can find any privacy, nighttime usually turns out to be petting time. There is nothing wrong with that. I'm sure this has been true since marriage began. The catch is that most people are exhausted at bedtime. Any woman who has been chasing a toddler all day, scrubbing floors, doing the wash, worrying about the family budget, checking the older children's homework—and possibly handling an outside job as well—is usually a very tired individual who finds it difficult to become an enthusiastic sexual partner, regardless of how much she loves her husband. When her husband makes amorous advances, she is usually unable to react as an enthusiastic mate. Any husband can easily misinterpret the situation as one of rejection; and serious consequences can follow.

On the other hand, the husband's day is probably beset with exhausting fatigue from either physical work or the mental anguish of a daily competitive routine, or both; and he might well find it difficult to demonstrate much imagination and enthusiasm in love-making, despite his going through the motions and performing to the point of orgasm.

When a couple establishes the habit of attempting sexual intercourse in spite of their fatigue, they are destined to have a disappointing experience at best. Even though they are willing to go through the motions, they are usually sorry that they bothered at all. Since the act was such a disappointment, it is not uncommon for people who have such an experience to interpret the lack of satisfaction as the partner's lack of love or as an indication of frigidity. In truth, it is neither. It is simply the wrong time. Many husbands accuse their wives of citing fatigue as an excuse for avoiding intercourse, and wives take offense at this. Before you condemn your wife as such a trickster, may I suggest that you give a good honest effort to setting aside a few private Sunday afternoons in which you do nothing else but fuss over each other? With adequate rest and time and with all the distractions of the world shut out for a while, just see how amorous you both are. The result should be a pleasant surprise. And even if no one complains of fatigue, you might find it an interesting experience to try daytime petting just for a change of pace.

Lack of Imagination in Love Play
Broiled steak is probably one of the most popular and one of the most expensive foods in the American diet; there is hardly anyone who doesn't enjoy it. Yet if every day we were served steak broiled exactly the same way, with exactly the same vegetables, it wouldn't be long before it would cease to be a treat. Most people, therefore, vary their diets and attempt to find new and interesting things to eat. The same is true, to some degree, of sexual intercourse. No matter how much two people love each other, or how much they enjoy sharing sex, they will find it begins to lack excitement unless they use some imagination and make the experience seem new and different from time to time.

I have already mentioned the value of enjoying sex at different times of the day. From time to time a cocktail or two before love play can also help to lower inhibitions and add a different atmosphere to love making. Private vacations without the children can also bring about a feeling of sensual closeness that be lacking in the daily busy routine. Remember, there is nothing that husband and wife can do together in sex play that is personally or morally wrong so long as it ends up in intercourse and gives mutual satisfaction.

Several years back, two middle-aged couples who were close friends had a combined tragedy. One of the women was widowed, and the husband of the other couple lost his wife—both from malignant disease. Within two years' time, the bereaved man and woman found themselves very much in love and were planning to be married. The woman confided to me that she was enthusiastic about the marriage but was worried because she had always considered herself to be sexually frigid. She stated that during her twelve years of marriage to her former husband, she had rarely enjoyed intercourse and had done everything she could to avoid it. And she thought it hardly was fair to subject her new husband to a frigid wife.

She asked me to discuss it with him prior to their marriage, so he would be sure that he knew what he was getting himself into, and she also requested that I offer guidance. The man was an earthy person who worked with his hands and spoke with his heart. When I told him of his future wife's problems and concerns, he said that they were no surprise to him because he had had occasion to discuss them with her former husband many times before his death; and he felt the problem was that she had never been adequately stimulated.

The wedding night turned out to be much as she had predicted it would be. She found it impossible to relax, was embarrassed about her predicament, and panicked at the idea of again suffering the humiliation of not being able to function as a satisfactory sex partner. She was terribly depressed about all this, but her new husband assured her that he loved her and was convinced that time and a little imagination would cure their problem. On the second night, as they were preparing for bed, she took her nightclothing to the bathroom to undress there as she had always done. She had always been very modest and frequently made mention of the fact that she had never permitted herself to be seen in the nude by her first husband. Her new husband was not about to put up with this however. In a bold tone, he declared, "Sally, your modest days are over, and so are your frigid ones. I'm going to come into the bathroom and give you a good shower!" She was horrified at the thought and raised a thousand objections. The husband paid no attention to any of them and proceeded to undress himself and then undress his wife. He then carried her into the bathroom and gave her the shower of her life!

Sally confessed to me later that it was like a baptism. It was the very first time she had ever experienced any sexual stimulation, and she was completely awed by the experience. Several years later, we were discussing the topic, and I asked her if she was at all troubled by frigidity. She blushed and said that it was a reverse situation now because she had found that sex was such an exciting and thrilling experience that she was at times even aggressive in their love making. When I asked her what had made the difference, she hesitated for a moment and said, "Well, my husband always makes it interesting. There are times when he gives me the feeling that he is so hungry for me that he would rape me if I were ever to say no. And who would ever want a greater compliment than that?" She went on to say that at other times "He makes me feel so feminine that I do all I can to live up to that image." "Didn't your former husband give you those same feelings?" I asked. She thought for a bit and replied, "Well, no. He was always so nice and polite and tolerant of my modesty that he left me with a feeling of guilt about my frigidity." In fact, she went on to say, instead of feeling as though she was about to participate in a mutually satisfying experience, she always had the feeling that she was simply paying him a debt.

Please bear in mind, this second husband was not an educated man. He had not studied psychology, nor had he read any elaborate texts on the anatomy and physiology of human sexual behavior. He was just a man who loved his wife, craved her, and knew how to show it.

Imagination in love play is partially the responsibility of the woman also. Many women are dull bed partners because they have been brought up with the idea that sexual intercourse is a man's thing and that the woman's role is to hold still and tolerate it as a duty. They also often have been taught that women of high moral principles are neither expected nor supposed to be aggressive about love play; and that their primary satisfaction from sex should come from giving their husbands pleasure. Such women pride themselves on the virtuous feelings they get from offering themselves to their husbands as sexual sacrifices.

The overall result is usually a very sad one. The mates go through the motions of sexual intercourse, including of course ejaculation by the male, but the experience is generally an empty one, lacking the thrill, excitement, and passion that should be part of the sex act. This is a disappointing and sometimes confusing letdown. The result usually is that the couple continues to have sexual intercourse, but the frequency declines, and general interest in the marriage falls to a low ebb.

Many couples simply resign themselves to believing that sex is not so important as the press and the playwrights make it out to be, and that they have to look for other forms of excitement in life. The sad awakening comes when one of the partners has an opportunity to have sex outside of marriage. If the partner has for long been frustrated, he or she is very susceptible to becoming intoxicated with the experience; and it is not uncommon for such a person to give up all the good sense and security of the marriage.

When this happens, family, friends, and relatives cannot understand how such a well-matched couple could have marital problems. What in the world could have ever lured the man or the woman to stray from what seemed to be such a good marriage? When it becomes apparent that one mate has strayed in pursuit of sexual satisfaction, he or she is often called a pervert and condemned for weakness and indiscretion. The faithful partner is often completely bewildered by the infidelity, and innocently states that it is hard to understand why there would be any reason to stray. Sex was never refused at home. Some also rationalize their plight with the explanation that they were not raised to be sexy, and that the only purpose of sexual intercourse is the procreation of children; and that the sensual aspect was simply a form of love that was of minimal importance.

This is a lazy and irresponsible approach to a very serious problem. If, as a woman, you consider sexual intercourse a chore that must be tolerated, you are missing one of the real highlights of marriage. If your participation in the sex act is limited to tolerantly holding still while your husband attempts to have intercourse with you, you are not only robbing him of the feeling of masculinity that comes from offering sexual satisfaction to his wife but also you are depriving yourself of one of life's most thrilling experiences. If you are the male partner who plods through sex mechanically with little communication or stimulation of your wife, you too are missing most of the thrill.

If this is your lot in life, get wise to yourself, and get in the act. Start by making up your mind to be a bit more aggressive. Lure your mate to bed once in a while. Fondle your partner's body, and permit yourself to become stimulated by being more of an aggressor. Put your own body in motion too during the act of coitus and just see if you don't get more out of it.

If you are not being adequately stimulated during the sex act, discuss it with your mate in a positive way. Experiment. Explore your body in private to determine your foci of stimulation and guide your mate to them.

Ears, axillae, inner thighs, mouth, breasts, and even the soles of the feet contain sensuous nerve centers as well as the genital organs. Vigorous, imaginative love play can at times focus on the total body—and it should.

It is wrong to expect that love alone is an adequate stimulus to produce a thrilling sex life. It helps, of course, but imagination, enthusiasm, experimentation, and communication are also necessary. Both husband and wife must be interested and participate. Anything that both partners find pleasurable is all right.

If at first you don't succeed, try, try, try again. If trying on your own doesn't help, read some books, talk to your mate, consult your family physician, and leave no stone unturned. If you are not being sexually satisfied, neither is your mate; and your responsibility to achieve satisfactory sexual adjustment in marriage is as strong as your responsibility for the care of your children. Work on it, and don't be satisfied till it's right.

Impotence and Loss of Libido

Inability to perform and loss of interest in sex can be caused by any of the physical and emotional factors discussed elsewhere in this chapter, but it can also be the result of alcohol, medications of many types, and systemic disease.

Regardless of what you think might be responsible for your difficulty, please consult your physician for a complete physical exam and laboratory workup.

I have attempted to prepare you to be your own marriage counselor with other problems, but this one requires professional help. So, please be completely honest with your physician. Tell him the whole story. With adequate interest and cooperation 80 percent of impotence and loss of libido is correctable.

Lack of Mutual Physical Attraction

Prior to marriage, a person's physical appearance and overall attractiveness are of primary concern. People with poor hygiene and sloppy personal habits are simply not sexually attractive. Unless they mend their ways, they become social wallflowers.

Unfortunately, pride in personal appearance and behavior often deteriorates after the marriage ceremony. Some people no longer feel the need to maintain their sexual identity, and take for granted that once they have acquired a mate—who has promised to "love, honor, and cherish till death do us part"—the deal is closed. Nothing could be further from the truth. Poor hygiene, bad manners, neglected health, and lack of pride in one's personal appearance are as objectionable in the married state as they are to the single person looking for a mate.

All the sex education in the world, even a course in the theatrical arts, cannot make a person a good sex partner with someone he or she does not find physically attractive. Granted, sex is more important to some people than it is to others, but if your own marriage lacks sexual satisfaction, take a good look in the mirror and ask yourself if you are the kind of person your mate should be proud of and eager for. Consider your own habits, particularly in bed. Body odor, bad breath, and neglected teeth will cancel out even the most virile libido. A face covered with greasy cream and a head full of curlers also present impenetrable obstacles against successful sexual advances. If you must play "beauty parlor," play "beauty parlor," but don't do it when you should be making love with your husband. Regardless of how attractive it might make you look during the day, it can't possibly be worth the masquerade act at night if it chases your husband away from you.

Physical and Mental Illness

Sexual performance is dependent upon the total physical and emotional well-being of both mates. If either mate is suffering from any physical or emotional upset, his or her sexual function is almost certain to be impaired. This is a very important fact from two standpoints. Number one, if your mate is temporarily physically or emotionally ill, don't expect much in the line of sexual performance until the condition gets straightened out. And number two, if you are the physically or emotionally ill mate, you owe it to yourself and to your mate to obtain proper medical care and resolve the problem as soon as possible. Almost no one would drive a malfunctioning automobile, and certainly no one would intentionally fly in a malfunctioning airplane. But for some ridiculous reason, some people have no hesitation about going through their daily functions in a malfunctioning body. This is unforgivable if a cure is available. Don't let it happen to you.

Old Age

The ability to perform sexually decreases as age advances. For practically every couple, there comes a time when sexual performance is completely impossible or just nor worth the effort. When most folks reach this age, they have usually become emotionally mature enough to realize that sex has had its day, and they are willing to express their love in other ways. Some people, however, don't give up that easily and become extremely depressed when they realize that their sexual careers have come to an end. This can produce a form of panic that sometimes drives males and females alike to extremes of sexually bizarre behavior. If this happens, please be aware of the fact that this is a medical problem, an illness. And as with all other illnesses, it requires understanding on the part of the other mate as well as good medical guidance by your family physician. This is a family problem, not just a personal problem; and so husband and wife should go for help together. Please do this before the bickering, embarrassment, and side effects of the condition destroy all that you have worked so hard for together. Sad as it sounds, this does happen.

Just recently, one of the nicest couples I have ever known came to me with a terrible problem. They were both sixty-three years old and had enjoyed thirty-eight years of devoted and successful married life, and had raised two fine daughters. Six months ago, the husband became sexually involved with his twenty-two-year-old secretary, and before long the wife was well aware of the situation, and became hysterical with rage and heartbreak. The husband stated that he just couldn't bear the thought of getting old. He said that even though his wife never refused him sexually, he found that he had a great deal of difficulty being aroused by her because she was now showing signs of old age. (As fate would have it, his sexual performance with the younger woman was also unsatisfactory.) The truth of the matter was that he was looking for a scapegoat to avoid accepting his own advancing age. He attempted to prove he was still young by demonstrating his masculinity to the younger woman. No one could say for sure, but if he had proper psychiatric guidance and the cooperation of his wife, the situation might have been resolved in a decent and amiable way. Instead, however, both mates became hostile to each other, and tragedy after tragedy ensued. Finally, it had absolutely destroyed both their lives and all that they had worked a lifetime to create. Sexual misbehavior in old age must be considered a matter of illness as much as, if not more than, a matter of immorality, and must be treated accordingly.

Advancing age was taking its toll at the same time on another couple—the same age—but in a different way. Bob and Lena were sixty-eight, had raised a nice family, and had enjoyed many years of peaceful marriage. It was Bob who came to me for help. He said that he was becoming irritable and depressed by the fact that his sexual performance was dwindling. His advances to his wife were 90 percent unsuccessful because of his inability to achieve and maintain erection. He would become embarrassed and upset, irritated and depressed. His wife was sympathetic and understanding but annoyed by the unpleasantness that ensued. "Why does it matter so?" I asked him. "In my ethnic culture, a man is not a man if he cannot perform sexually with his wife," he replied. My answer was, "But not forever; it just is not made to last beyond a certain age. That age varies from person to person, but everyone has his time when the sexual performance ceases." "That's what my wife has been saying, but I had a hard time accepting it," he replied. This reassurance on my part helped a great deal. I then offered the suggestion that he stop trying so hard to prove himself sexually, but rather to approach his wife only if he were spontaneously aroused, and not try to make it happen. I also told him that sex careers were significantly longer in men who do not use alcohol. His wife told me three months later that they were much happier. Without the pressure to have sexual relations, they were occasionally possible and satisfactory; but more important was the fact that they were enjoying the other aspects of marriage without worrying any longer about sex.

Infidelity as a Cause for Sexual Maladjustment
It is unreal for any married couples to expect consistent sexual satisfaction if one of the mates is unfaithful. This is so obvious that it should not need elaboration, but it is a very definite problem. Let's face it, if the infidelity is due to lack of sexual satisfaction in the marriage, and if the person is repeatedly having extramarital affairs, it is almost certainly because it provides more pleasure than sexual relations at home. If things were bad enough in the beginning to precipitate infidelity, they are certainly going to get worse as time goes on. It will be worse because their original problem, whatever it was, is compounded by the unfaithful partner's comparison of the mate to the lover. Once infidelity has reared its ugly head, the couple must call upon every ounce of forgiveness and maturity, and even seek professional help, in order to rebuild the marriage and rekindle the sexual fascination.

If infidelity has occurred in your marriage, do your best to rekindle the flame of fascination, and don't just settle for peaceful coexistence. Marriage that is repaired for the purpose of satisfying responsibility is destined to fall apart again and again, and not really be worth the effort.

In summary, there are many causes for lack of sexual satisfaction, and frigidity is neither a curse nor a bad word. Lack of sexual adjustment is only a symptom. It must be studied and analyzed to determine the underlying cause. And once the truth is known, it can and should be treated like any other disease of the mind or body. The prescription is usually a large dose of interest, enthusiasm, humility, love, and understanding administered in generous daily doses forevermore.

Part III

Golden Rules of Marriage

Introduction

If anyone else has ever written a rule book for the game of marriage, I have never seen it. I have stated elsewhere in this text that no two marriages are the same and no two people should expect to find marital happiness by the same route. However, I would like to offer the following list of what I consider to be the golden rules of marriage. Some of the rules will overlap, but the redundance is intentional for the purpose of emphasis. A few people might get by and find happiness in marriage even though they break almost all of these rules; however, I feel very strongly that any couple who keeps all of these rules will be more certain to find happiness, regardless of what hardships they encounter.

The best way to make use of these rules after you read them through the first time is to assign yourself one rule a day as a daily project and try to make it a part of your life. Take the rules in the order they are presented. When you have finished, start over again, and again, and again.

Perhaps you would like to add some rules of your own. That's great! Write them down and add them to your notes.

Rule 1
Keep the Marriage Dynamic

Human beings are restless and curious creatures. They seek security, but they are also usually bored. Unless man has a constant challenge, constant new experiences, a constant something to look forward to, he becomes restless, irritable, and dissatisfied. The needs and desires of people vary with various phases of life; therefore, it is wise to constantly assess your needs and those of your mate.

Always keep a project of some sort going, whether it be fixing the house, learning something new, pursuing a hobby, cultivating new friends, enjoying new experiences with your children, or helping someone in need. Always keep something interesting going on as a husband, wife, and family. If one member of the family is going out alone for his kicks in life too frequently, evaluate carefully whether he or she is getting enough kicks at home to be fulfilled. Keep your eyes open; keep your mind flexible; and for God's sake, don't let yourself fall into any lazy ruts, particularly the "television rut."

The first rule then is to KEEP THE MARRIAGE DYNAMIC!

Rule 2
Be Courteous at Home

Be courteous at home. No one will question that a man's home is his castle and that he deserves to be free and comfortable there. Likewise, a woman deserves no less. But this does not relieve either husband or wife of the responsibility to be courteous and respectful. "Please" and "thank you" make the difference between a request and a command. A request is almost always granted with enthusiasm; a command is almost invariably resented. If parents are gentle with each other and are respectful and courteous, the children usually turn out to have these same attributes.

BE COURTEOUS AT HOME!

Rule 3
Never Belittle Your Mate

Did anyone ever belittle you, either in private or in public, in your presence or behind your back? If he did, do you remember how bitterly annoyed and resentful you were about being so treated? If someone for whom you had little regard belittled you, chances are you would take minor offense and guard against taking him into your confidence or having him for a friend. If the person meant a great deal to you, however, it might cause you to feel absolutely crushed and sap you of all your self-confidence. It would also leave you feeling hostile and possibly resentful to the point of taking revenge and counterattacking with similar behavior when the opportunity arose.

If this is what happens when someone belittles you, why in the world should you belittle someone else, particularly if it is someone you love? If you had a favorite piece of furniture, you wouldn't intentionally scratch it. If you had a new automobile, you wouldn't intentionally hammer a dent in the front fender. Why in the world would it be justifiable to deprecate a loved one? Some people may get a feeling of superiority by belittling someone else, but that surely is a high price to pay for a short-lived experience of inflated ego.

Others use the excuse that they are simply pointing out their mate's faults in hopes of effecting an improvement. This is hard to believe. I don't know that I have ever seen a need for humiliating any person in public or private to get a point across. I have never seen anyone benefit from this type of humiliation.

Constructive criticism is fine. We all need it most of the time, but if it is stripping your mate of his or her dignity and self-confidence, you are definitely on the wrong track. You had better quit it before you create problems that even the most well-directed constructive criticism cannot remedy.

Let me say it again, NEVER BELITTLE YOUR MATE. It is never funny and it never accomplishes anything other than the generation of hostility. It makes you look like a fool in the eyes of the people who hear you do it. You have everything to lose and nothing to gain by this practice. NEVER BELITTLE YOUR MATE!

Rule 4
Always Let Your Mate Be Number One

When you marry, you agree to take "this man" or "this woman" to be your lawful spouse; to have and to hold; for richer, for poorer; for better, for worse; until death do you part. The other person becomes a part of you. If your mate is to assume this responsibility, he or she must be made to feel that he or she is number one with you.

We all love our children and our parents, and have a responsibility to them; however, this is a responsibility that must be fulfilled without infringing on the priority status of our mates. If your mate resents your attentions to anyone else, then such attentions must be set aside until your mate feels adequately satisfied. Most often a reassurance of this priority status is the cornerstone upon which a solid marriage rests. But unless your mate feels that he/she is NUMBER ONE, it won't be long before he becomes so resentful that you won't continue to be first with him (or her) either. It is easy to be distracted by other interests and responsibilities; therefore, you should always be on your guard.

ALWAYS LET YOUR MATE BE NUMBER ONE!

Rule 5
Call Your Mate by Name
or a Pet Name

It is an accepted fact that any person's favorite word is his own name. Psychologists have noted that when a person hears his name, he perks up and devotes his whole attention to what is being said in the form of a reflex response. We see this in pets too. For example, when a dog hears his name he comes running with his tail wagging and is obviously delighted with the acknowledgment. People aren't quite that demonstrative, but the basic feeling is nevertheless present. If this be so, and if you desire to please and hold the attention of your mate, use your mate's name frequently. It sounds so obvious, doesn't it? But for some reason, many couples succumb to a "Hey you" way of addressing each other that subconsciously offends. Think about it a bit. If you find that you rarely call your mate by name but rather use phrases like "Get me that," "Do this," and so forth without including the person's name with a tone of affection, try my suggestion and see if it doesn't bring some favorable results. A little flattery never hurt anyone and costs nothing.

CALL YOUR MATE BY NAME OR A PET NAME!

Rule 6
Don't Hesitate to Praise Your Mate in Public

After several years of marriage, people have a tendency to take each other for granted and get out of the habit of issuing direct thank you's and praise for a job well done. Unfortunately, this is most often interpreted as a lack of appreciation and, therefore, leaves one wondering whether or not the extra effort is worth bothering with. Public acknowledgment of your mate's strong points is well worth trying if you are not already in the habit of doing so.

Some time ago, my wife and I were having dinner in a fine restaurant, and I couldn't help but overhear the conversation at the next table where two couples were dining together. As one of the men looked over the menu, he saw *Beef Wellington* listed as one of the entrées and commented that his wife had made *Beef Wellington* during the past week and that it was delicious. A few moments later I heard the wife comment that she enjoyed putting extra effort into her cooking and other family chores because her husband appreciated it so much. It was obvious that this was a couple with a solid marriage.

A year or so ago, we visited the home of another family. We commented that their home seemed to reflect a great deal of themselves. In spite of the fact that it contained many interesting pieces of furniture, which I'm sure were quite expensive, the wife took us to a corner of the room to show us a rack of shelves and very proudly stated, "John made this one Sunday afternoon, and I'm just so happy with it. We could never find one like this in a store that would serve the purpose so well. It's so nice to have a man interested in his home." The husband never said a word, but his expression of contentment spoke for itself. The acknowledgment that his wife had given him at that moment was reward enough to ensure new enthusiasm for new projects for many years to come.

Let me say it again, DON'T HESITATE TO PRAISE YOUR MATE IN PUBLIC!

Rule 7
Resolve Today's Problems Today

In preparing this section of the text I arbitrarily chose ten couples whom I considered to be extremely well-adjusted, and who manifested little outward marital problems during my experience with them. I asked them each what they considered to be the secret of their compatibility. Eight out of ten replied that it was a family rule that they would never go to bed with an unresolved problem. One woman told me, "We discuss a problem until everything has been said about it, and then we agree on a course of action. We might not be convinced that it is the best course; however, we are convinced that nothing more could be said about it at the time that would improve the situation."

If you think about it a bit, this is exactly what happens in business and politics and in all controversial matters. The matters are discussed completely. The differences of opinion are aired; a decision is made; and those who professed a course of action which differed from the decision are committed to embrace the accepted policy.

If this were not so, life would be filled with so many unresolved problems that compatible progress would be an impossibility.

RESOLVE TODAY'S PROBLEMS TODAY!

Rule 8
Bend But Don't Break

If your mate has a really strong feeling about any particular subject, you should do everything you can to understand this point of view and adjust your own thoughts accordingly. No two people are of identical cultural backgrounds, and no two people have the same interests; therefore, a great deal of flexibility is required to mold two separate individuals into a solid partnership.

This is not to say that you must bend your code of principles and morals to the point where you lose self-respect doing so. There are certain basic principles of right and wrong that must be adhered to. For some reason, these are things that people rarely disagree harshly about. The disputes are almost always about minor issues which are hardly worth the dignity of controversy.

Strength of character is to be admired, but stubbornness is ridiculous.
BEND BUT DON'T BREAK!

Rule 9
Plan Ahead

There are two major factors which determine a person's level of achievement. One is how hard he works, and the second is how good a plan he has. This is also true of all facets of marriage. The degree of success we attain in marriage depends on how hard we work at it and how good a plan we have.

It has been my experience that there are very few things that are not attainable in our present world of opportunity, provided couples work hard enough at it and plan well enough ahead for what they want. Whether it be a new home, special things for your existing home, new satisfactions in recreation, new economic achievement, new social experiences, or whatever your heart desires—plan ahead, select reasonable goals, work toward them, and your life will not be lacking.

Anyone who spends any substantial amount of time complaining about his lot in life without spending at least twice that amount of time working toward a solution is simply being lazy and irresponsible and has only himself to blame for his misfortune. PLAN AHEAD.

Family planning has been discussed elsewhere in this text, so I will not take space to elaborate on it further at this point—except to say that each married person has the responsibility to establish a sensible plan for the sake of everyone concerned. PLAN AHEAD!

Work careers are satisfying only when people attain a level of achievement that approximates their maximum potential. Only a good plan and hard work can accomplish this. The earlier a good plan is conceived, the more likely it is to succeed.

So please, PLAN AHEAD!

Rule 10
Avoid Sore Points

Nobody enjoys being embarrassed, particularly by a loved one. We all have our sore points that predictably bring annoyance. For some people it's a physical trait, such as a big nose or obesity or being too tall, too short, or too anything. To others the embarrassment comes from the criticism of a family member, especially the black sheep, or an irritating trait of one of their parents. Still others are sensitive about their lack of education or some embarrassing episode in their past. We all have these sore points and they are almost always obvious to those who know us well. Since exposing them will invariably produce annoyance and hostility, why do it? If you really love your mate, prove it by overlooking his shortcomings and, if the point comes up, simply offer serious reassurance that it is of little concern to you. Never take for granted that if a person smiles and shrugs off this type of embarrassment, it is something that he or she doesn't really mind. Everyone is sensitive and must be respected accordingly.

AVOID SORE POINTS!

Rule 11
Stay Attractive

Helena Rubenstein, one of the pioneers of the cosmetic industry, is credited with having said, "There is no such thing as a homely woman, only a lazy one." She proved her point over and over again by taking women with the least natural potential and teaching them how to fix themselves up and make the most of what they had.

If this is possible with women, it must be even more so with men, because men have less grooming to do. There is no excuse for sloppiness and neglect, which are the usual characteristics of the unattractive person.

If you have a cosmetic imperfection or deformity, such as a scar, mole, cyst, and so forth, which bothers you or your mate, consider having simple corrective surgery. Such minor surgical procedures usually can be performed by your family doctor right in his office; they are painless, and covered by most health insurance policies. Face lifts and corrections of nose and ear deformities are a little more complicated and must be performed by a plastic surgeon, but these procedures too are usually covered by health insurance and are well worth the effort.

Look in the mirror each day. Are you happy with your hair, your weight, your speech, your posture, your hygiene, and your teeth? If you don't consider yourself attractive, how could your mate consider you attractive? And if you are not attractive to your mate, your entire marriage may be in potential jeopardy.

STAY ATTRACTIVE!

Rule 12
Be Reliable

If you enter into any relationship with any other person that involves a mutual agreement, the one most important factor is the reliability of the person making the agreement. This is so whether it be the matter of the basic marriage contract or the simple matter of promising to take out the trash at the end of the day. Whatever you promise, keep that promise. Whatever the agreement, live up to your end of it.

It is very difficult to respect someone who is not reliable. It is very difficult to like someone you do not respect. It is nearly impossible to love someone you do not like. Therefore, to ensure your love and make your marriage a solid one, BE RELIABLE!

Rule 13
Never Promise More Than You Can Produce

As father and husband, we all like to consider ourselves the grand provider of all things. Our pride in ourselves as men makes it almost a personal insult if we have to deprive our loved ones of anything; yet we all have our limitations. Our families learn to rely on our commitments to them and plan their own lives accordingly. When we cannot produce to the level of our promises, they are disappointed and resentful. Fathers and husbands can get the feeling that they are preyed upon to an unfair degree; however, in many cases, the reason that so much is expected of the husband is that he promises more than he can produce. It is far more pleasant to surprise your loved ones with something that they did not expect, than to promise them something and then disappoint them when it is not possible to keep the promise.

Women today are often put in an impossible situation, particularly if they are employed. Just being a consciencious wife and mother has always been regarded as a full-time job ("woman's work is never done"), but the woman employed outside the home accepts a second full-time responsibility in addition. If this is your predicament, be realistic about your limitations. Get help at home if it is needed. Do not accept a job that requires more than you can give, even if you must compromise on income and prestige. It is better to do a lesser job well and happily than strain your limits and those of your family with one that is too demanding.

Even the full-time "at home" wife and mother can make the mistake of attempting the impossible by trying to make things "too perfect." It is unrealistic to expect a house with young children to be impeccably kept. Likewise, when domestic responsibilities exceed your capabilities, be wise and ask for help. Don't heroically destroy yourself trying to accomplish the impossible.

You will have a better and happier life if you NEVER PROMISE MORE THAN YOU CAN PRODUCE!

Rule 14
Admit Your Own Shortcomings

By the time most couples get to the point of committing themselves to marriage vows, they are quite aware of each other's shortcomings. But even if they are not, I daresay it would be hard for either partner to hide any shortcomings for more than three or four weeks of married life!

If you are willing to accept this as a fact, doesn't it make sense to admit your shortcomings, confess them, and learn to work around them rather than go through life pretending that they don't exist? If mates have accepted each other in spite of their shortcomings and inadequacies, they have obviously agreed to live with them and to help in their resolution if possible. The types of shortcomings and idiosyncracies I am referring to are things such as claustrophobia, homesickness, fear of pregnancy, fear of responsibility, bad temper, tendency to depression, fear of illness, lack of self-confidence, and so forth. If you have your own personal hang-ups, you would do much better to bring them out in the open and discuss them with your mate rather than hide them.

ADMIT YOUR OWN SHORTCOMINGS!

Rule 15
Be Pleasant

A pleasant attitude and pleasant remarks seem to create such good feelings in people that it seems a shame to deny them. We all see examples of this every day when we meet people who smile and greet us with a cheerful "Good morning." We have no choice, whether we are in a good mood or not. The automatic response is to smile back and say "Good morning." And everyone feels better for having done so.

For years I had my car washed at a very impersonal local car wash. They washed the car and took my money; I got in the car and drove off. Scarcely anyone acknowledged my presence. Recently, however, a new car wash opened, and I decided to go there simply because they were not so busy and the lines were not so long. I was surprised to be greeted by a young man who said, "Good morning; it's good to see you." He opened the door for me to get out. The car went through the same car wash procedure as it had always done at the old place, but when I paid the money, the cashier smiled and said, "Thank you ever so much." When I got in the car to leave, another young man said, "Thanks for coming. Have a good day now." At first I thought the enthusiasm was due to the fact that the place was new, but after I had returned several times I got to know the owner, who told me that the three people I commented on had been carefully instructed to greet the customers in this way and that he found it accomplished two basic purposes, (1) it made the customer feel comfortable and glad that he came, and (2) it helped the employee enjoy his job more. This man's psychology certainly worked on me because not only do I find that I use his establishment exclusively, but that I am having my car washed twice as often, simply because I enjoy having people tell me they are glad to see me.

If this works in business, it should also work in marriage. If you are not already doing so, get into the habit of kissing hello and kissing good-bye. Also make it a habit to share the pleasant moments of the day with your mate in the evening. If you find that you don't smile enough around the house, have a long talk with yourself and admit that no one enjoys seeing a grouch, and that it is even less of a pleasure living with one.

BE PLEASANT!

Rule 16
Be Appreciative

Marriage is full of sacrifices. If the sacrifices are appreciated, they are worth making. If they are not appreciated, they become a chore.

Acknowledge the sacrifices made in your behalf and you will benefit a hundred times over.

If your wife or your husband makes a good dinner, acknowledge it! Acknowledge the extra effort put into the dinner and show how much you appreciate it. If your husband or wife paints the living room, acknowledge it and demonstrate just how much you appreciate it. Discuss how nice it looks, and they'll be more willing to do it the next time.

A fellow told me the other day that he had spent the weekend painting his house. Out of curiosity I asked him what his wife's comment was about his efforts. He smiled and said, "She told me it was about time and pointed out a dozen other jobs that need doing too!"

"Did she thank you for doing it?" I asked.

He looked at me and said, "You must be kidding!" Needless to say, they had problems.

BE APPRECIATIVE!

Rule 17
Give Enough of Yourself to Your Family

It is never an acceptable excuse to say that you are too busy to have enough time for your mate or your children. This is your primary responsibility and everything else must come second. In my opinion, any person who has a successful career but is a failure in marriage is a failure as a person. Newspapers are full of stories of successful, well-known people who married and divorced many times and finally committed suicide as a conclusion to what turned out to be a lifetime of tragedy.

It is practically impossible to find complete happiness in life if a person does not find happiness in marriage. Therefore, put marriage first! Give it enough time and interest, even if your career must suffer to some extent! If you have enough of the essentials of life to get by, the extra effort put forth can only be for luxuries, so make sure they are worth the sacrifice and do not compromise too much family time to GIVE ENOUGH OF YOURSELF TO YOUR FAMILY!

Rule 18
Don't Play with Temptation

The old adage holds that if you play with fire, you will eventually get burned. This also applies to excessive familiarity with a person of the opposite sex.

Whenever someone gets involved in a relationship with a person of the opposite sex, and tries to justify it by saying that it is "just a harmless friendship," I have been inclined to ask, "How would you feel if your mate were involved in a friendship of equal magnitude with someone else?" The answer is usually a nod of understanding. As a rule, no one intends to become involved in an act of infidelity at the outset of any relationship, but anyone who fools around long enough is bound to end up with troubles.

Since you would almost certainly get burned, DON'T PLAY WITH TEMPTATION!

Rule 19
Don't Expect Your Mate to Be Something that He or She Is Not

A person's basic personality changes very little after he reaches adult life. If a person is of average intelligence and appearance prior to marriage, there is no reason to expect him or her to become a razzle-dazzle whiz kid afterward. As a matter of fact, it would be more likely to expect the pressures of marriage to weigh somewhat heavily and sometimes make life difficult. Therefore, do not expect your mate to be something that he or she is not.

If your husband never demonstrated an interest in the ballet, don't be so unfair as to expect that he ever will. Likewise, if your wife has never had any interest in sporting events, it is quite unfair to expect her to ever be excited about buying a season ticket to the local professional football team. If your husband has never been interested in dancing or if he has two left feet, this must certainly have been apparent to you before marriage, and it is unfair of you to punish him for this inadequacy. If your wife lacks the facility of stylish taste and has always dressed herself in a simple fashion, it would certainly be unfair to punish her for not having the facility to keep up with the Joneses.

Mind you, I am not saying that there is no obligation for people to do their best and stay on a self-improvement campaign; however, you must love your mate, although sometimes you may not like him or her, for what he or she is and beware of magnifying inadequacies or idiosyncrasies. DON'T EXPECT YOUR MATE TO BE SOMETHING THAT HE OR SHE IS NOT!

Rule 20
Keep Yourself Interesting

Evaluate yourself from time to time. Are you an interesting person? If you are not an interesting person to yourself, you can hardly expect to be an interesting person to your mate. After marriage it is very easy to get in a rut and become overburdened with the responsibility of a job, keeping house, and raising children. Just getting the day's work done seems to be all that many people can manage. If it has gotten you to the point of not considering yourself interesting, however, then you must make changes in your life.

Read the newspaper daily and see what is going on. Always try to keep a book going so that you have something to discuss. Try not to let yourself be satisfied with idle gossip and television, but rather try to cultivate a continuous source of new ideas and new plans for making life interesting and keeping your mate on his or her toes to keep up with you. Give your mate something to look up to. If your table conversation is dull, give some thought during the day to what would be an interesting topic to discuss and prepare yourself accordingly.

If you are not in the habit of doing these things, it will not be easy at first. But once you work on it, you will find it makes your marriage more interesting, and it will make you more interesting to yourself. KEEP YOURSELF INTERESTING!

Rule 21
Don't Neglect Your Sex Life with Your Mate

Sex has been described as not being a building block of marriage but rather the mortar that binds the building blocks together, and fills in for some of the missing blocks of the foundation.

It is true! If you are young and healthy enough to be capable of sexual performance, it is important to enjoy it as often as possible.

The excuses that I hear for the neglect of regular sex in marriage have been discussed in Chapter 25. They are all understandable and curable. Review them! If your own sexual life is unrewarding, work aggressively toward solving the problem. If you cannot solve it on your own, get help from your family physician. But at all cost, do not neglect sex. Do not assume, because your mate is not outwardly complaining about the infrequency or lack of satisfaction of sex that he or she does not care. He or she may be an understanding person or may have given up for any of the reasons that have been discussed. But I doubt that anyone in this predicament would not care.

If you are not enjoying sex with your mate regularly, take heed, work on it, and solve the problem. Your bonds of marriage will be reinforced manifold.

DON'T NEGLECT YOUR SEX LIFE WITH YOUR MATE!

Rule 22
Be Tolerant of Your Mate's Interests and Recreation—Within Reason

When a friend of mine heard that I was writing this book, he asked, "Do you really think it will help anybody to know what to do about their problems?" I said I certainly hoped it would because this was the purpose of writing it in the first place. "O.K. then," he replied, "what about this? I like to go bowling once a week, and my wife gives me a bad time about it. What does it say about that?"

The more I thought about it the more I realized that this was an extremely difficult question to answer. It all depends on how much time the bowling takes away from family responsibilities and whether or not it involves excessive expense which jeopardizes the family economic security. As I reviewed the situation, however, I found that the condition is fairly self-limiting. Husbands and wives certainly know what is right and what is wrong for them. If the recreation is a healthful one and does not take an abusive amount of time or family resources, it should certainly be condoned. As a matter of fact, I've had wives tell me that they are delighted to have their husbands away from home one night a week, for bowling or whatever, because they are ever so much more pleasant and interesting on the other days. Sometimes, if they don't go out occasionally, men seem to develop a sort of "cabin fever." Women too have a necessity to be among other women for their own development as women.

Tolerate your mate's outside interests and recreations as long as they do not infringe upon family security—but not beyond that point. Many recreations can become addictive and compete with family responsibility to the point of jeopardizing the marriage. Whenever either mate feels that this point has been reached, the distraction must cease until the marriage is stable. Only then should it be resumed to any degree and only with the most extreme caution so as to never infringe on family happiness and security.

BE TOLERANT OF YOUR MATE'S INTERESTS AND RECREATION—WITHIN REASON!

Rule 23
Do Not Permit Yourself
to be Unhappy in Your Job

When a person is unhappy in a job, it often leads to resentment of a great part of his or her life.

If you dislike your job, take an objective look at the situation. Are you putting enough personal effort in it to get the most out of it? Is the job the problem, or are you the problem? If you do not have a good attendance record, a change of jobs would not necessarily be your answer. If you are antagonistic toward your employer, be careful, because you may be inclined to carry your hostilities and bad habits with you to future jobs.

If you have decided that you are miscast in your job, however, take action and do something about it. In this day and age, even in times of recession, there is hardly ever justification for anyone to be unhappy in his or her work. Educational opportunity is such that initiative and perseverance can prepare practically anyone, in his spare time, to get almost any job that he would really consider a goal. Even though necessity might force a person to keep an undesirable job for a short period of time, there is no need for anyone to persist in an unsatisfying, unpleasant job for the balance of his work career. It is not fair to you; it is not fair to your mate; it is not fair to your employer. If you are unhappy in your job, demonstrate some initiative and work toward something that would make you happy.

DO NOT PERMIT YOURSELF TO BE UNHAPPY IN YOUR JOB!

Rule 24
Keep Healthy

Illness is a great deterent to personal happiness. The best way to avoid illness is to maintain good personal health care—which means avoiding body abuses such as over fatigue, excessive smoking, excessive drinking, obesity, and so forth. Good dental care and good periodical physical examinations are also in order. Most important of all, of course, is to consult your physician at the first symptom of any physical discomfort or illness.

The services of a good, interested family physician are one of the biggest bargains that you can possibly invest in. In spite of the fact that a great deal is written about the cost of medical care, I doubt that there are more than five families in my own practice that spend more money per year in my office than the average family of smokers spends on cigarettes. Almost any illness, if it is diagnosed and treated early enough, is curable; so why deprive yourself of the privilege of feeling well?

You wouldn't drive your car with a miss in the engine or a shimmy in the front wheel or malfunctioning brakes. Neither should you expect your body to function with headaches, nervousness, frequent colds, coughs, or any other persistent illness regardless of how minor. So take care of yourself and see your doctor with regularity.

KEEP HEALTHY!

Rule 25
Work Toward Providing Your Family with an Adequate Home

A home need not be fancy to be adequate; however, the basic security, growth, and development of each individual in your family is largely dependent upon the home's comfort and adequacy. If possible, a home should provide the following:

1. Adequate space for each person to have privacy and a means for self expression in his quarters. This means that each child should have his or her own bedroom. If this is not possible, and if the children are forced to share a bedroom, it is of vital importance that the room be divided in such a way that each child has a specific section that is his and only his to enjoy and to take care of. Under no means should children be permitted to share any part of a bedroom with their parents; it has been proved over and over again that it is emotionally unhealthy for parents and child to sleep in the same room. Parents and children should each have their own private quarters—even while they are still infants.

2. A home should provide adequate recreational facilities. In some cases recreational facilities could be just a place to read quietly, or a place to spread a jigsaw puzzle, or to play cards or chess; or a nearby place to play catch with a ball. Other people require greater space for more elaborate recreation.

Regardless of the recreational interests and talents of your family members, they should each have a place to work on their own projects and enjoy themselves.

3. The proper neighborhood for your family. Regardless of what a bargain a house might be, or how ideal the house is physically, you'll never find happiness there unless your family is suited to it and to the neighborhood. Anyone who has experienced the misfortune of raising children in a neighborhood where there are no other children knows what I'm talking about. Likewise, if you are meticulous about the care of your home and live among neighbors who are slipshod about their home maintenance, you can certainly understand the hardships that would result. The reverse is also true. If you are not particular about the fine points of gardening or home repair, you might find it very uncomfortable living in a neighborhood where people pride themselves in these matters. It is important to evaluate the people among whom you would be living. Do you think you would feel comfortable in this group? If the differences in your cultures would be too great, it might be worth considering a different neighborhood where you might adapt more readily. Whatever your particular criteria for an adequate and comfortable home, look carefully to find them and establish your family in an environment that suits them best.

Once you have established a happy home, don't part with it easily. A family that moves about from place to place at the slightest provocation is deprived of the security that comes with being a solid member of any society and community. They have no opportunity to develop *esprit de corps* or lifelong friendships. The result is usually insecurity, and instability with nothing to hang on to.

WORK TOWARD PROVIDING YOUR FAMILY WITH AN ADEQUATE HOME!

Rule 26
Don't Nag

"Man convinced against his will is of the same opinion still."

Nagging might on occasion get you your own way, but it is rarely worth the hostility and annoyance that it generates. That is such a self-evident fact that very few would contest it. However, many people develop the habit of incessant nagging about some of the most insignificant things and make themselves absolutely obnoxious as a result.

It does not make sense because any two people who love each other will stand a much better chance of understanding and solving problems with discussions and decision making rather than nagging.

If, after discussing a matter and deciding on a course of action, your mate does not follow through with a commitment, discuss it again and see whether he or she has any intention of doing so. If he does, try to establish a specific time and place to get it done (participate in the task yourself, if possible) and try to resolve the problems one at a time this way. If there is too much resistance from your mate on the matter, consider doing it yourself, or find another solution, or drop the matter entirely, but DON'T NAG.

If you consider yourself a nag, or if you have ever been accused of being a nag, get wise to yourself and give up the habit, because the hostility generated just is not worth it.

DON'T NAG!

Rule 27
Never Criticize Your Mate's Family

Long before you knew each other, you and your mate each had a family that raised you from infancy until the time of maturity. Therefore, you owe great debts to your families and should demonstrate a substantial amount of allegiance to them.

But at the time of marriage it is clearly understood that a person's primary responsibility is transferred from his family to his new mate. However, it is unreasonable to expect any person to be willing to reject his family to the point of tolerating out-and-out negative criticism of them. Most people have too much pride and family loyalty for this and would respond with resentment and hostility if you were to attack any member of his family.

Families may fight unmercifully among themselves but demonstrate a remarkable degree of cohesiveness when they are attacked from the outside. Therefore, if you attack your mate's family, you have everything to lose and nothing to gain. Do not be misled by thinking that since your husband or wife may criticize his or her own father or mother, you could get away with the same criticism. If your mate is criticizing someone in her own family, you can listen patiently, and if you like you can even comment (taking the part of the person being criticized), but never ever make the mistake of joining in on the criticism.

Regardless of the conditions, regardless of how justified any criticism might be, NEVER CRITICIZE YOUR MATE'S FAMILY!

Rule 28
Keep a Little Spice and Surprise
in Your Life

For most people, the two favorite days of the year are their birthday and Christmas or Chanukah. The reasons are obvious. These are days they can look forward to in a very special way—days when they can anticipate pleasant surprises. It is a wonderful custom to have such days set aside to be special, and it has obviously been so well accepted that the tradition has lasted over centuries. Even people who don't believe in Christ, for the major part, embrace the spirit of Christmas.

If this custom has been such a success for two days out of the year, why not add a little spice to the other 363 days with surprises for your loved ones and frequent acknowledgment of the special place that they have in your heart? Surprises of this type can come in many forms—the husband who brings his wife a new nightie as a surprise on his way home from work because he saw it in a store window. The wife who surprises her husband with his favorite menu or extra special treat. The husband who sends his wife special valentines in October. The wife who suggests that she and her husband go to a football game on Saturday afternoon, when he knows that football is really his favorite pastime rather than hers. The husband who suggests taking his wife out to dinner in the middle of the week to break the monotony. The wife who packs a picnic dinner on a nice day.

All of these are delightful surprises. For those of us who have been on the receiving end of such surprises, we know that unexpected things are often the most appreciated, and it isn't long before we are thinking of ways to reciprocate for the special kindness.

Don't wait for Christmas or a birthday to greet your mate with a surprise. You can have a Christmas any day of the year, even today.

KEEP A LITTLE SPICE AND SURPRISE IN YOUR LIFE!

Rule 29
If You Love Your Mate and Children, Tell Them So Frequently

The backbone of all marriage is love. It is the most important building block in the foundation and the single most important stimulus for the sacrifice and sharing that makes marriage work. A great deal is spoken about it during courtship and at the time of the wedding, but it is my experience that many people proceed to take that love for granted from the wedding day on.

As one man told me several years ago, "If my wife ever told me that she loved me with half of the forcefulness that she uses when she points out my mistakes, I would think that I was the most loved person in the world." I have seen so much neglect in this area that there are times when I am inclined to think that not only is love blind, but it must be deaf and dumb as well.

It is really a shame that this situation exists, because the reassurance that comes with the verbal expression of love is so very pleasant and contagious. Not only is it important for mates to express their love for each other, but it is equally important for parents to express their love verbally for their children. It has been my experience that parents who do verbally express their love frequently to their children are rewarded with affection and cooperation in return. It seems that children who feel loved cherish that feeling and do their best not to lose it. Without that feeling of love, however, children have a tendency to be defiant and rebellious to their parents and to the world around them. For many people there is a shyness about verbally expressing love, but once the habit is established of kissing good morning and kissing good-bye, and tacking on an "I love you" at the end of each kiss, it becomes very easy. Try never to take it for granted that your mate and your children know that you love them. It doesn't always work that way.

Very often in my office, I have occasion to ask people, "Does your mate love you?" or "Do your parents love you?" Many, of course, will respond with a very sincere, "I do not know." So, please, please, do not take it for granted.

In summary, then, there is everything to gain and nothing to lose. IF YOU LOVE YOUR MATE AND CHILDREN, TELL THEM SO FREQUENTLY!

Rule 30
Permit No More than
One Family per Home

The healthy family is made up of one husband, one wife, and the children that result from their love. The roles of husband and wife and father and mother are vital and the children depend on the rules and guidance of the parents for their development. If more than one family has to occupy the house and attempt to function as a more complex unit than has been described above, it is nearly impossible for each member to function within the structure of his or her appointed role.

If a young couple lives with the parents of either member, they are still subject to those parents as their children. It is impossible, therefore, for the husband to be the head of the home when indeed his father is. It is impossible for the wife to be the heart of the home when indeed the mother is. It is extremely difficult for the young couple to cultivate their roles in marriage to produce the necessary mutual respect to make a solid union.

In all of my experience, I have never seen a healthy marital relationship exist in conditions where a couple was living with parents or any other couple. It is understandable that there could be very brief periods when a family might be absolutely required to live as the guests of another family for a month or less during a time of extreme emergency, but any period of cohabitation beyond that time is destined for trouble. The trouble might just exist in lack of satisfaction rather than any actual confrontation, but that too is trouble. Even if your home temporarily must be a single room in someone else's house, keep it separate and private.

Regardless of how humble it may be, it is better to have a home of your own than to live as guests in anyone else's. To those of you who say you are only going to live with your parents for a few years, until you can save enough money to buy a fine home of your own, I say settle for what you can afford now! When you can finally afford that fine home of your own, you may not have much of a marriage left to enjoy it with. To those who would justify living with parents by saying that your parents need you, I say that your first responsibility is to your own family and your responsibility to parents must be secondary. To those of you who say your parents must live with you because of economic circumstances, I say that this is indeed a difficult problem, but try to find a way to maintain privacy or make one. To those of you who say that you prefer to live with family because you are happier that way, I say "HOGWASH!"

PERMIT NO MORE THAN ONE FAMILY PER HOME!

Rule 31
Keep Your Bad Moods to Yourself

We all have our bad days—days when we are so irritable we are literally not fit to live with. Many people admit that on such days they can't even stand themselves. Since this is a symptom common to so many people, it might be considered an understandable and excusable situation. What is not understandable and excusable, however, is why anyone would choose to inflict the wrath of his hostility and bad temper on his or her mate. For unfortunately, it is the mate who usually must bear the brunt of foul moods and irritability.

If you recognize this, and if you have any control over yourself during that period, for goodness' sake, leave your poor mate alone and keep your bad mood to yourself. Any loving mate would understand an explanation like, "Please excuse me, dear; it's one of my bad days." But if the mate observes the inconsiderate, hostile behavior of the ill-tempered member for long enough, it won't be long before he resorts to retaliation.

If you happen to be married to a person who is subject to frequent foul moods and uncontrollable temper (particularly if it is in the form of premenstrual tension, or the reactions to business pressures, and so forth), insist that medical help be sought, so that personal control might be better.

It might also be a good idea to keep your distance during these times rather than retaliate and precipitate a real family squabble.

If you have a bad temper and are subject to "bitchy" moods, keep it to yourself and if at all possible seek medical help and guidance.

KEEP YOUR BAD MOODS TO YOURSELF!

Rule 32
Don't Abuse Alcohol

A good old reliable rule as to how much alcohol a person can consume is that you may drink until you feel good, but you may not drink until you feel bad. I consider a worthwhile corollary to that rule to be that you may drink so long as you behave in an amiable and responsible fashion, but you may not drink if you behave in an intolerable and irresponsible fashion.

Those of us who love each other as mates are only as secure as our mates are stable. If a mate is unstable, we are dreadfully insecure and there is no such thing as a stable drunk. In fairness to your mate and in fairness to yourself, you must not abuse alcohol.

How much is enough? How much is too much? If your mate (or anyone else for that matter) ever tells you that you're drinking too much, then you can, in truth, accept the fact that you are indeed drinking too much and you should stop. Alcohol has a definite place in setting a party mood and on occasion in relaxing inhibitions to overcome stiffness that can predispose one mate to frigidity. However, if alcohol in any way causes you hardship rather than pleasure, it is too much and you must stop it entirely. (If one mate has a problem, both mates should abandon the use of alcohol.) If ever you reach the point of drunkenness, you have indeed committed one of the sins of social abuse and you must reconsider your standards.

DON'T ABUSE ALCOHOL!

Rule 33
Be Optimistic

Life in general, and married life in particular, can have so darn many discouraging facets that only love can make it tolerable and only love plus optimism can make it worthwhile. No matter how well things are going for you, if you have a pessimistic outlook, it is possible to paint anything black. Likewise, if you have an optimistic outlook, it is possible to bring faith and hope to the most dismal of situations. We all have our limits as to how much misery we can tolerate, and no one can gracefully come home to gloom day after day.

Descartes is credited with saying, "I think, therefore, I am." He used this as the basic premise of his philosophy and elaborated all things from that point. In daily life we might think of this as, "I am as I think I am," or to put it differently, if I think I am miserable, I am miserable. If I think I am happy, I am happy. If I think I have a future, I have a future. If I think I am going to hell, I am on my way to hell.

Life isn't worth living if you are willing to see only the pessimistic side of it. I have seen so many people in my experience miss the pleasures of the sunny days of life because they seem to have an ever-prevalent concern over the possibility of a rainy day tomorrow.

The result is that they experience the misfortunes of life three times over. First, in endless worry over misfortunes that are constantly anticipated; again, if and when they experience the misfortunes; and finally, in spending endless hours reviewing the misfortunes after they have been resolved. Whether we like it or not, into each life some rain must fall, but why call it a flood?

Optimism, progressiveness, and happiness are all kissing cousins; therefore, force yourself to BE OPTIMISTIC!

Rule 34
Don't Intentionally Bore or Irritate Each Other

In every marriage there are some things that please and interest one member but completely bore or irritate the other. If it is a point of major interest to the member who chooses the topic to discuss, then the other member should do everything possible to understand and share the interest. However, if it is a petty matter like gossip or the discussion of something that would be completely out of the realm of the interest of the other member, it should be avoided.

I am put in mind of one woman who chooses to bore her husband with incessant chatter about her mother, her mother's neighbors, and so forth. Her husband tells me that he dreads mealtime because he knows that he is going to be sentenced to another chapter of "Mother and Friends."

Another woman recently told me that her husband chatters endlessly about his work on engine design. She said that she is delighted that he is interested in his work and gets satisfaction from it, but that she has no comprehension of the subject and might just as well be spending the evening with someone who only speaks Chinese.

A man tells me of his wife who persistently tells stories of all the things her brother-in-law can afford to buy her sister, things which they themselves cannot afford. He says this has put him in such a constant state of humiliation and envy that he can no longer stand the sight of her brother-in-law and sister, nor the mention of their names, in spite of the fact that they are very nice people whom he would otherwise like very much.

It is so terribly irritating. The wife knows it's so terribly irritating, and yet she has never developed the good sense and discipline to avoid the delicate subject.

Doubtlessly, you and your mate have your own lists of irritating or boring subjects that you would prefer to avoid. Why not write them down and discuss them openly for once and forever and then avoid them forevermore.

Review the list from time to time and add to it as you see fit.

DON'T INTENTIONALLY BORE OR IRRITATE EACH OTHER!

Rule 35
Make the Most of Your Time Off

We all work hard for the privilege of having some time to ourselves to enjoy with our families; but all too often this precious time is a complete waste and a bore to everyone concerned.

If you don't have a good plan to make good use of your time off, you will completely forfeit the rewards that you worked so hard for. Unfortunately, most people can function well when they are directed by an employer toward some prestructured plan; but when they are given freedom they grind to a nonproductive halt. Whether you enjoy home-improvement projects, sports, games, sightseeing, theater, travel, reading, walking, picnicking, swimming, skiing, dancing, visiting friends, having guests, or whatever, DO IT; and do it with a plan, so that you make the most of your time off. Do not wait for your days off from work to think about what to do—plan ahead. You will enjoy the anticipation as well as the event.

MAKE THE MOST OF YOUR TIME OFF!

Rule 36
Never Compare Your Mate with Anyone Else

All of us have our strong and weak points, and if we are to be compared to anyone else, regardless of who it is, there are many ways in which we would compare favorably and many more ways in which we would compare unfavorably.

When you marry, each of you is committed only to be yourself and to do your best. We are all proud, and we are all sensitive about our weak points, and most of us are not able to shrug off the humiliation that comes from a direct comparison with any other person, especially if the comparison is made by our mate.

No matter how much money your husband makes, you can be sure that there is somebody who makes more. No matter how much effort your wife puts into housekeeping or raising the children, you can be sure that someone else does it better. No matter how nice your home is, or how fine your neighborhood, there is always a better one. So why make yourself miserable about all of that? Work hard for personal improvement, but never downgrade your mate or yourself by making unfavorable comparisons with other people.

NEVER COMPARE YOUR MATE WITH ANYONE ELSE!

Rule 37
Always Consult Your Mate Before
Making an Important Decision

Legally, as well as practically, mates are partners. Any major decision made by one affects the other and therefore both members should be in reasonable agreement on a decision about any serious matter. That is common courtesy and good sense.

It is certainly conceivable that both members might not always agree, and that the final decision would have to be a condition in which one member must impose his will on the basis of superior experience or knowledge. It should be understood though that the decision is binding. Regardless of this, however, both members should be well informed so they can be prepared to cope with the consequences of any major decision.

ALWAYS CONSULT YOUR MATE BEFORE MAKING AN IMPORTANT DECISION!

Rule 38
Never Criticize Your Mate
Without Acknowledging
Your Own Inadequacies at the Same Time

If you have a problem that involves the need for a change of behavior on the part of one or both of you, it is obvious that the only way the change can come about is through discussion. In discussing the problem, however, never make the mistake of criticizing your mate without first acknowledging shortcomings of your own that might be playing a part.

It is natural to resent direct criticism, but far more possible to respond to a request for cooperation in curing a difficult situation if the approach is a humble one.

A common example of this is the couple who find themselves economically overburdened. It would seem to be the natural instinct for the husband to tell his wife that she was just going to have to cut back on her spending because she has been too free with their money and has put them in jeopardy. Any woman told this could not help but feel resentful. The husband would do better to say, "Our budget is out of order, and I feel that we have been spending too much money. I have probably been the main offender because I have bought several things for myself and possibly spent a little too much on my recreation and I intend to cut back some. Would you please cooperate by limiting your expenditures too?"

A woman receiving this sort of solicitation might not enjoy it either, but she receives the message loud and clear without being offended or feeling as though she is being accused of being negligent or irresponsible. NEVER CRITICIZE YOUR MATE WITHOUT ACKNOWLEDGING YOUR OWN INADEQUACIES AT THE SAME TIME!

Rule 39
Always Acknowledge Your Mate's Efforts and Improvements

The greatest stimulation to progress and improvement is appreciation. Modifications of personal behavior and concerted efforts for personal improvement are not easy for anyone. It is certainly ever so much easier to have an attitude of "like me as I am or forget it."

If you are fortunate enough to have a mate who is working for self-improvement and improvement of your marriage in general, the best way you can be ensured of its continuation is ALWAYS ACKNOWLEDGE YOUR MATE'S EFFORTS AND IMPROVEMENTS!

Rule 40
Keep Current Friends and Interests

As we go through life, we meet friends and cultivate interests at every stage. Since people and their interests are in a state of never-ending change, it is sometimes difficult to live today's life with yesterday's friends.

If your husband has a different job from what he had five years ago, and his friends and interests are different, make an effort to get to know them and enrich your lives by sharing experiences on a current basis. If your wife has become extremely interested in a civic organization or in a career, make an effort to get to know her new associates. You will enrich your own experience by so doing.

When we become completely dependent on old friends and cling to the old cultures and traditions of our families, we limit our progress and have a tendency to become dull. The more friends we have, the richer our total lives are, and the more varied friends we have, the more complete our total experience will be.

Always KEEP CURRENT FRIENDS AND INTERESTS!

Rule 41
Live within Your Means

Almost every man would like to drive a Cadillac. Almost every woman would like to have a mink coat or maybe two or three. With today's marketing and credit buying, the purchase of almost any of these items is within the realm of possibility. Paying for them is something quite different.

If a couple does not use mature discretion about their purchases, they can end up overspending their income and creating a constant state of economic tension. The unfortunate part of this is that most people who end up in economic jeopardy do so for the purchase of items which they do not need and very frequently do not enjoy.

It is said that all things have a price. The price of economic security is good judgment, common sense, and restraint. DO NOT OVERSPEND YOUR INCOME. LIVE WITHIN YOUR MEANS.

Rule 42
Avoid Violence at All Cost

The culture of yesteryear established woman as a second-class citizen who had no right to vote or speak up in any way. Her husband was her master, and it was his privilege and duty to beat her and discipline her if she got out of line. Fortunately, modern times have reversed this, and women and men are completely equal. Every once in a while, however, I still see men come in with their battered wives after they have put on a home performance of the "Cave Men" play. There are well-organized programs in most communities to aid battered women and attempt to rehabilitate the marriages in which violence is a problem. If you have such a problem, I urge you to seek help at once. A call to the local police department will direct you to the proper agency for help.

Physical violence is obviously wrong and needs no further mention. However, the more common form of violence these days is the violence of words that pass between husband and wife when they become incensed. When two people have screamed violent vulgarities at each other, they completely strip each other of all dignity and respect. Even though they go through the act of making up, I have never really seen anyone who was capable of forgetting the insults that were screamed at him by the person he is supposed to love. Neither have I ever seen anyone who was completely capable of forgiving such a performance.

If anything angers you to the point of becoming violent or hostile toward your mate, do yourself the favor of separating yourself from your environment until you can get your thoughts together and take a sensible and sane approach to the problem. Violence and temper will do nothing but make it worse.

AVOID VIOLENCE AT ALL COST!

Rule 43
Insist on Privacy in Your Family

Privacy has been discussed at numerous places in this text, but it cannot possibly be overemphasized. Having an unwelcome or uninvited guest is about as annoying as anything could be. Likewise, having the private matters of family life become common knowledge among friends and relatives is a nuisance to even the most tolerant mate.

Over my years of experience, I have found that when marriages fail and end in divorce, they have done so with great aid from well-meaning third-party confidants who offered advice that turned out to be more detrimental than helpful.

Last week a thirty-five-year-old divorcee with three children, whom I have known for many years, came to my office to discuss plans for remarriage and to ask my advice. I asked her why she felt her first marriage had failed, and she replied, "Whenever I had a problem with my husband I would go home and talk to my mother about it. Mother was so interested and sympathetic that she said she didn't understand how I could have tolerated such abuse, and invited me to come home for shelter until I could get straightened out. The more I told mother my problems, the more horrible they seemed, and by the time I was done with the whole story, I had convinced her and myself the whole marriage was beyond repair."

When I asked her what made her feel she could make a go of the marriage she was now planning, she thought about it for a bit and said, "I think I have become mature enough to learn to keep family problems all at home and maintain privacy." She went on to say that had she the maturity and good judgment to maintain privacy during her first marriage, she felt it certainly would have survived.

When private matters become public, they lose dignity and become common gossip which helps no one.

HAVE MORE RESPECT FOR YOUR HOME! INSIST ON PRIVACY IN YOUR FAMILY!

Rule 44
Never Hold a Grudge

The very nature of humans is to have inborn frailties which predispose us all to indiscretions, bad judgment, and even self-destruction. This has been recognized since the beginning of time and has served as the basic tenets for most religions.

Even to this day, confession and the forgiveness of sin are a vital part of most faiths; and, for that matter, they almost all promise the forgiveness of sin by God, provided the person who committed the sin is truly sorry. Forgiveness—and not carrying a grudge afterward—is an absolute essential following an indiscretion if your marriage is to be a solid one. The person who committed the sin, or the indiscretion, would find life very difficult if he were to consider himself permanently labeled as a wrongdoer. If this is the case, and he is deprived of his sense of pride, there would be little reason for him to try to live it down and make things better. On the other hand, if he felt that all was forgiven and forgotten, he would stand a much better chance of starting over again.

For the person holding a grudge, it means suffering many times over for something that has long since run its course. Nothing is ever to be gained by perpetuating an impossible situation. So why bother?

NEVER HOLD A GRUDGE!

Rule 45
Go to Bed at the Same Time

Though it seems natural that husband and wife should go to bed at the same time, I never cease to be astonished by the large number of people who tell me they do not. The reasons are many, but the legitimate excuses are few. The most common reason is that either husband or wife will be addicted to some late-night television that keeps him or her up beyond the other's bedtime. This is an absurd habit because unless the couple goes to bed together, they miss a time of communication, which is as essential as it is at mealtimes. In many ways, it is more essential because it is the one time when husband and wife can be alone to discuss matters and communicate without interference from the children or anyone else. The impediment to sexual adjustment caused by going to bed at different times is also so obvious that it does not need amplification here. Let me say it again plainly and simply, GO TO BED AT THE SAME TIME!

Rule 46
Share Your Successes
and Glories with Your Mate

Chapter 6 in Part Two was devoted to unequal development between mates. One of the frequent causes of unequal development is the situation in which one mate will experience accomplishments on an individual basis and become so bemused by his own importance that he isolates that portion of his life from his mate. This is indeed a shame, because if there is real glory in achievement, it comes from having someone with whom to share it. Don't be afraid of experiencing any humility in sharing your glory. People have been doing it publicly for years. This is equally important whether the success is that of the husband or the wife.

Certainly you must be aware of this every time you see a virtuoso performer. After bowing to the applauding audience, the star immediately holds his hand out to the orchestra and acknowledges that they too were responsible for the successful concert.

I visited a home recently where the wife had done an absolutely magnificent job in decorating. She acknowledged my compliment to her efforts and was quick to acknowledge her husband's contribution by saying, "It's easy to select nice things if you are fortunate enoughto have a husband who can provide the funds to pay for them." The husband was obviously very pleased at the acknowledgment and returned with, "My wife has such good taste that she could make a fire hydrant look like a work of art."

Needless to say, they are happy because they share their successes. The best example of this that I can think of is the husband who openly states at the time of his own success, "My success is mostly the fruit of my wife's sacrifice." Is this not true for most of us? Why not acknowledge it?

SHARE YOUR SUCCESSES AND GLORIES WITH YOUR MATE!

Rule 47
Live Each Phase of Life
to Its Fullest

There is a time to be a child, a time to be an adolescent, a time to be an adult and "put away childish things," a time for maturity, and a time for old age. Each and every phase of life, and likewise, each and every phase of marriage, has its joys and satisfactions. I urge you to enjoy each phase for what it is; do not pretend that you can keep the pages of the calendar from turning. We all know people who foolishly go through that pretense because they missed some of the essential satisfactions of an earlier phase. This subject is dealt with in great detail in Part One of this text; and if there is any question about any of it, I would urge you to reread the text on the phase that you question. Every phase of life and marriage is potentially beautiful.

LIVE EACH PHASE OF LIFE TO ITS FULLEST!

Rule 48
Don't Put Off the Decision About
Having Children Too Long

It was not until the middle of the twentieth century that satisfactory, reliable birth-control methods were developed—enabling couples to decide when to have children, and how many. Prior to then, nature took its course, and fate determined the number of children a couple would have—and when.

Since adequate birth-control methods have become available, however, it has been my experience to learn that many couples find it difficult to decide about the number and timing of children. They often procrastinate until the ideal age span in which to bear and raise children has passed. To be sure, it makes good sense not to have children until you have ample marital security, and enough economic security with which to provide them with an adequate home. It is common sense also to not have more children than you can afford. But I implore you to be realistic about your decision. If you decide you want to have children, set a realistic timetable and allow enough leeway to compensate for the possibility that it may take a year or more before conception occurs. Make up your minds early enough to be sure that you don't wait too long to be able to enjoy your children while you yourselves are still young. Again I say, plan early for the number and timing of your children.

DON'T PUT OFF THE DECISION ABOUT HAVING CHILDREN TOO LONG!

Rule 49
Be Willing to Give 90 Percent
in Hopes of Getting
10 Percent in Return

Whoever first said that marriage must always be a fifty-fifty proposition must never have been married, at least not happily so. How could he be if he insisted on absolute equality at all times? The truth of the matter is that the only way a marriage can be happy and successful is when each mate is willing to give at least 90 percent in hopes of getting 10 percent in return.

It is true! If one were to insist on equality at every turn, the daily inequities would drive one crazy. I have seen many cases in which one partner would carry almost the entire load for many years while the other partner was going through difficult times. Eventually, however, most good marriages result in mutual happiness, which is really the best reward that any of us could ask for as payment for our sacrifices. If you love your mate and want to enjoy life to its fullest, avoid the immature pursuit of equality.

BE WILLING TO GIVE 90 PERCENT IN HOPES OF GETTING 10 PERCENT IN RETURN!

Rule 50
Keep Some Fun and Good Humor in Your Marriage

We all enjoy having fun and good humor. They add spice and flavor to our lives. The most common answer I get when I ask young people why they have chosen the mates they have is that he or she "is the one I had the most fun with." After the wedding ceremony, however, all too many people become so overwhelmed with their problems of marriage and parenthood that they neglect fun and good healthy humor. Don't let it happen to you. If you see a cartoon in the paper that amuses you, cut it out and show it to your mate. If something funny happens, share the experience with your mate. If there is some fun to be had in your community, join in, take part in it. Why not? Isn't that part of what you got married for? For most of us, it is. So don't take life so seriously. KEEP SOME FUN AND GOOD HUMOR IN YOUR MARRIAGE!

Rule 51
Keep Physically Active and Fit

The reasons to keep physically active and fit are several:

1. People with physically fit bodies are obviously healthy and are certainly more attractive to the opposite sex.

2. Physically fit people feel better and therefore enjoy richer, longer, and more satisfying lives.

3. Physically fit and active people are significantly less prone to nervousness. The reason is that emotional fatigue without physical fatigue can precipitate anxiety, insomnia, irritability, lack of interest in sex, depression, and a host of other very unpleasant side effects. It is true that one of nature's most effective tranquilizers is physical fatigue induced by strenuous physical exercise.

Ideally, this form of physical exercise can be a social activity as well. Tennis, golf, handball, jogging, bicycling, swimming, dancing, and hiking are all excellent examples of sporting activities in which couples can participate for both physical and social benefit. If you cannot share in any of these activities, an exercise program or a very simple hobby, such as gardening and home maintenance, will often suffice. Regardless of how you do it, I urge you, for yourself and the sake of your marriage, to KEEP PHYSICALLY ACTIVE AND FIT!

Rule 52
Never Hesitate to Admit Your
Mistakes and Apologize For Them

It's embarrassing and upsetting to make a mistake; but in most cases, it is also both understandable and forgivable. To knowingly make a mistake, however, and stubbornly attempt to justify it is irritating, disrespectful, and downright stupid. And yet, I have seen so many people do just that. They're wrong; they know they're wrong; but they won't admit it. It just DOES NOT make sense, because any couple who plays this sort of game finds that their marriage degenerates into a chaotic fiasco. If this is a problem in your marriage, be honest about it and do everything within your power to rectify it. Admit your mistakes. You will find that it is a contagious courtesy after a while, and if your mate is subject to the same bad habit, he or she might correct it as well. Thus you will save yourselves a great deal of unpleasantness.

I have heard people say that they hesitate to openly admit mistakes for fear of appearing weak. To this, I say, "It takes a person of strength to recant and you will ultimately gain more respect for having done so."

I'll say it again, NEVER HESITATE TO ADMIT YOUR MISTAKES AND APOLOGIZE FOR THEM!

Rule 53
Make Love Not War

The secret of a happy marriage is having a partner whom you love, and loving each other for the rest of your lives. Arguing, bickering, and offending each other is a direct contradiction of the principle and purpose of true love and true marriage; and if you are one who would do these things to someone whom you are supposed to love, you are actually doing them to yourself and hurting yourself.

There is no such thing as winning a battle with someone you love. MAKE LOVE NOT WAR!

Rule 54
Consider Having a Family Pet

Not all people are pet people, and I am not suggesting that every family must have a pet. It is, however, a subject well worth considering. Pets have a way of giving a house a very homey atmosphere. A good pet gives unlimited love, yet asks very little in return. A pet creates a lighthearted atmosphere that tends to cheer people up in difficult times. A dog, although it needs a lot of space and perhaps more attention than other pets, has always been known as "man's best friend." Cats require very little space and attention and yet give a great deal of amusement, affection, and pleasure. Parrots particularly are readily available these days and offer endless amusement and companionship; yet they demand the very minimum of care and living space. Think about it. Consider it seriously, and if both mates are in agreement, CONSIDER HAVING A FAMILY PET!

Rule 55
Reevaluate Your Marriage Every
Six Months and Plan Improvements

At least every six months (sometimes even more frequently if it is indicated), reevaluate your marriage. Ask yourself, "Am I happy? If not, why not? Is my mate happy? If not, why not? Am I considerate? Do I ask too much? Do I give enough? Have I developed any habits which irritate my mate? Has my mate developed any habits which irritate me? Is our marriage interesting enough to keep both of us from being tempted to go astray? Is our sex life satisfactory?"

In your reevaluation, it would also be worthwhile to consider rereading this text in its entirety at least once every two years and specific sections at various intervals when specific problems arise. A subject of only casual interest to you now might be of vital importance in several years to come. Even though you may get the background of a particular problem at this time, you will be able to appreciate the problem in depth only when you are in the midst of it.

You will also find that your opinions about things will change as your experience grows, and likewise your judgments of the thoughts and suggestions presented in this text might take on different meaning.

Write your plans down in your notebook so you can refer to them the next time you do a six-month reevaluation. They will be very helpful. Fill out the questionnaire at the beginning of this text every six months and let it guide you to keeping your marriage healthy.

REEVALUATE YOUR MARRIAGE EVERY SIX MONTHS AND PLAN IMPROVE-MENTS!

Rule 56
Eliminate Your Irritating Traits

We all have traits of one sort or another that are irritating to other people, particularly to our mates and our children. It is not very difficult to recognize our irritating traits because they usually represent the key issue in marital disputes, nagging, failures in life, loss of friends, breakdown in rapport with family members, and sometimes personal tragedy. There are times, of course, when one mate nags the other so incessantly about a specific trait that it is natural to turn a deaf ear or to falsify the complaints as being an exaggeration of reality. I urge you to be humble enough to evaluate every criticism you receive and carefully consider doing something to correct it whether the criticism be something major, such as irresponsibility, poor hygiene, bad manners, or disorganization, or something as minor as chewing on a toothpick, picking your nose, or burping in public. Accept criticism gracefully and you will find that your life will be a happier one when you ELIMINATE YOUR IRRITATING TRAITS!

Rule 57
Consider Having an Adequate Spiritual Life

Modern Americans are probably the freest society in history. The United States Constitution has been interpreted in such a way that a person's personal freedoms are protected at all costs. For a while, even the binding rules of traditional religion were challenged to the point where church attendances have fallen off considerably. In an effort to appeal to the desires of the people, many church groups have liberalized their rules and modified their activities.

It is not my purpose to comment on the pros and cons of this liberalization; however, I do feel it worthwhile to acknowledge the importance of having a satisfactory spiritual life in your family. It is essential that people who take on the tremendous burden of marriage and parenthood have the benefit of a belief in God and a way to appeal for His help in times of need. It is equally important that children be taught the love and respect of God to guide them to maturity with morality. If you are a couple fortunate enough to share a strong religious affiliation, I urge you to guide your children in a continuation of the family tradition. If your background is one in which formal religion was not a strong part of your culture, find out what your community has to offer and select a church group which seems to fit you best. Embrace it and enjoy it. If the idea of church does not appeal to you, perhaps just personal, private prayer on a regular basis might suffice. Whatever it may be, I suggest you maintain a satisfactory spiritual life in your family. It always seems to me that life goes much easier for people who do.

CONSIDER HAVING AN ADEQUATE SPIRITUAL LIFE!

Rule 58
Have a Regular Date Night

Any fellow who does not take his best girl out on a date at least once a week really does not deserve her. Likewise, any girl who would not accept at least one date per week from her favorite fellow could hardly consider herself an adequate partner in romance. Why should life after marriage be any less?

Even though married couples share many responsibilities and pleasures in their homes, there is a definite need for regular distraction together outside of the home—without the children.

It does not matter whether the date is going out to dinner, a show, a picnic, a visit with friends, or just a long walk together. The important thing is to be together to devote your attention to each other and to have fun. After all, isn't this what attracted you to each other in the first place? So why deprive yourselves of these pleasures now? No one is ever too old for dating, so HAVE A REGULAR DATE NIGHT!

Rule 59
Select an Interested
Family Physician and Be a Faithful Patient

Finding a physician who knows how to diagnose and treat tonsillitis or appendicitis or diabetes is as simple as finding someone to repair your washing machine. All you have to do is look in the yellow pages of your telephone directory, and any physician listed and licensed would be almost guaranteed to be a reliable person for this job. Finding a family physician interested in treating you as a family and taking a warm and understanding interest in all your problems—medical, emotional, social, economic, and so on—is quite something else.

Where does one find such a person? I know many people who insist that such a physician is no longer available in our current society. I will concede that it is more difficult now to find a family physician with these qualifications than it used to be; however, they are indeed still available if you look carefully and offer yourself as a faithful patient.

If you are looking for a family physician, the first step is to ask your friends and neighbors which family physician they use. Ask them if he or she is interested in them as a family. Ask them if they feel comfortable discussing intimate, personal matters with their doctor. Does the physician have a well-equipped office? Is his practice arranged in such a fashion that someone will always be available in the event of an emergency? And does he seem well-trained to give sound advice?

Once you have located a physician, by reputation, who seems to have all the qualifications you are looking for, seek him out and make your own judgment as to whether you will feel comfortable entrusting your family's health and welfare to him.

Once you have located and committed yourself to your chosen family physician, let him be the captain of the team. Be faithful by going to him with all of your medical problems and let him be the judge as to whether or not specialty consultation is in order. Be honest enough to follow his recommendations and keep your appointments as he advises you to do. You'll find that if you establish such a relationship, you will be free to call him on the telephone to get advice about minor problems. He will also be willing to take time to discuss marital problems or the behavioral problems of your children, or the emotional problems of any of the other family members as they arise.

Just think of it—where else could you go and find any other person who is willing to devote his time and be interested in only you and your problems at the moment? If you deny yourself the privilege of having a family physician, you are cheating yourself out of one of the basic essentials of life. A true family physician becomes a real and important member of the family, so, SELECT AN INTERESTED FAMILY PHYSICIAN AND BE A FAITHFUL PATIENT!

Rule 60
Never Give Up Hope

No problem is beyond solution; no true marriage is beyond repair, so long as both mates are willing to try. If you were to evaluate your marriage on just how things are today, you might be discouraged; but if you take heart in the fact that marriage is a continuous story, and not just one page in a book, and that the story is filled with joys and heartbreak, you will appreciate the fact that any problem, regardless of how bad, is tolerable with understanding—and solvable with a good plan and lots of love.

NEVER GIVE UP HOPE!

Conclusion

In this text I have attempted to offer an understanding of marriage and its problems and a list of rules for the pursuit of happiness in marriage. This text, obviously, is not the last word on anything but rather the first step toward understanding what marriage is all about from the benefit of one family physician's experience. The real solution, however, is founded on each person's basic cravings for happiness and the sense of fair play in the treatment of the ones he loves.

Humility and compassion, blended with love and understanding, are the basic ingredients in any prescription for the cure of marital problems—and the pursuit of happiness.

In closing, I would like to offer you the prayer embraced by Alcoholics Anonymous as their members struggle with themselves to make happy and fruitful lives and overcome chaos and despair.

> *God, grant me the serenity to accept the things I cannot*
> *change, courage to change the things I can*
> *and wisdom to know the difference.*

GOOD LUCK!

Michael C. Venditti, M.D.